Christian Mi
In Western Society

CHRISTIAN MISSION IN WESTERN SOCIETY

PRECEDENTS, PERSPECTIVES, PROSPECTS

Edited by
Simon Barrow
and
Graeme Smith

CHURCHES TOGETHER
in Britain and Ireland

Published by
Churches Together in Britain and Ireland
Inter-Church House
35-41 Lower Marsh
London SE1 7SA

Tel. +44 (0)20 7523 2121 / Fax +44 (0)20 7928 0010
E-mail: info@ctbi.org.uk OR <team>@ctbi.org.uk
www.ctbi.org.uk

Registered charity number 259688

ISBN 0 85169 246 X

Editing and production: Carla J Roth
Cover design: Mark Whitchurch
Printed in England by The Cromwell Press Ltd, Trowbridge, Wiltshire

Further copies available from:
CTBI Publications
31 Great Smith Street
London SW1P 3BN
Tel. +44 (0)20 7898 1300 / Fax +44 (0)20 7898 1305
E-mail: orders@ctbi.org.uk
www.chbookshop.co.uk

Contents

Contributors

JOE D. ALDRED is a bishop in the Church of God of Prophecy and director of the Centre for Black and White Christian Partnership, Birmingham.

ALLAN ANDERSON is coordinator of the Research Units for Pentecostal Studies and for New Religions and Churches in the Centre for Missiology and World Christianity, University of Birmingham.

SIMON BARROW is secretary of the Churches' Commission on Mission, part of Churches Together in Britain and Ireland. He is also an assistant general secretary of CTBI, based in London.

WILLIAM EGGEN is a member of the *Societas Missionas ad Afros* (SMA). He has worked in Ghana and the Netherlands. Recently he has been lecturing in missiology and anthropology at the London Missionary Institute (Roman Catholic).

DUNCAN B. FORRESTER has recently retired as professor of theology and public issues at the University of Edinburgh. He has written extensively in the field of Christian political ethics and mission.

ADRIAN HASTINGS is emeritus professor of theology at the University of Leeds. The author of many books on African and world Christianity, he recently edited the *Oxford Companion to Christian Thought* (OUP, 2000).

BERT HOEDEMAKER is emeritus professor of ecumenics and mission at the University of Groningen, Netherlands, and a minister of the Uniting Church in the Netherlands. His books include *Secularization and Mission* (Trinity Press International, 1998).

JAY KOTHARE is an Anglican priest in Manchester, and formerly worked in Thamesmead and Southall. He is from Bombay and has an active concern for faith in an urban, multireligious environment.

HONG JUNG LEE is a Korean missiologist and pastor. Formerly director of the Centre for North-East Asian Mission Studies at the Selly Oak Colleges, Birmingham, he is now ecumenical officer in the Presbyterian Church of Seoul.

ANN LOADES is a professor in contemporary theology at the University of Durham. She is a past editor of the journal *Theology*.

MICHEAL MACCRAITH, a historian, is professor and academic director of Irish studies at the National University of Ireland, Galway. He has taught and carried out research in Edinburgh, Rome and Louvain. His interests include Celtic Christianity, the Renaissance era and contemporary Gaelic literature. He has published extensively.

LYNNE PRICE has worked and taught theology in Birmingham. She is the author of *Faithful Uncertainty: Leslie D. Weatherhead's Methodology of Creative Evangelism* (Peter Lang, 1996).

GRAEME SMITH is senior lecturer in social and cultural theology at Oxford Brookes University, England. He has carried out research in the areas of missiology, ecumenism and political theology. He is co-editor of the journal *Political Theology*.

WERNER USTORF is professor of mission at the University of Birmingham. His many books include *Tales of Post-Christendom in Europe* (SMT, 1999).

ANTONIE WESSELS is professor of the history of religion and missiology at the Free University of Amsterdam. He has written extensively on Islamics, Christianity and culture, including *Europe: Was It Ever Really Christian?* (SCM, 1994).

JANET WOOTTON is a Congregational minister at Union Chapel, London. She is co-editor of the journal *Feminist Theology* and is involved in the Women in Theology network.

Foreword

As a past moderator of the Churches' Commission on Mission (CCOM), the part of Churches Together in Britain and Ireland that links the mission departments and agencies of the churches in England, Scotland, Wales and Ireland, I am delighted to commend to you this stimulating collection of essays on *Christian Mission in Western Society*.

There are a number of obvious attractions to a volume such as this. For a start, the contributors all possess considerable expertise in their fields, and they all seek to engage with practical and scholarly concerns. The book includes a mixture of well-known writers and newer voices, men and women, people from different backgrounds and cultures, and from a variety of church traditions and theological stances.

What holds them together is a common concern to explore creatively (and sometimes provocatively) the past, present and future of Christian mission in the West. All contributors, to some extent, reflect a positive desire to inculturate the gospel authentically and to open up a productive dialogue between mission theology and Western societies.

Yet there is a strong critical edge, too. For the gospel is not just concerned with individual spirituality or the extension of the church, but with human flourishing in the life-giving presence of God. Where injustice, poverty, racism, sexism and discrimination exist, Christ is dishonoured and the mission of transformation, learning and conversation carried out in his name is marginalized or disfigured.

Christian Mission in Western Society amounts, then, to a clarion call for the refiguration of the life and practice of church institutions on these islands and across our rich but divided continent and region. More than that, by enriching our perception of the complex web of tasks in Christian mission, it focuses our attention more widely on the coming commonwealth of God as the ultimate horizon of human hope – even in the midst of despair and greed. For that reason, this book presents a challenge not just to engage riskily with Western society but also to accept our responsibility for larger changes in the global order.

The Revd Dr Janet Wootton

Acknowledgements

Thanks are due to many people for involvement in this publication. Graeme Smith was the originator of the idea and has remained involved throughout. The individual contributors, together with the Centre for Missiology and World Christianity of the University of Birmingham (formerly part of the Selly Oak Colleges), the British and Irish Association of Mission Studies, based in Cambridge, and the international Council for World Mission, based in London, gave permission for the use and adaptation of significant conference papers.

While the editors have made every effort to update material and references where feasible and appropriate, the authors and the production editor bear no responsibility for any resulting omission or unevenness. In particular, given that much of the material in this book originated from oral presentations, a decision was taken to retain the different approaches to references and to keep publication titles in the language of the original citation. The bibliography contains a selection of material from the endnotes and from other recent sources.

Particular thanks should be extended to Jocelyn Murray and Carla Roth for production and copy editing over a long and sometimes difficult gestation period. Others who have given invaluable assistance at different stages include Colin Davey, Mary Houston, Mark Whitchurch (cover design), Anne van Staveren, Jane Allcock, James Anderson, David Brain, the staff of the Churches' Commission on Mission and CTBI's colleagues at Church House Publishing.

Please note that the views expressed are those of the individual contributors and not necessarily of CTBI, its commissions or its member bodies.

Simon Barrow

Introduction: Reviewing Mission in Western Society

Werner Ustorf of Birmingham University highlights a central issue for this important collection of essays on the future of Christian mission in Western society when he suggests, contrary to much popular assertion, that an overview of the history of Christianity in the West does not lead to the conclusion that there has been a failure of inculturation. People in western Europe are not waiting to be told of a previously unknown saviour, Jesus Christ, nor are they waiting for an introduction to previously unknown churches. In fact, the opposite is the case. They already have a variety of opinions about Jesus Christ and the churches, however erroneous the churches themselves may think these are.

What this means for mission is that western Europeans have already located Christ and Christian faith in their schema of values and meaning, mainly in a safe place within a kaleidoscope of prejudices, instincts, values, superstitions, beliefs and purposes that make up their cultural identity. Christianity is already inculturated, and the churches do not approach western Europe with a new message.

Facing the challenge of mission in the West today

How are the churches to respond to this successful inculturation? One response, which Ustorf examines critically, is to suggest that the churches' mission now is to sweep away modern Western culture. This culture that so effectively contains Christianity may be seen as an obstacle to the spreading of the gospel, the product of an Enlightenment outlook inimical to the churches' message. It should therefore be replaced. It might be said that this confrontational response seeks to colonize western Europe – to rid the Western 'heathen' of their accumulated false beliefs and to write the 'true gospel' upon this freshly created *tabula rasa*. In short, the private opinions of Western modernists are to be superseded by the public truth of the gospel message.

This recolonization model is substantially indebted to the nineteenth-century European missions. It is still current in sections of the Gospel and Our Culture movement associated with the late Lesslie Newbigin. It also finds echoes in the 'new Christendom' ideologies of some parts of the Roman Catholic and Orthodox churches. As the writers in this volume demonstrate, it is based on a very broad and unsustainable generalization about the homogeneity of Western culture.

A second approach is more generous to at least some features of the culture of the West. It proceeds by asking what mission might look like when aspects of that culture are appreciated and valued. How can we be 'missionary' if we accept and treasure elements of the society within which Christianity is already inculturated? This is a qualified, not an uncritical, appreciation. It does not praise all things Western, but neither is it the outright condemnation associated with the first response. It may acknowledge many political, economic and social problems associated with Western society, both internally and in relation to other parts of the world. However, this does not mean mission can begin from the premise that such a society must somehow be conquered. There is a critical conversation to be had between the churches and Western culture – a conversation in which both partners will learn, grow and develop. In fact, some aspects of Western life can inform and reform the churches just as much as the churches can infuse and transform society.

This book leans strongly towards the second of these mission models. Through its different essays, some of the questions and issues that surface as a result of understanding mission as a critical conversation with Western society's culture(s) will be highlighted and discussed. For this reason, *Christian Mission in Western Society* is divided into three parts. The first, 'Precedents', looks at some historical examples of how mission has endeavoured to take aspects of indigenous culture seriously. In this section we perceive the impact of strong local cultures on Christianity as it has spread throughout Europe and other parts of the world. Often the Christian religion has been changed as a consequence of these encounters.

The second section, 'Perspectives', explores some of the challenges that arise for mission theology if elements of Western culture are taken seriously. In particular, it examines questions about the relationships between truth(s), Christianity and society, especially in the context of what has become known as postmodernity. One prerequisite of taking culture seriously is recognizing that it, as well as the churches, has significant understandings of human beings and society to impart.

The final section, 'Prospects', seeks to reflect some of the contemporary examples of mission activity that value and appreciate the contributions of cultures from within Western society. Included in this portion of the book are articles on inner-city religion, Black theology and globalization. Bert Hoedemaker's paper, first delivered to a consultation organized by the Council for World Mission, is especially important in defining the wider relationship between mission, (post)modernity, religion and eschatology. In this section we gain some insight into how aspects of Western culture have reformed Christianity or are seeking to bring about new orientations within it. For while it is obvious that much of this culture is sexist, racist and unjust, it is equally important to recognize that there are also elements of it which seek to challenge these injustices and inequalities. It is these aspects of the culture of Western society, along with insights from other parts of the world, that can inform the life of the church. In this way Christian communities rightly become the recipients of the missionary activity of God, not simply its promoters.

Western Christianity revisited

Before we look further at how the individual contributions to this book fit together, it is important to spell out the double context in which they arose. *Christian Mission in Western Society* primarily comprises revised papers from two conferences held during the summer of 1997. The first was hosted by what was then the School of Mission and World Christianity at Selly Oak, Birmingham. The second was held under the auspices of the British and Irish Association of Mission Studies (BIAMS) at Maynooth theological seminary in Dublin. Both were addressed by prominent theologians, missiologists and scholars.

The aim of the first symposium, 'Mission in Western Society', was to examine whether Antonie Wessels' chief hypothesis – that the historic spread of Christianity in western Europe can be understood as a process of ongoing inculturation – was applicable in the contemporary context. Wessels, from the Free University of Amsterdam, delivered the first keynote address outlining this proposal. A response was made by Werner Ustorf.

The thesis was then explored through the lenses of three current Christian movements: political theology (Duncan B. Forrester), feminist theology (Ann Loades) and Black theology (Joe D. Aldred). These were selected because they were the movements in the Western churches believed most likely to exemplify the process of continuous inculturation described by Wessels. The hope was that such movements could illuminate missiological thinking, not that they should be appropriated by missiologists! Each was examined on a particular day, with responses made by members of the School of Mission and World Christianity. Hong Jung Lee (Korea) and Allan Anderson (South Africa) were included here, as well as contributions from current and past students such as Lynne Price.

That this symposium took place in the Selly Oak Colleges is highly significant. The staff and students of the colleges were drawn from a wide range of countries and churches. This meant that the question of mission in Western society was addressed in an international and ecumenical context. One key missiological question that arose from formal and informal discussions was whether, in fact, Western society can be saved. Just how enduring and comprehensive is the racism, economic inequality and sexism analysed by many of the speakers? This question is especially apparent in the chapters by Joe Aldred and Hong Jung Lee. It is not far from the truth to suggest that many at the symposium doubted whether there was much to praise or value in Western society. This tension remains central for those who refuse to condemn the West in a blanket manner yet recognize the many endemic problems associated with it.

In 1997, we also commemorated the 1400th anniversary of the arrival in Britain of the Roman monk Augustine (on 27 May) and the death of the Irish monk Columba (on 9 June) – two key missionary figures intimately connected with the Christianization of these islands. To mark these anniversaries, the British and Irish Association of Mission Studies held a conference in Dublin to examine their continuing resonances. Scholars and practitioners were brought together to look at the contributions of Roman and Celtic Christianity to the Western church, and to investigate where and how Christian mission might move from here.

The keynote addresses were given by Adrian Hastings and Micheal MacCraith. They examined, respectively, the relationship between these two forms of missionary movement and the romantic notions that have grown up around, especially, Celtic Christianity. On the basis of these bold reconstructions, papers were given that sought to reflect the legacies of Augustine and Columba in a changing context. Jay Kothare (inner-city, multicultural spirituality) and William Eggen (narrative and itinerancy between the West and Africa) were two of the most challenging contributions here.

Overall, it should be noted, the emphasis in both these colloquia was on western Europe. But since the history of Europe is tied inextricably with 'the West' as a general way of denoting post-Enlightenment, post-colonial, (post?)-industrial societies in their globalizing phase, it seemed appropriate to keep the horizons as wide as possible. Both conferences also sought to place the challenge of the West in a critical world context. It is our hope that the editors and the individual authors have made clear the different specific contexts that constitute and shape the overall designation 'Western society', and that the book as a whole reflects a purposeful openness to the critique of the Two-Thirds World. The concluding chapter, by Simon Barrow, also mentions the transatlantic challenge to the European paradigm.

The missionaries

Turning to the essays themselves, the first section of this book looks at the general and individual activity of missionaries. It explores examples of how Christianity has spread effectively while taking elements of the local cultures of western Europe (and in Lynne Price's case, Africa) seriously. Antonie Wessels begins by asking whether the history of the expansion of Christianity in western Europe can offer lessons for the contemporary missiologist He suggests it can, especially if the movement of Christianity is understood as a process of ongoing inculturation. By this he means that as it spread Christianity adopted and transformed elements of local cultures, in particular the beliefs and stories associated with certain holy people and places. This contrasts, according to Wessels, with a prevalent negative approach to myth illustrated by the 'demythologization' project popularized by the noted German biblical scholar, Rudolf Bultmann.

Wessels wants to encourage the church to relate positively to the myths and stories of her time. Myth has been an instrument for the transmission of the churches' message – the churches adopted and transformed the cultural myths that they encountered. Wessels offers a number of examples of this, an outstanding one being the inculturation of the goddess Brigit as the Holy Brigit, which 'provided a continuity on a popular level for long and widely held beliefs'. Wessels shows how the churches can learn from such examples as they seek to relate to contemporary cultures. He illustrates this with reference to, among others, Leo Tolstoy, James Joyce, Vincent van Gogh and the rock band Oasis.

But are there negative myths to which the churches should not inculturate? Wessels believes there are. Some stories can become dangerous ideologies. The twentieth-century inculturation of romantic Germanic mythology within Nazism is an obvious example. Some criteria are required to decide between good and bad myths, and Wessels offers two stories to help discern the righteousness of a myth. These illustrate remarkable self-sacrifice and the importance of hope.

Whilst Wessels is concerned with the processes of missionary activity, Adrian Hastings' priority is the differences between two Christianizing traditions, Celtic and Roman, whose representative figures were St Columba and St Augustine. Here we see how one popular religious culture could not easily be swept away by a new set of beliefs and practices. There is a more integrated relationship between the Celtic and Roman Christian traditions than is often supposed. Hastings doubts the extent of the division often portrayed between Celtic and Roman Christianity, but he also recognizes that they were not the same in ethos and priorities. He attributes the disagreements described at the Synod of Whitby to Bede's overstating of the case. The Roman date of Easter had been accepted by many in Ireland prior to Whitby and was accepted by others afterwards with relative ease.

The differences between the two traditions centre on the diocese and the monastery. The dioceses of the fourth and fifth centuries had largely disappeared by the sixth century, says Hastings, wiped out by the incoming Saxons. Bishops did survive in Wales and Ireland but they were inevitably based in monasteries. By contrast, when Augustine arrived his intention was to establish an ecclesiastical structure of provinces and dioceses – something both more ancient and more modern than the

Celtic pattern, Hastings notes. More ancient, in that active dioceses had existed prior to the Saxon invasions; more modern, in that Augustine intended a structure that emphasized the central place of Rome. The Roman model was based on an ecclesiastical structure that was hierarchical, territorial and legal, offering control and universality. However, before the differences between the Roman and the Celtic traditions are over-stressed, Hastings notes that the 'clerical cadre' available to Augustine, from which he might select a diocesan clerical order, was principally monastic.

This 'different but not divided' pattern is also apparent in relation to monasticism. Augustine and his followers were mostly monks, but not the same type of monk as the Irish. The Irish monks tended to look for remote and wild locations, were not likely to construct many buildings besides a church and were much given to *peregrinatio* (wandering), seen as a blessed state. There was also a close link between monastery and kindred and a preoccupation with a saint's genealogy. In contrast, the Romans – following the Rule of St Benedict – adapted to the urban needs of Rome. The emphasis was on stability in monastic life, illustrated by Bede himself. The Benedictines stressed the communal life and the virtues of obedience and moderation. Seventh- and eighth-century British life undoubtedly benefited from the mutual enrichment of these two traditions. Hastings concludes that 'one cannot imagine that either movement alone could have done the job with the panache with which together they managed so well'.

The continuing enrichment to be found in the Celtic tradition is the subject of Micheal MacCraith's contribution. MacCraith examines the relevance of the life of St Columba for Christian living in our own day, stressing the importance of a proper appreciation of historical-critical questions concerning the sources for what we know of Columba's life. Such historical work is important, MacCraith argues, because the image of the Celt is a construct that developed at the beginning of the eighteenth century during the reaction against the rationalism of the Enlightenment. MacCraith attributes the content of the construct to three writers: Matthew Arnold, Ernst Renan and James Macpherson. For Arnold, there was a stark dichotomy between the Celts and the Anglo-Saxons, and this has survived as part and parcel of popular perception down to our own day. Further, in their hands the Celts are the 'feminine' romantics whilst the Anglo-Saxons are the 'masculine' rationalists.

Having analysed some of the romantic notions that have become attached to the idea of 'Celtic' religion, MacCraith then looks at areas in which the example of St Columba offers guidance for contemporary Christians. These include involvement in political life, a positive attitude to learning, and engagement with the creative arts.

Lynne Price then brings us up to date by looking at two twentieth-century missionaries, Florence Allshorn and Leslie Weatherhead. Price asks the question, 'Do we have any alternative precedents for helping us move from a largely discredited colonial missionary approach to one that is relevant and effective?' She refers to these alternative precedents as missionary 'maggots' and asks whether there are any 'maggots that may have slipped into the missionary luggage' brought back to these islands. Maggots historically have had a role in healing, she notes. She thinks there are such beneficial intruders and illustrates this through the moving story of Florence Allshorn, the crisis she suffered on an African mission station, and her subsequent acknowledgement that 'the heart of the missionary enterprise was human relationships' not the perpetuation of ecclesiastical machinery.

Equally, Leslie Weatherhead – the well-known Methodist preacher, writer and sometime minister at the Congregational City Temple, London – exemplifies for Price a creative methodology of evangelism that she calls 'faithful uncertainty'. Weatherhead's approach was dialogical, discursive rather than apologetic. He shared his own ideas but also invited his listeners and readers to engage for themselves in the experience/reflection process and to take responsibility for their lives. The lesson to be learnt from these missionaries, says Price, is the need for critical self-reflection in mission. By taking us into the area of dialogue in Christian mission, Price leads us into one of the issues of the second section of the book, on mission theology. She also introduces some constructive critique of the Decade of Evangelism and of the Gospel and Our Culture movement.

Issues for mission theology

The second section of *Christian Mission in Western Society* tackles such key questions as: How far should the churches identify the Christian message with decisive truth and proclamation? Can mission survive the end of the metanarrative, the idea of one overarching 'story' into which all else must be fitted? Need the churches necessarily oppose increasing relativism? These are huge issues that require pinning down to specific practical situations.

Duncan Forrester begins the discussion with his exploration of 'speaking truth'. His approach is historical, starting with Augustine of Hippo who, says Forrester, 'saw speaking truth to power as public confession of the faith, an essential aspect of the mission of the church'. This meant not explaining or justifying the existing order, but rather interpreting history in the light of the gospel. Forrester moves on from Augustine to the ambiguities of the Christendom project whose 'conscious intention' he describes as 'the proclamation and manifestation of the truth of the gospel'.

Recognizing the problems of this totalizing model, Forrester is reluctant to endorse either Oliver O'Donovan's attempt to rehabilitate Christendom or Alasdair Kee's denunciation of it as 'unqualified apostasy'. Instead he analyses its problems as a transformation of mission. In Christendom the church is 'speaking truth *from* power' not *to* power. In the Enlightenment, however, truth and church are separated and secular reason dominates the public square. Here Forrester draws on Søren Kierkegaard's critique of the Enlightenment project, which argues that 'truth is not something to be comprehended, controlled, used or appropriated. It is rather to be indwelt, lived out in action and witnessed to.'

The modern missionary movement, based on 'Christocentric universalism' is, according to Forrester, a typical Enlightenment/modernist project. But we live now in an increasingly postmodern society. Some see this as a predicament. Forrester argues that with its 'concern with the concrete, with action and existence, with freedom' as well as its 'suspicion of grandiose and impersonal schemes and systems', postmodernity presents both opportunities and challenges to the church. These will not be grasped by a hoped-for return to Christendom – the contemporary world is too fragmented. So the Christian task is to 'witness to the truth in a world in fragments'.

How can this be done? Forrester, having accepted that the contemporary context is postmodern and atomized, suggests an equally postmodern, fragmented response. This means that the church 'if it is true to its calling and its mission, does not look back wistfully to an unrecoverable past, but looks forward with expectation to God's future, and meanwhile offers its fragments as a contribution to the common store and seeks to embody its insights in its life'.

A response to Forrester is offered by Hong Jung Lee. He addresses two questions: first, the extent to which we actually live in a fragmented world, and second, whether it is possible for us to locate a source for truth. For Lee, questions of truth are intimately bound up with ethical considerations. He agrees that we live in an increasingly postmodern society whilst also emphasizing that the contemporary world is experiencing a process of globalization. It 'has been brought under the dominion or hegemony of cultural forces such as CNN, the Internet and Hollywood, which dictate values, symbols, lifestyles, aspirations, morals and identities'. The process of globalization has negative consequences as human life becomes defined more and more in terms of economic principles and market realities. This situation requires, Lee argues, a restatement of social ethics that sees the local context from a global perspective and the global context from a local one. Such a restatement of Christian political discourse should 'resist the hegemonic methods of other disciplines, setting out new rules of the game'.

Lee discusses the concept of the *oikoumene*, or household (*oikos*), drawing upon the work of Konrad Raiser, general secretary of the World Council of Churches. There are two possible renderings of *oikoumene*, one that can be characterized as militarily secured, politically administered, economically organized and scientifically planned. This follows a logic of total control that stifles life and threatens to make the earth uninhabitable. The other, biblically based perception of the *oikoumene* is a liberating impulse founded on relationships rather than structures. The division is between death-dealing and the living interaction of *oikoumene*. For Lee, the understanding of a life-offering *oikoumene* is found in the stories of the Minjung, the suffering peoples of Korea colonized by the West. These stories 'contain messages or wisdom that can be theologized as a part of God's mission in which Minjung suffer and struggle for their own dignity, subjecthood, and liberated and sanctified life'.

What this means is that 'the stories of the people, in a sense, reveal the ultimate purpose of God's mission in history and show the way in which all realities can participate in God's mission'. This defining role for the Minjung, their central place in history, can be interpreted as a challenge to Forrester. For while he is postmodern in desiring to offer fragmented truth, Lee is more modernist – suggesting an unambiguous source for the truth about global-local society. One implication of this might be that the division between modernity and postmodernity can sometimes be a division between the West and the South.

The question of truth and postmodernity appears again in the chapter by William Eggen. Eggen, a Dutch missionary theologian, is aware that many liberation theologians are suspicious of theories about inculturation and the dialogue with non-Christian religions because they seem to hide proselytizing intents or to abdicate social involvement. To examine this concern, Eggen turns to the stories of Jesus to clarify the concept of a narrative approach to mission. He finds that Jesus' life was characterized not by 'revealing immutable essences' nor by 'preaching some transcendent eternals' but by showing 'how God's word is in the revitalizing of people and in the outmanoeuvring of evil spirits' and by 'harnessing the creative forces of life'. For Eggen, this means that liberation theologians should accept that Jesus is primarily interested in the personal life story, that the narrative is more important than the metanarrative. This is not in opposition to the concern for liberation, because the personal story in which we encounter God is a story of struggle for liberation, of the search for God's liberating presence. Eggen argues that mission in postmodern times is 'the hard labour of purifying the listening ear and seeking eye that search for God's face and for the miraculous narrative of creative presence in people with their daily ecological, social and communicative struggles'.

Eggen's hypothesis is a form of the missiological paradigm *missio dei*. It is concerned with the search for the activity of God in the world. The same approach is discernible in the contribution by Werner Ustorf. Ustorf begins by asking what kind of West, or Western culture, we are talking about. He contends that the West is in a state of transformation that 'concerns less the religious side of the human longing for the infinite, as such, than the way the religious quest is expressed'. Western Europeans have embarked upon a search for more democratic, non-institutional religions, a kind of emigration in an inward direction 'or to non-orthodox and non-institutionalized free spaces, at any rate places where religious control and initiative are in the hands of the people'. Any decline in institutional church life is not necessarily a cause for concern but can be understood 'positively, as the emancipation of religious symbols from the control of religious institutions'. Ustorf goes on to list issues he has heard arising from this new context, such as the question of how we respond to the view that Christianity continues to be important long after it has ceased to be true. Or the fact that, today, all texts – religious or not – tend to be seen as products of culture and history, as fiction. What of the belief that 'the kingdom of God is within us', or people's reluctance to believe if that means 'to *force* their own souls into believing'? There seems to be a 'methodology of permanent suspicion in relation to one's own motivations, constructions and even experiences'.

Ustorf then asks, 'How ought the church to understand this new "post-Christian" situation?' The first major response he outlines is associated with Lesslie Newbigin and the Gospel and Our Culture project. This analyses contemporary culture as 'hostile', the Christian tradition *cannot be inculturated*, and so believes that Christian proclamation will succeed only after the formation of what Emil Brunner called a new 'culture humus'. The second response is Barthian. Again there is a gap between gospel and modern culture, but this is a gap between gospel and culture *in principle*. 'Indeed', Ustorf says, 'Barth does not offer anything of how we might bridge this gap.' Ustorf, however, doubts this separation of gospel and culture; for him 'the promise of salvation is always borrowed from its old owners and is appropriated by the new inhabitants of the tradition'. Like Wessels, he states that 'the appropriation and transformation of a religious tradition is legitimate in principle'. Christian mission is about the translatability of the gospel, both linguistically and culturally, which means that the Christian faith will both 'feel at home in a living and specific culture' and at the same time 'always remain fragile and alien'.

Where does this leave Christian mission in western Europe? Ustorf resists the temptation to offer a pithy, 'sound bite' definition of mission. Nor, as mentioned above, does he believe that 'the problem of European history is to be explained in terms of a failure of inculturation'. Instead he offers three reflections generated by the quest for mission. The first is reminiscent of *missio dei*: 'The church takes part in God's mission, it does not own it; the church works towards salvation, but she herself does not save anyone.' This means that 'all the forces and traditions in European culture that are, in their own fashion, influenced by Christ's way – extra-church and non-church as they may be – must be acknowledged as associates and equals in their attempts to liberate our life from the powers and principalities, and their competence needs to be recognized'. Related to this is the idea that 'God, the source of life, is also in places where the church is not yet or no longer. Western Christianity, therefore, needs a theological approach that allows reflection on the coming and going of the church and the trans-historical presence of God.' Third, and not so obviously related, 'What Christianity has to offer is a *space* where people get the chance to reconstruct and re-create themselves before God.'

The assumption of Ustorf – as also of Forrester, Lee and Eggen – is that mission is not simply concerned with proclaiming the truth about God to an otherwise corrupt order. In different ways, they emphasize the importance of aspects of Western culture for understanding God's involvement in the world. That may mean discerning and speaking of God in fragmented ways, in the work of the Minjung for liberation or within life-enhancing initiatives outside the churches. Whichever we select, we can perceive elements of Western culture being appreciated and valued. In Section 3 of the book, this insight is explored in more depth by looking at specific examples of how the churches have engaged with features of Western culture – contemporary illustrations of mission activity.

Missiological engagement with the contemporary

The first contribution in the final section examines inner-city spirituality from the perspective of Celtic Christianity. The next consider how the churches can be affected by feminist and Black theology, which have been strongly influenced by movements for change in wider society – both in the West and through liberation struggles in the Two-thirds World.

Jay Kothare's contention is that Celtic spirituality is at home in the inner city and that, to a certain extent, it is lost when it is hijacked by an exclusively White, middle-class, university-educated and mostly clerical audience. His chapter highlights a series of parallels between the situation of the Celts and that of the inner city, so that Celtic Christianity acts as a tool for analysing inner-city religious life. For example, Kothare states that 'the spirituality of the inner city stems directly from the Cross and so does the spirituality of the Celtic peoples, who themselves have had a long, gory history of conquest, occupation, marginalization, forced emigration and ethnic cleansing'. He examines the three kinds of martyrdom identified by the Celts: red, white and green – the destruction of people, the imposition of conformity and the loss of environment. The Celts were a people on the move just as inner cities are made up of migrant communities. Likewise the Celts venerated their very own home-grown saints, while those in the inner city – Rastas, Buddhists, Muslims, Hindus, Sikhs and Christians – have their own territorial saints.

Kothare depicts a spiritual and religious life outside of the institutional churches. He states that 'the ancient Celts and inner-city folk share the heritage of a lay, non-ecclesiastical, communal, domestic and family-orientated spirituality'. God is discovered 'at the heart of the multifaith contemplative spirituality ... blossoming in the inner city'. Kothare is resistant to the criticism that this is 'old-fashioned apolitical mysticism', because 'to the people in the inner city it is a way of nurturing self-esteem, self-worth, self-confidence and self-awareness'. In fact, interestingly, he argues that 'the inner city is the prayer zone of our post-Christian society'. It is possible that Kothare could be accused of romanticizing the Celtic tradition, but there is no doubting that his experience of the inner city in its religious, political, social and cultural dimensions is vibrant.

The second example of a contemporary missiology is that of feminist theology. Ann Loades is concerned with the manner in which feminism can impact on the life of the churches and the Christian tradition. She speaks from within the Christian tradition, although she is aware that many, such as Daphne Hampson, find that 'Christianity is both untrue and profoundly unethical in its devaluation of women'. Loades is sympathetic to Hampson's critique of Christianity. She says, 'The tradition is powerfully ambivalent for women, both (in some ways) affirming women and (in other ways) diminishing their worth and value by treating the male as normative.' However, she is equally critical of Hampson's use of Enlightenment rationalism. Loades hopes that it will, nevertheless, be 'possible to inculturate feminist theology within the Christian tradition that has given it birth and within the lives of women outside the tradition at present, though this will be a long haul in both cases'.

Loades then examines some of the other issues that the Christian tradition needs to address. One is 'the unease ... about the association of the female and the feminine with the godlike and the divine'. Related to this is the way in which Christian theology 'has "genderized" appropriate ways of thinking about and actually experiencing divine presence and immanence as well as transcendence, sacramental or otherwise'. For Loades 'one objective of feminist theology must be to find some social and political "edge" to make an impact on long-term change in society as well as in ecclesiastical institutions'. An example is the way that 'theology has been concerned with the "unborn" and with adolescent sexuality and its control, but remarkably little with the lives of actual children as responsibilities of both their parents – rather than, for example, as merely appendages of their mothers'.

The concern that patriarchal churches should inculturate with the feminist tradition is mirrored, although in a separate and distinct manner, in the critique of the churches as racist. Joe Aldred voices this critique when he states that 'Black people of every generation and of every location know, either by instinct or by experience, the repercussions of White missionary activities that over centuries have ridden roughshod over Black cultural heritage'. Aldred articulates an understanding of the mission work of Black communities in Britain, particularly that carried out by people from the Caribbean since the 1950s, as a way of exploring a new approach to mission, since 'the model of the last five hundred years [in Europe] offers us little by way of a suitable example'.

Aldred begins by looking at the nature and purpose of Black missionary activity in Britain. He argues that, in terms of mission, 'what has driven

Black Christians ... has been their innate sense of love for God and loyalty to their denomination, which were and are distinguishable by a particular liturgy, theology, doctrine and cultural norm'. The 'expressed aim of Black mission was to meet the salvific needs of Black people', not least because there was a danger in Britain of what Io Smith calls falling by the wayside. Black mission emphasizes spiritual and social care for individuals together with 'a high level of loyalty [that] is extended and expected in many areas of both the church's and individual's lives'. Particular challenges confronting the churches, according to Aldred, include the need for White-led churches to recognize the dearth of Black ministers. Likewise the Black-majority churches need to take cognizance of the small White presence within their ranks, although the more significant issue is generational – the question being 'will the pioneering generation, still with us, allow the emerging generation of aspirants to theologically and missiologically remould the Black church in their image'.

South African missiologist Allan Anderson, in his critical response, picks up Aldred's generational point by citing the work of Robert Beckford, which illustrates how 'this form (post-1950s African-Caribbean) of Black Pentecostalism may not be sufficiently addressing the Black community's context of the 1990s'. Anderson offers an alternative analysis of the remarkable growth of Black Pentecostalism. He notes that Pentecostalism is the 'fastest-growing section of Christianity and one of the most extraordinary religious phenomena in the world today'. This famously lead Harvey Cox to reverse his well-known position on secularization.

Anderson stresses that Pentecostalism's roots in the African-based slave religion of the United States, along with its emphasis on freedom in the Spirit, 'rendered it inherently flexible in different cultural and social contexts [and] made it remarkably successful at inculturation'. Some of the main features of the spirituality of African-American slave religion are 'an oral liturgy, a narrative theology and witness, the maximum participation of the whole community in worship and service, the inclusion of visions and dreams into public worship, and an understanding of the relationship between the body and the mind manifested by healing through prayer'. Anderson concludes by analysing the significance of the power of the Holy Spirit for Pentecostal churches in Africa. This finds expression in healing and protection from evil, which are 'the most prominent features of the proclamation of these Pentecostals and are probably the most important part of the liturgy in their evangelism and church recruitment'.

Christianity as pluriform and ec-centric

These illustrations of a contemporary missiology are not complete. In fact, they raise as many new questions as they address old ones. What they do illustrate, however, is the ever-growing number of manifestations of the Christian tradition in Western society. Within one continent, Europe, there are now a plurality of 'Christianities', and these stretch far beyond the limit and control of the churches. Alongside the feminist and Black theologies mentioned above could be added other movements that seek to resist racism and sexism. Then there are those who seek to challenge unjust economic orders, political oppression, discrimination based on sexuality and environmental damage, all of which have an important impact on theological thinking. We are confronted in western Europe with a pluriform Christianity of which the traditional churches are but one expression. The question, of course, is what holds these different streams together, if anything. Are they all Christian, even when they are sometimes mutually incompatible – for example, those on opposing sides of the debate on the rights and ordination of gay and lesbian people? Are there limits to the identity of Christianity, and if so, what might they be? If there are limits, who sets the boundaries? In spite of renewed attempts at control from the Vatican and other institutional church sources, it is not clear that the churches are still the regulators of orthodoxy.

It is probably unfair to suggest a consensus emerging in the rich contributions you are about to read. However, I am left with one strong impression. This is that the identity of Christianity and Christian people are not *of themselves* important questions. We do not need to define who is Christian and who is not, nor what Christianity can or cannot be. Indeed we appear to have reached the end of the usefulness of the terms 'Christianity', 'churches' and 'gospel' in defining association with the life of God. What can be meant by any of these terms is now either so broad as not to be helpful or so limited as to imply a series of political and theological judgements that cannot command useful consensus. (For a different view, however, see Simon Barrow's contribution.)

The appellation 'Christian' is at best a request to be listened to by a certain group of people. Mission theology is concerned with a series of issues not dependent on whether someone can or cannot be called a Christian. These include whether a movement is liberating or oppressive, whether human life is enhanced or degraded, whether people find spiritual regeneration, whether the diversity of human society is celebrated, and much more. My impression is that, in the chapters which follow, *these* are often the defining criteria for speaking about the work and life of God. It is not that certain people, because of their association with churches or so-called doctrinal orthodoxy, are in or of Christ. The divine is already incarnate in Western culture in myriad forms, bringing about full human life in society. God does not need an introduction – or reintroduction – to western Europe. There is not a necessity to speak about God to people 'in the dark'. Furthermore, Western culture does not need to be swept away to make room for God. The missiology explored in this book is not a lamentation of the failure of inculturation, but instead a critical exploration and celebration of successful inculturation, and how it may be developed.

Graeme Smith
February 2001

Precedents ~
The Missionaries

The Inculturation of Christianity in Europe

Antonie Wessels

In this chapter I want to address questions and issues that arise from understanding Christianity's historical movement as a process of ongoing inculturation.

I do not pretend to be a church historian; I am, rather, a historian of religion and a missiologist. I am interested in the way in which the church, in her Christianizing of Europe, integrated into European culture. What interests me most is the question of whether we can learn from the history of the (early) Christianization of Europe ('how the West was won', so to speak) and draw lessons from that history in order to communicate the gospel in the de-Christianizing situation of secular Europe today.

Very important for my approach – as worked out in my recent books on the topic – is Mircea Eliade's idea that the church was successful in her early mission work in Europe because she knew how to relate to the myths and stories of Europe. If this is true, one can question whether the demythologization programme (Rudolph Bultmann) was the wrong thing to do in the twentieth century. Did the church rob itself of the very tool (the mythic vehicle) it most needs to communicate the gospel?[1]

When one looks at the way in which Europe was Christianized, one can basically distinguish two methods. One was the use of the axe, as in the case of Boniface (d. 754), the Apostle of Germany, when he cut the Oak of Donar at Geismar. Another example would be Charlemagne, who fought the Saxons in 772 and destroyed their central sanctuary, formed by trees that were regarded as the pillars of the world. He wanted to prove that the god of the Christians was more powerful. The second method was that chosen by Augustine of Canterbury, who at the beginning of the seventh century followed the instruction of Pope Gregory the Great to redeploy ('recycle') the temples rather than destroy them. These two approaches could be compared to two of the five models Richard Niebuhr discussed in his well-known *Christ and Culture*: 'Christ against culture' and 'Christ as transformer of culture'.

Since the 1991 world assembly of the World Council of Churches in Australia and the contribution of Chung Hyun Kyung dealing with Korean culture – the appeal to the spirits – the relationship between gospel and culture is again very much on the ecumenical agenda. Culture forms the voice that answers the voice of Christ (as was stated at the WCC world mission conference in Bangkok in 1972). 'No culture is closer to Jesus than any other culture.' One knows the gospel only in its intimate relationship of culture to culture, including European culture.

Again, my concern is to understand how the church in Europe communicated the gospel in the past and what we can learn from these examples in order to communicate the gospel in Europe today. My interest is not so much to account for or justify the Christian faith *vis-à-vis* reason. Religion can be expressed on different language levels: the mythic-narrative, the religious-confessional and the argumentative-reflective.[2] Without denying the importance of the other language fields (levels, games), I will focus primarily on the first. Which mythic-religious language was used in the past, and which can be used to communicate the gospel today?

After saying something about myth in general, I will give some examples of the positive inculturation of the gospel in the European context in the past. Then, inspired by these examples, I want to look for a similar connection or link with contemporary European culture. I will be dealing mainly with literature, art and music (having, in earlier writings, dealt more extensively with visual culture). Finally, I want to raise the crucial question: does 'anything go', or are there criteria on the basis of which one can decide whether something is an authentic or inauthentic (what was called in the past syncretistic) contextualization of the Christian faith?

Myth

Myth has taken on an ambivalent meaning in our languages. On the one hand, it is seen as a story that is not true; on the other, it is viewed as a story with a plot or clue.

Mythic thinking is spontaneous, imaginative and creative; scientific thinking is systematic, rigorous and logical. One of the four functions of myth mentioned by Joseph Campbell is the pedagogical: myths can teach one how to live a human life under whatever circumstance.[3] The plot of a story is an invitation to participate in a fundamental discussion about one's own life. A plot is always told against the background of a greater story. Finally, it is the story of the community wherein the story is told. When one abandons the myth, listeners will not understand. Telling is building the community. To tell the story (or stories) is a building stone for the continuation of the community of storytelling in other and new situations. Each story conveys norms and values that the narrator finds important for the continuation of the community, for the sake of its children. Each story re-creates the community. Biblical stories still form the main part of the 'mythological universe' of Western civilization.

The first, negative, meaning of myth I mentioned – a story that is not true – is the most prominent these days. In the twentieth century there is a growing animosity towards myth.

A personal observation: in 1995, I happened to read a book on Celtic myths which quoted the opinion that for some people myths are 'highly poetical talk about the weather'.[4] At the time, Holland was threatened by overflowing rivers. Something similar, but more serious, had happened about forty years earlier. But interestingly, a considerable shift had occurred during the intervening years. While the flood of February 1953 was seen in the context of God's providence, the serious flooding that threatened to break through the dikes in January and February 1995 was interpreted in a completely secular way. Now it was the governments in The Hague and Bonn who were held responsible! Were those myths perhaps dealing with something more than the weather?

This negative approach to myth also seems to have been characteristic of the church of the early centuries in Europe. Myths were seen as 'pagan'. The church related more to philosophy and made use of it as an instrument to defend and present her faith. The church, with gratitude, used the philosophers' criticism of Graeco-Roman mythology for its own purpose.

In recent decades, the one-sidedness of this negative approach and its implicit dangers have been hinted at. The German theologian and psychoanalyst Eugen Drewermann, for instance, has referred to the negative aspects of the demythologization approach with regard to communicating what the gospel is really about.[5] He even goes so far as to say that the psychological consequences of this approach were to create the conditions that allow the gospel to be denied today.

I have stated above my opinion that this animosity towards myths and mythology in the old church was significant. But that is not the full story. The old church did, in fact, relate to the myths and stories of her time in all kinds of ways. Myth was used as a vehicle, as an instrument for the transmission of her message. That approach is my main concern. A theologian such as Johan Georg Hamann (1730–88) was already, at the beginning of the Enlightenment, opposed to this one-sided emphasis on reason alone.[6]

Inculturation

If one looks at the history of the Christianization of Europe, one can find numerous examples in which the church related her message to the Indo- and Old European culture of pre-Christian religion. One can mention many examples of the 'lifting of the pre-Christian religion and culture up to a new level' (*aufheben*). Examples of this 'successful' inculturation are the way in which the church related to the myths of former holy places, times and persons – sometimes all three at once.

Some examples: the 'church year' is seen, rightly, by some as one of the most brilliant inventions of Western (and, I suppose, not only Western) culture. From the fourth century, Christmas was connected with 25 December, the festival of the truly 'invincible sun', replacing the festival of Mithras. In the north of Europe, where the midwinter festival was originally celebrated on that date, this earlier festival contributed to the popularity of the Christian festival. In Scandinavia the feast is still named after the pre-Christian one: Yule.

The other date in the year connected to the turning of the sun – 21 June, the beginning of summer – was linked by the church with the predecessor of Christ, John the Baptist (born half a year earlier, according to Luke 1.26).

This feast is now celebrated on 24 June, in connection with the pre-Christian festival. In many areas of Europe, including the Netherlands, the feast is celebrated with a procession at places where there are chapels of St John the Baptist. The words in the Gospel of St John, 'He must increase, but I must decrease' (John 3.30) were reinterpreted with reference to the increasing and decreasing of the sun. For Christ was seen and spoken of with the word of the prophet, as 'the sun of righteousness' (Malachi 4.2).

In connection with the cutting-down of the holy oak at Geismar, mentioned earlier, it is interesting to note the example of a basilica in Scherpenheuvel, in the Netherlands, built on a spot where a German oak supposedly once stood. In the church, one finds a replica of the oak. And near Antwerp, Belgium, there is a place called 'Jesus-oak'.

There are, by the way, historians who question the rather militant image of Boniface and Willibrord. Willibrord, for example, was not the destroyer he is sometimes depicted as. The hammer of St Martin with which he is supposed to have knocked down holy images was more of a liturgical object. The copy on display in the museum in Utrecht does not show any trace of any actual use as a hammer![7]

Columbanus the Younger (d. 615) used the ruins of a temple of Diana for the rebuilding of his monastery church. St Columba spoke of Christ as 'my druid'![8] The archangel Michael replaced Thor in many places, such as Glastonbury. Is it more than a coincidence that Hercules banned wild animals for Crete and St Paul did the same?[9]

In due time St Mary, the mother of Jesus, took over the role of Isis, Cybele and Diana as the great mother of all life and nature. It is no accident that at the end of the fourth century and the beginning of the fifth Mary is pictured in the very same position as Isis, divine mother of Horus. The cult of Isis had a large influence on that of Mary. It was only in the sixth century that the temple of Isis in Egypt was closed. Between 400 and 500, the temple of Isis in Soisson in France was dedicated to the holy virgin Mary. The temple of Athens, the Parthenon, became between 500 and 600 a church of Mary. It is sometimes said that in the Holy Spirit the Old European goddess Mater Matuta continued to live: 'In the third person of the Trinity the goddess of Old Europe has taken a fixed abode.'[10] Ephesus was the place of the cult of Cybele/Demeter, the virgin mother, symbol of Mother Earth. She is venerated under many names: Gaia or Gaea, Rhea, Cybele, Hera, Demeter, Maia, Anna Perenna, Don, Dana, Anna. Is it a great wonder that the mother of Mary received the name Anna?[11]

In the popularity of the Grail in England and Wales, as well as on the Continent, one finds a continuation of the old Celtic tradition of the miraculous food-producing chalice. The stories became popular when the importance of Christian communion and the veneration of Mary increased.

In Christian art, one is struck by the continuity with pre-Christian images: the apostles are depicted as *rhetors oratots*; Christ as the good shepherd is like Hermes, who carried a ram; the Madonna with child takes over pictures of Isis and her son Horus; the bearded Christ (the earliest depictions being of a shaven young man) may go back to images of Asclepius and Zeus.

In the transition from paganism to Christianity in Ireland and Wales, one finds female saints whose powers and character are very similar to those of earlier goddesses. Some writers of *vita* gave the saints the status of gods. These were transformed into holy women. Some pagan gods and heroes of Celtic myths were transformed into saints.[12] The inculturation of the Holy Brigit and the associations with the goddess Brigit are an outstanding example of this: 'As a native saint with culturally familiar characteristics, she provided the church of Kildare with a means of entrenching Christianity in Irish society and provided a continuity on a popular level for long and widely held beliefs.'[13]

From this evidence, one may conclude that the church in the period of early Christianization related to existing holy places, times, persons and stories. It took on the colour of its environment. Like any religious community, Christianity has, in its rituals, made use of existing myths and symbols and integrated them into a new order. The church interpreted her message as she transmitted it within the new European context, retaining many resonances with the past.

One might ask, then, why people were so much in need of holy places, holy times and holy persons. Is this need felt less today, at least in the

West, than it was in the past? In my opinion, these examples show that men and women throughout the centuries, even today, need holy places, mountains, rivers – even if it is only a certain corner of one's own house. For spiritual survival today, we need to set aside certain times, places and exemplary figures in order to be able to continue our pilgrimage in life.

Gospel and culture

My next concern is how we can learn from these examples and relate them to contemporary culture – particularly to literature, art and music.

Literature

It is often said that we are now living in a time of the end of the great narratives, in the sense of those systems that could give us overall answers to all questions. In what way did the church previously make the connection with literature, and how can we relate the great story to the myths and stories of today?

Every mythology, however traditional it may be, is changed by the alchemy of the writer. The true writer is always somebody who changes myths or invents them. 'A book must be like an axe to break the ice of the soul,' Franz Kafka said. What George Steiner, in his book about the Antigone legend, said of Sophocles' drama is true for any great piece of art: there are eternal themes of conflict between divine and human law, between the individual conscience and public demand, between old and young, between woman and man, between respect for history and what is newly ordained, and so on.[14]

Literature is important for the church in many ways. 'One can learn more theology from creative writers than from the study of religion.'[15] According to the Dutch theologian K. H. Miskotte, the modern person looks in such books for what was once found in 'the dusky, upwards-directed vaults of the churches. He does not kneel down anymore; he reads the riddle of his unasked-for existence.'[16]

Many biblical stories are mirrored in contemporary world literature.[17] Different examples could be given to illustrate how the connection between gospel and literature can be made. Not as two opposed entities, not gospel *or* literature, but gospel *and* literature – and sometimes, perhaps, literature as gospel.

Some examples: the most important myths in the work and personal lives of Tolstoy and Dostoevsky were, according to George Steiner, religious. Throughout their lives, both writers were, like Jacob, wrestling with the angel and demanded that this angel reveal a coherent myth about God and a verifiable story about God's role in the fate of humanity. Tolstoy and Dostoevsky were *religious* artists in the same sense as the builders of the cathedrals were, or Michelangelo when he made the image of the eternal in the Sistine chapel. They were possessed by the idea of God and traveled their lives as if on the way to Damascus.[18]

In Dostoevsky's *The Brother Karamazov*, Ivan (the atheist) mainly talks, but Alyosha (the Christian) acts. Dostoevsky was convinced that, in the last analysis, rational arguments were powerless to answer theological questions: 'Therefore Alyosha does not reason with Ivan, states Zosima, nor with the old Karamazov, nor Christ with the great inquisitor, but they answer again and again with an act of love. No arguments are put over against each other, but manners of existence.'[19] An important part of Dostoevsky's fiction was an explanation of the New Testament.

Novels such as Joseph Conrad's *Heart of Darkness*, Thomas Mann's *Mountain of Purification* and James Joyce's *Ulysses* are often quoted as modern literary examples of the quest.[20] Joyce carried the vision of his home and the emotion of his earlier faith everywhere with him from his native Dublin. He called his short stories and sketches about Dublin 'epiphanies', using this religious phrase for a sudden insight into the life of an artist. He looked continually for myths that transcended time and were part of the life of people everywhere. 'People in general, not people in particular, are Joyce's subject.' Leopold Bloom in *Ulysses* is a Dublin Jew but also the wandering Jew, and Stephen Dedalus, the Dubliner poet, acts out the eternal search of fathers and sons to find one another.[21] 'Stephen is the image of Lucifer, an outcast out of free will and irreconcilable until his last gasp. Bloom is Christ (or, as the book says, another, a stranger).'[22] Joyce's pilgrimage and his effort to built an *ecclesia* for civilization ended partly, according to Steiner, in frustration.

Gospel and art: the example of Vincent van Gogh

I would like to defend the thesis that Vincent van Gogh, who started out as an evangelist in his youth, remained one as an artist and painter. He did not give up his Christian faith, but it changed.[23]

Was there a break with his Christian faith, as is often suggested? Is there discontinuity between the first, 'active', part of his life (1870–80) and the second (1880–90)? Did he begin to despise the God of Scripture and of the pastors, and did he turn to the god of nature? Did he want to establish a new community (cf. the *ecclesia*, like Joyce), 'the yellow house', under a new god, the sun of the Midi in southern France?[24] Did the 'sun' take the place of Christ? Did father Millet (the painter) and father Michelet (the writer) replace his own father, the pastor? Is literature (French literature, for example) replacing the Bible? Is art replacing religion, or did art *become* his religion?

To me these are false dilemmas. As an evangelist and as a painter, Van Gogh wanted to bring consolation to people. Like Jesus, he was moved by the worn out, the poor, the bruised ones of the 'hard times', as Charles Dickens would call the situation of people in nineteenth-century England. One example that illustrates my point is his painting *Still Life With Open Bible*. It shows a large, 'dark' copy of the Bible. There is an extinguished candle and, in front, a shining yellow copy of Zola's book *La joie de vivre*, with the title clearly readable. 'Here you are,' some people say: the dark, written-off Bible, the light extinguished and instead the yellow light bringing the joy of life that literature provides. However, I would like to argue with that interpretation. This Bible is the Bible that belonged to his father, who had passed away just a few weeks before. The extinguished candle refers to the extinguished life of his father, not to the Bible.

Van Gogh knew the contents of the Bible very well. He was an ardent reader of the Bible in his youth, but also spoke of it with appreciation in his later life. In this painting, the Bible lies open at Isaiah 53, one of the so-called 'hymns of the suffering servant of the Lord'. It is unthinkable that Van Gogh intended to play down the significance of this passage. Several times in his letters to his brother Theo he refers to this passage. It is striking that while in the Hague where he was taking care of Sien, as she is called, a prostitute with her child, he drew her literally in her naked misery – giving this etching the title *Sorrow*. Can we not say that he intended to show her as a 'woman of sorrows'?

Next to the Bible is the book by Zola. To suggest that it replaces the Bible is incorrect. On the contrary, it is this book which he uses to interpret the Bible. In one of his letters to Theo (161), referring to the authors Jules Michelet, Harriet Beecher Stowe, Thomas Carlyle and George Eliot, he writes that the Bible remains eternally, but these authors – like many others – rather than stating that the gospel is not of value any more, show how it can be applied in our time. Six years later, in 1887, he writes to his sister telling her to read works by Guy de Maupassant, Francois Rabelais, Henri Rochefort Goncourts, Voltaire's *Candide*, books by the brothers Edmund L. A. H. and Jules A. de Goncourts (*Germinie Lacerteux en La Fille Elisa),* Zola's *L'Assommoir* and *La joie de vivre,* and the writings of Jean Richepin, Alphonse Daudet and Joris-Karl Huysmans. He then continues: 'Is the Bible not enough for us? In these days I believe that Jesus himself would say to those who sit down in melancholy, "It is not here, get up and go. Why are you looking for the living among the dead?"'[25]

Still Life With Open Bible affirms that significant novels express the truths of the Bible for a contemporary audience. Vincent saw in one of the figures in Zola's novel, Pauline Quenu, like the Servant in Isaiah, an incarnation of renunciation, sacrifice and charity. 'But it was fitting that Zola expressed the servant mission for a new age in the form of a new age.'[26]

The gospel and music

In what way did the church relate in the past to music, and how could it be done today? Music is a means by which we may express feelings more accurately than by words, as Felix Mendelssohn said.

The revelation of God on Mount Sinai was related to music (a very loud trumpet blast, Exodus 19.16). The walls of Jericho fell through a liturgical, musical conquest (Joshua 6). Elisha was prophetically inspired by the help of music: '"Now bring me someone who can play the lyre." And as the musician played, the hand of Yahweh came on him' (2 Kings 3.15). King Saul's evil spirits were exorcized by the music of the young shepherd David on the harp (1 Samuel 16.23).

Early Christian gatherings were sober but also inspired by the psalmody of the synagogue, which was soon introduced in the church. Ambrose introduced hymns. St Augustine (d. 430) was in favour of hymnody. In the West, Gregorian music was developed.

Hildegard of Bingen, who founded religious communities, composed music and wrote liturgical songs. She saw herself as an instrument of the divine spirit, 'the sound of the trumpet, of the living light'.[27] She drew much inspiration from The Song of Songs. Psalms and hymns remind us of the bliss of the uncorrupted state at the beginning of creation and make us receptive to the presence of God. For Hildegard, there was a connection between word and the humanity of Jesus, while music related to the spiritual and harmonic unity of the divine Trinity. Martin Luther saw music as a gift and a servant of God, as a working of the Holy Spirit, and therefore an essential element in worship and preaching.

One could refer in this context to the importance and use of the organ in church. Once an instrument in the secular marketplace, it was drawn into the church. Certain secular tunes were 'lifted up to a new level' in the time of the Reformation. Charles Wesley asked why the devil should have the good tunes. 'Moody and Sankey favorites' were very popular; a clown in a London circus about a hundred years ago once mocked these songs, whereupon the audience started to sing one and then another until the clown was forced to leave the ring.

Popular music[28]

Music is very important for young people in our societies. The one who does not feel completely at home on this earth, not settling anywhere but making a pilgrimage, is the one who finds solace in a song. Music brings life into a mortal existence. Many are talking about the wholesome work of music. Penetration, participation and transcendence happen in music through the miracle of hearing. The ear makes another reality possible; the other reality of music 'enters, penetrates my inner being and I become a citizen of the space of music'. Pop artists are in the middle of the mystery of life, wrestling with it, seeking to confront the dark, deadly forces in their search for real life. Rock fans do not sit down in laziness; the music makes them get up and go out into the adventure of life. Such music invites one to confront one's own feelings, one's own love of life (or weariness with life), one's disappointments and one's pain.

The best music both tears down and builds up. The stories of Joshua from the Bible and Amphion from Greek mythology illustrate this function. One knows the story of Joshua and the conquest of Jericho: the walls tumbled down at the sound of the ram's horn trumpets (Joshua 6). Amphion, on the other had, played his magic lyre in order to get stones moving to build a wall. Rock music unites the forces of Joshua and Amphion. This happens in any concert: with the passion of the horn blowers of Jericho the old environment is pulverized, and with the magic of Amphion the new enclosure is created in which one is taken up. Musicians are doing with sound what painters are doing with images.

Criteria

Is it possible in this relating of gospel and culture (literature, art, music) to single out criteria for what is or what is not acceptable?[29] How does one develop such criteria? When are myths true, and when are they false? How does one relate myths or stories from the Bible to the stories of people today?

One has to be conscious of the ambivalence of each culture, including European and Western culture. Myths and stories can become empty and shallow; they can become dangerous ideologies. Do you understand what you read, do you understand what you see? In both cases you need an interpreter.

In the ecumenical movement, the dominant paradigm became Christo-centric universalism.[30] I would prefer to use as a model for Europe 'Christ-centred syncretism' (M. M. Thomas).

The church father Jerome (d. 420) can be quoted as an example of how the church wrestled with the question of relating to culture, in his case to classical secular culture. He was, of course, known as the translator of the Bible into Latin, the Vulgate, and was a pupil of the Roman grammarian Donatus, author of an extensive commentary on Roman literature, especially the writers of comedies such as Terence and Virgil. Jerome became, in turn, an interpreter of the Bible. According to him, it was possible to build a bridge between secular learning and the gospel. Not everything had to be rejected; elements of Graeco-Roman culture could be used in the service of spreading and deepening the Christian faith. Did not St Paul also, according to Jerome, make use of classical authors (he had several direct quotations from secular literature)?

To explain the way in which he made use of classical literature, Jerome used the image of bees, which take honey from some flowers and fly past others. When the Jews left Egypt, they robbed the Egyptians of gold and silver, which they melted to make vessels for worship. Jerome follows a fixed scheme: secular examples and authoritative statements precede biblical and Christian ones. In his argument, classical writers have a certain weight but the Christian examples are the main point. Jerome does, however, contrast the eloquence of pagan literature and the truth of the Christian faith: 'We are pupils of the *piscatores* [fisherman] not of the *oratores*!'[31] Christians who had had some education were, to a certain extent, bored by the fisher language *(sermo piscatorius)* of the Bible.[32]

Characteristic of Jerome's life was the tension he felt. His life was dominated by a dream. He saw himself standing before the throne of Christ, where he was reproached for being more Ciceronian than Christian: '*Ciceronianus es, non Christianus.*' He then took an oath not to read any more secular authors, and stuck to it for the rest of his life.[33]

Culture, even modern European culture, is ambivalent. One should be careful to distinguish authentic and inauthentic ways of contextualization, and the points at which the gospel differs from aspects of modern culture. Some modern myths are false, and one has to combat them. There are negative myths. One has to be critical of the image culture, video games (media coverage of the second Gulf War in 1991 is a case in point). There are victims of the image culture.

A modern Dutch writer, Renata Dorrestein, wrote a book whose title was taken from the words of Christ at the Last Supper, 'This is my body.'[34] Some people found it blasphemous, but in reality she wanted to expose and attack modern Western culture, in which everybody seems to venerate the body (the fitness centre, beauty parlours) and humans are seen as the makers of their own lives.

In the 1930s, K. H. Miskotte related – and rightly so – the revived German paganism and the gospel, in his book *Edda en Thora* (a comparison of the German and Israelite religions).[35] Alfred Rosenberg's book *The Myths of the Twentieth Century* has been called the slide negative of *Edda en Thora*.[36]

A Dutch literary figure, C. Rijnsdorp, tells of how he was influenced, at the age of 15, by two booklets by Felix Dahn: *Odins wraak* and *Odins troost* (*Odin's Wrath* and *Odin's Consolation*). Both books were steeped in romantic admiration of Germanic mythology. He tells us that he was in a romantic pantheistic period and remembers how, after reading the books, he was at a crossroads between paganism and Christianity.[37]

I have mentioned positive ways in which the church related in the past to music and could do so today. Yet we know how music was used, or rather misused, in the time of the Nazis, as described by Günter Grass in the novel *Die Blechtrommel*. The wordless myth of music can in our culture – a culture 'after the word' (Steiner) and without myths – also express spiritual longing, consolation and inspiration.

'Religion disappears but God remains,' the French writer Victor Hugo claimed in the nineteenth century. If this was true then, is it true today? Voluminous books have been published about the 'history' (Karen Armstong) and 'biography' (Jack Miles) of God. The latter called his book a 'topper', an end point. Is one allowed to speak again about Him or Her?

But how does one speak about the 'most soiled of all human words: God', as Martin Buber once said?

We live in a time of secularization. There seems to be minimal knowledge of iconography and symbolism. Many people are living in a kind of religious-symbolic vacuum,[38] where a kind of agnosticism reigns as far as symbols are concerned. Is it because of lack of knowledge, lack of will or lack of interest that people today do no want to deal with these issues? Not necessarily. We in the Netherlands live in a very flat country and possibly, as some have suggested, this makes us also flat, superficial people. A century ago Vincent van Gogh warned in his letters:

> For look, one thought that the earth was flat. That is true today from Paris to Asnières, for example.

> Yet science shows that the earth is round, which nobody denies today. Despite that, today one thinks that life is flat and runs from birth to death. But life is probably round and *qua* extent and *qua* possibilities much greater than the hemisphere that we know today.[39]

If one wants to speak today about this subject, one needs to clear out a lot of accretion in order to understand what really matters. The author of *God: A Biography* sees himself as someone who cleans the soiled stained-glass windows of the cathedral in order that the sun can shine through again to illuminate the treasures that are there.

If one can take down the barriers of lack of knowledge of, indifference to and unwillingness to study the religious message, what contribution could one make in order that the gospel message would be more understandable and imaginable in our contemporary world?

In the West, we have constructed a wall between word and image whereby a painter such as Van Gogh is disqualified as a theological source. 'The Western prejudice in favour of "God as Word" has probably led to the avoidance of one who took seriously God as Image.'[40] Jan Willem Schulte Northolt, the Dutch poet and scholar, commented in his last lecture, 'About God and Me', that when he wanted to know who God was, he did not take refuge in theology but in poetry. He did not penetrate the secrets of existence with the help of philosophy but of poetry.[41] In theology – the theology of Karl Barth – he did not find room for further imagination.

In art, literature and ordinary life, one can find again and again, like Jesus in the parables, imaginative stories and telling images. I would like to relate such a story:

Friday, 26 April 1996, was the tenth anniversary of the disaster at the Chernobyl nuclear reactor. I saw a programme on Dutch television that consisted of an impressive interview with one of the survivors. He was brought into the picture with the wounds that require daily care. Only with the help of a drive in Germany to raise funds for exorbitantly expensive medicine had he been kept alive. Most moving was his account of what had happened the day of the explosion. When it took place, he was off duty. He could have stayed away, but without any protective clothing – which was not available – he had entered the plant in order to save friends. He found a wounded and dying friend and carried him on his shoulders out of the nuclear reactor. At the place where the body of his friend had rested, the deadly radiation entered his body.

Is this not a modern, new and authentic story, an icon through which one hears and sees what the real service of God – which is always at the same time service of humanity –means? No one has greater love than he lays down his life for his friends (John 15.13).

In another Dutch television programme, about Jesus and images of him today, the title song contained the phrase 'description unknown'. But one can ask, 'Is he really unknown?' Or is it indifference, lack of interest, unwillingness that make one want to get rid of this telling example? Any child could see how the face of this man from Chernobyl lit up. Does not the world remain in existence because of just such people?

This story also reminds me of a song by the group Oasis that deals with indestructible hope. In it, one hears the protest against the internal and external powers that make young people let the dreams they had be washed away by the gods of this century, in particular, love of money. As a child, according to this song, you wanted to become a spaceman, but it was taken from you and you were appeased with money in order to give up on your dreams. But the song ends by making it clear that it is not too late:

> It's strange how your dreams change as you're
> growing older
> You don't wanna be no spaceman, you just want
> gold,
> All the dream stealers are lying awake.
> But if you wanna be a spaceman,
> It's still not too late.

The world becomes a hell when there is no longer any hope. According to Dante in *The Divine Comedy,* there are people in hell who can no longer use verbs in the future tense: 'One can speak of eternal damnation when we are not able to use the grammar of the future anymore, that is, the grammar of hope.'[42] But why should we not be able, if we have forgotten that grammar, to learn it anew?

NOTES

1. See my *Europe: Was It Ever Really Christian?*, London, 1994, and *Secularized Europe: Who Will Carry Off Its Soul?*, Geneva, 1996.
2. See Dorothee Sölle, *Opwellingen van moed: Aanzet tot een andere manier van denken*, Baarn, 1994, p. 139.
3. Joseph Campbell, *The Power of* Myth, New York and London, 1988, p. 39.
4. Roger Sherman Loomis, *Celtic Myth and Arthurian Romance*, London, 1993, p. 39.
5. Eugen Drewermann, *Tiefenspsychologie und Exegese: (Band II) Die Wahrheit der Werke un der Worte, Wunder, Vision, Weissaguing – Apokalypse, Geschichte, Gleichnis*, Olten und Freiburg, 1986, p. 127.
6. See Sölle, p. 147.
7. I owe this information to Adriaan H. Bredero.
8. See William Reeves, *The Life of St Columba, Founder of Hy, written by Adamman, ninth abbot of that Monastary*, Dublin, 1857, p. 74. I owe this reference to Jacqueline Borsje.
9. See Jacqueline Borsje, *From Chaos to Enemy: Encounters with Monsters in Early Irish Texts – An investigation related to the process of christianisation and the concept of evil*, Turnhout, 1996, p. 146, Note 345.
10. See Gerard de Haas, *Publieke religie: Voorchristelijke patronen in ons religieus gedrag*, Baarn, 1994, pp. 106–7.
11. Hubert Dethier, *De beet van de adder: Deel 1 De leerstoelen der deugd – Heterodoxen en ketters in de middeleeuwen*, Brussels, 1994, p. 58.
12. Miranda Green, *Celtic Goddesses, Warriors, Virgins and Mothers*, London, 1995, p. 190.

13. Dorothy Ann Bray, 'St Brigit and the fire from heaven', *Études Celtiques* (1992), p. 112.
14. Quoted by Jacques De Visscher in George Steiner, *Heeft de waarheid toekomst? Essays*, Baarn, 1991, p. 16. See also George Steiner, *Antigiones: The Antigone Myth in Western Literature, Art and Thought*, Oxford, 1984.
15. Robert W. Brockway, *Myth from the Ice Age to Mickey Mouse*, State University of New York Press, 1993, p. 100.
16. Quoted by Erik Borgman, *Alexamenos aanbidt zijn God: Theologische essays voor sceptische lezers*, Zoetermeer, 1994, p. 117.
17. See for instance T.M. Gilhuis, *Nu dan, luister: Bijbelse verhalen nieuw gehoord (Listen Well: Biblical stories heard in a new way)*, Kampen, 1990.
18. George Steiner, *Tolstoj of Dostojevski: Een oefening in de oude kritiek*, Amsterdam, 1992, p. 243.
19. Hans Küng and Walter Jens, *Wereldliteratuur en religie: Pascal, Gryphius, Lessing, Hölderin, Novalis, Kierkegaard, Dostojewski, Kafka*, Hilversum, 1986, pp. 225, 229.
20. Some find this motive in John Updike's *Rabbit Run* and William Burrough's *The Naked Lunch* (Brockway, p. 105).
21. *The Reader's Companion to World Literature*, Mentor, 1956, p. 239.
22. Steiner 1992, p. 319, who quotes Blackmur in *Anni Mirabiles*.
23. For a more extensive treatment of this theme see my *A Sort of Bible: Vincent van Gogh as Evangelist*, London, 2000.
24. Tsokasa Kodera, *Vincent van Gogh: Christinanity versus Nature*, dissertation, University of Amsterdam, 1988, p. 163.
25. Cliff Edwards, *Van Gogh and God: A Creative Spiritual Quest*, Chicago, 1989, p. 51.
26. Edwards, p. 50.
27. Marjolein de Vos, 11 October 1996.
28. I am using insights from Jan Koenot, *Voorbij de woorden: Essays over rock, cultuur en religie*, Baarn, 1996.
29. Eugene L. Stockwell, 1988, quoted by Bert Hoedemaker, 'Evangelie en cultuur: Kantekeningen bij een voortgaande oecumenische discussie', in H. S.

Benjamins et al., *Evangelie en beschaving: Studies bij het afscheid van Hans Roldanus*, The Hague, 1995, p. 172: 'If we take seriously the theological assumption of the Gospel transforming cultures from within, and if the Gospel cannot be considered independent from its various cultural expressions, how can we single out universally applicable Gospel criteria?'

30. Hoedemaker, pp. 174–5.
31. G. Bartelink, 'Evangelie en profane literatuur in de brieven van Hiëronymus', in *Roldanus*, pp. 95 , 97, 100–102, 104–6.
32. Danny Praet, *De God der Goden: De christianisering van het romeinse Rijk*, Kampen, 1995, p. 111.
33. Bartelink, p. 100.
34. *Want dit is mijn lichaam*, Zutphen, 1997.
35. K. H. Miskotte, *Edda en Thora: Een vergelijking van germaansche en Israëlitische religie*, Nijkerk, 1939.
36. Willem van der Meiden quoted in C. D. van Troostwijk, J. Beumer and D. Stegeman (eds), *Wij willen het heidendom eeren Miskotte in de nieuwe tijd*, Baarn, 1994, p. 58.
37. C Rijnsdorp, *Laatste gedachten*, Kampen, p. 570.
38. Jacques De Visscher, *Een te voltooien leven: over de rituelen van de moderne mens*, Kampen, 1996, pp. 15, 17, 187.
39. Letter nr. 635; letter to Emile Bernard B8.
40. Edwards, pp. XV, 189.
41. JanWillem Schulte Nordholt, *Verzamelende gedichten*, Baarn, 1989, quoted by E. L. H. M. van de Loo and others, *Kunst van geloven*, Baarn, 1996, p. 148.
42. Quoted in Steiner 1991, p. 46.

Between Augustine and Columba[1]

Adrian Hastings

On 27 May 597, the Roman monk Augustine and his companions, dispatched by Pope Gregory I, landed on the coast of the Kentish kingdom of Ethelbert to restart the Christian church in what was becoming England. Thirteen days later, on 9 June, Columba, the dominant figure in the Irish evangelization of what was to become Scotland, died on the island of Iona. The church of Augustine spread northwards from Canterbury to London and even York. The church of Columba spread southwards from Iona to Lindisfarne.

Contrast and coalescence

In many ways the Christianization of the greater part of Britain in the hundred and fifty years from the age of Columba to that of Bede can be interpreted in terms of the relationship between these two movements. How far did they differ, how far coalesce? Why did they differ at all, and what, if anything, can one learn from the tensions between them?

A picture of contrast is easy enough to draw, and has been time and again, beginning with Bede's account of the argument at Whitby. The nodal point does, of course, lie there. The Synod of Whitby was held on the Northumbrian coast in 664 to settle the date on which Easter should be observed. No issue was, in practice, more important. A religious community is held together by its ritual, and Easter was the central festival of the Christian church.

With a shortage of priests and very considerable distances, most of the Northumbrian laity can hardly have attended mass very regularly. Easter Sunday was the occasion when king and people gathered together to assert commitment to their new faith. But in the Northumbria of King Oswy, that had become a most painful moment of division. While he was celebrating Easter on the Sunday favoured by Bishop Colman of

Lindisfarne and his Scottish (or Irish) monks, Queen Eanfled was only at Palm Sunday and still keeping the Lenten fast.

Eanfled was the daughter of Ethelberga and granddaughter of the King Ethelbert of Kent who had received Augustine. When Eanfled's father, Edwin, the first Christian king of Northumbria, was killed in battle, Ethelberga returned to Kent with her daughter and Paulinus, the Bishop of York. From there Eanfled had returned to marry Oswy.

Northumbria was, by this time, the point where the Roman and Ionan missions had come to overlap, a little confusingly. Oswald, Oswy's predecessor, had been in exile in Scotland during Edwin's reign. There he had been baptized, and from there he had later brought missionaries to Northumbria, led by Aidan. Bernicia, the northern part of Northumbria, had been evangelized principally from Lindisfarne, the Iona of northern England. But the Christianity of Deira, its southern half, was focused on York, where Paulinus had been bishop, following Pope Gregory's instructions to revive this ancient British see as the metropolitan for the north.

Under Oswy, Bernicia and Deira were united and Northumbria's two Christianities merged. So the celebration of Easter – and, of course, all the rest of the calendar, which depended on Easter – had turned into a continual source of irritating division. It could not go on. Oswy called a great meeting at Abbess Hilda's monastery at Whitby for each side to put its case. Colman led the one side, Bishop Agilbert, a Frenchman, the other.

As Agilbert's English was none too good, he asked Wilfrid, the rumbustious young Abbot of Ripon and one of the fiercest upholders of the Roman view, to speak in his stead. Colman appealed to the tradition of Iona and the authority of John the Evangelist. Wilfrid replied by suggesting that the Scots were stupid and that anyone who resisted 'the decrees of the Apostolic See' by clinging to the outdated practices of a few oddities in a corner of a remote island was clearly guilty of grave sin. Even if 'your Columba' really was a saint, how can he be compared with the Prince of the Apostles? 'Thou art Peter, and upon this rock I will build my church.'

King Oswy found this argument irrefutable, and henceforth Northumbria held to the practices of Rome while Colman retreated sadly enough with a group of his monks, both Irish and English, first to Iona and then to Ireland. Bede, writing about all this seventy years later, was wholly convinced that Wilfrid was right: Roman authority must not be challenged, and the Irish way of computing Easter was just wrong. Bede was a fanatic for computation, but he was as conscious of his Irish monastic heritage as of the Roman. The great strength of his history was the attempt to do justice to both, and he stresses the gentle charm, the austerity and the good sense of Colman and his predecessors, Aidan and Cuthbert above all. They are, in a way, the favoured heroes of his whole story.

Grand as Wilfrid was, he does not come across half so attractively. The Cardinal Manning of the seventh century, as he has been described – not unfairly – Wilfrid was the upper-class, international-minded bishop, thoroughly at home in Rome or Lyons, who picked up property as fast as Aidan had given it away, loved a large retinue and engaged in acrimonious law suits. He felt it incumbent on him to imitate, in all its worldly impressiveness, the episcopal style he had observed in Lyons. Yet his religious and evangelistic activities extended from Hexham to the Isle of Wight and even to Frisia.

Two ages of the Western church

A contrast between Wilfrid and Colman as representing our two missionary traditions could be striking enough, and yet it would be a very misleading one, hugely overstating the differences. Wilfrid was *sui generis* in the English church of his time, and yet within the Irish tradition we can actually find a not unfair comparison, with Columba himself. Both were great saints, towering above their contemporaries in ability to combine monastic commitment with a dominant, if at times insensitive, role in public life. Columba was of far grander blood than Wilfrid, and one feels throughout his life the tension between the scholarly ascetic and the ecclesiastical politician who became more or less the acknowledged leader of the Irish of western Scotland and continued to exert a powerful influence on the Irish mainland. Certainly he was, in this, no more typical of Irish monasticism than Wilfrid was of Roman monasticism.

The conflict as it appears from the story of the Synod of Whitby should not be overdone. Bede's personal fascination with the Easter issue perhaps made him play it up as a central point in his history a good deal more than was really justified. In fact, most of Ireland had already accepted the Roman dating well before Whitby, and most of the Irish party at Whitby – not only King Oswy but also Bishop Chad and Abbess Hilda – adopted it easily enough. St Cuthbert, an English monk and prior of Melrose by the time of Whitby, transferred from the one system to the other and became a bishop at the insistence of Archbishop Theodore, but was manifestly always within the Iona tradition.

The interfertilization of Ireland, England, France and Rome at this time was continual and mattered far more than any element of dispute. Many an Englishman studied in Ireland. Wilfrid began his religious career at Lindisfarne. There were Irish monks not only in Northumbria but in Sussex. At no point was there any lasting disagreement of principle between the two traditions and yet, undeniably, there was a considerable difference in ethos and priorities, an understanding of which will throw light on the strengths of both.

In a way, they belong to two distinct ages of the Western church. The Irish model grew naturally out of the way things had been in the British Christian church, the old dioceses of London, York and doubtless others in the fourth and fifth centuries. The British church can have been little different from that of Gaul or elsewhere in the West. It consisted of town-based dioceses, each led by a group of clergy, around a bishop, most of whom will have been elderly married men – devout butchers, bakers and candlestick-makers who had, all the same, been through the schools of their town.

Few were of much distinction or theological erudition; they are as anonymous as almost everyone else in late Roman Britain, but they kept the church going and quietly expanding, grounded on the urban culture of the late empire. Patrick's father was a deacon, his grandfather a priest, doubtless fairly typical members of the early fifth-century clergy. When faced with an outbreak of Pelagianism in the 420s and 430s, the clergy of Britain may have been only too aware of their own theological limitations, so they appealed to the church of Gaul to sort out their doctrinal confusions and two bishops, Germanus of Auxerre and Lupus of Troyes, came over to affirm – in an Augustinian way – the necessity of grace.

From the early fifth century, the old-fashioned ministry of British Christianity was being supplemented in another way, too, again via Gaul. In the year 386, Augustine of Hippo, at the time a professor in Milan, was told an exciting story by a civil-servant friend, Ponticianus, who had recently come from Trier, about the effect of reading Athanasius' *Life of Antony* on some friends of his in Trier, who had immediately decided to join a group of monks. Although at the time Augustine had never heard of this new form of Christian life, the incident was more than twenty years after Martin of Tours had begun the first monastery in Gaul. Monasticism was spreading everywhere and it would be amazing if it did not spread into Britain, too. A fifth-century church in the town of Canterbury was already dedicated to Martin, as was that of Ninian in Whitehorn. The latter was most likely itself a monastery. We can best see Ninian, a contemporary of Patrick, representing both the expansive and the monastic dimension in British Christianity, carrying it into Pictish territory just before its principal base in the east of the country was overwhelmed by pagan Saxon invaders.

The monasticism that must have been carried via Gaul to Britain in the fifth century, to spread in Wales and Ireland in the sixth, was exactly the monasticism of Antony, Martin and the like. It was not purely or principally eremitical, but it was not very fully coenobitical either, more resembling what in the east was called the *Lavra* – a group of monks sharing a church and a measure of common life but spending much time on their own and fairly free to wander. Extreme asceticism, the selection of remote places for habitation, but also a good deal of to-ing and fro-ing characterized this kind of life. Celtic monasticism was basically simply oriental monasticism, replacing the desert with the rocky islands of the Atlantic seaboard.

In the Gaul and, undoubtedly, the Britain of the fifth century, monasticism in no way replaced the existing church structure of the urban diocese, though there probably developed an understandable tendency to choose for bishop not an ordained local lawyer – or whatever – but a monk with a reputation for holiness. And this could be followed, as in the case of Augustine of Hippo, by the monk-bishop bringing a group of monks to live with him beside the diocesan cathedral, at once transforming the ethos of the local church.

But then something far more decisive happened. The towns of Britain themselves were almost swept away. Most probably a small community of Christians always survived around the shrine of Alban at Verulamium; quite possibly another group kept on praying in the little church of St Martin on the east side of Canterbury. But the old sees disappeared, because the urban communities and culture on which their clerical ministry was founded had been wiped out by the incoming Saxons. Bishops survived in Wales, Ireland and Galloway, but they came inevitably to be based in monasteries – or, more precisely, the remote community of the monastery remained the only viable core institution for a Christianity deprived of towns.

That did not mean, in theory, that abbots were superior to bishops, just as the considerable isolation of the Celtic churches from the rest of Europe did not mean that, for instance, the authority of the see of Rome was not accepted as pre-eminent. But, in practice, the Welsh and Irish churches were forced to develop a shape that suited their society, a shape in which we hear much of monks and monasteries, but little of bishops and dioceses, and in which monastic life remained a rather solitary pursuit.

The Irish pattern

In other ways, however, Irish and Welsh monasteries followed a line of development similar to that going on elsewhere in the West. Thus, in the absence of any other kind of school, they became the principal centres of learning and of the transcription of manuscripts. Comgall's Bangor in the late sixth century, Hadrian's school at Canterbury a century later or Bede's Jarrow were alike distinguished for their classical erudition. Columba himself was famous as a transcriber of manuscripts – Latin manuscripts. But it looks as if the remoteness of Ireland from any larger Latin-speaking society stimulated its monasteries (as those of Wales) to lead Europe in the development of a vernacular literature. If English literature began with Caedmon at Whitby in Hilda's time, then it may owe its origin to the Irish example.

In much of this Columba represents the Irish pattern remarkably well. He was an abbot but never a bishop, he came to dwell on a remote and rocky island, he was both a poet and a scribe. But the great Welsh missionary of a generation earlier, St Samson, may represent it even better. A disciple of St Illtyd and abbot for a while of a monastery on Caldey Island, he moved on to Cornwall, to the Scilly Isles and finally to Dol in Brittany. What dominates the pattern of his lifestyle is the island monastery and the habit of *peregrinatio.* He ends his life as 'Bishop of Dol', though it seems that there was no regular diocese there until centuries later. He was primarily an abbot.

Peregrinatio was a form of asceticism rather than an expression of evangelism. It could be fulfilled by settling on the uninhabited Skelligs. Nevertheless, it prompted evangelism because the wandering monk saw it as a Christian duty to share his faith with what inhabitants there were. Major monasteries effectively developed a *paruchia* of dependent monasteries, churches and congregations, some sort of quasi-diocese unrelated to any specific territorial delimitation. No *paruchia* proved more enduring than the Columban.

When Augustine and his 40 companions landed at Thanet, they carried with them a form of ecclesiastical culture in some ways older than that of the Irish, in other ways more modern. The older ways were somewhat as follows: they were far more diocesan-conscious. Though mostly monks, their instructions were to set up sees rather than monasteries, and sees in urban areas. Pope Gregory knew his history. He knew that there had once been bishops in the towns of London and York, the principal cities of Roman Britain, so he decreed that as soon as possible those two sees should be restored and become metropolitans for two provinces, each of twelve dioceses.

The fact that these and all the Roman towns of Britain now lay in ruins in no way affected the theoretical model or, less than one might imagine, even its implementation. Angles, Saxons and Jutes had probably tended to occupy these cities rather more than we realize. King Ethelbert was clearly well established in Canterbury when Augustine arrived. London and York certainly continued to be inhabited to some extent and proved quite reasonable places for bishops to occupy. They and other former cities probably continued to shelter larger populations than other areas of comparable size. Moreover, they were conveniently linked by the old road system, which continued to be used. A handful of Roman cities could, then, provide the skeleton for the new ecclesiastical order even if, when Archbishop Theodore came in the second half of the seventh century to establish a viable diocesan network right across England, it had to be based in many areas on tribal divisions and the existence of monasteries rather than on the location of towns.

Even in London and Canterbury, however, a Roman type of civic life, on which the old sees had effectively depended for their clerical cadre, no longer existed – in this being quite unlike Rome or Lyons. There a social basis for the old diocesan clerical order still survived; here it did not. The principal available clerical cadre was now a monastic one, something able to provide the vital force for the advancement of the church.

In this the Romans and the Celts at work in Britain were not in reality far apart, but the Romans clung nevertheless to the older model as far as they could. By no means all of Augustine's 40 companions were monks from Rome. Some were clergy who had joined his party in France, and it would seem that it was these non-monastic priests who actually staffed the cathedral at Canterbury while Augustine's monks lived in a separate monastery, though he himself will have belonged to the cathedral community. The early English bishops – Ithamar of Rochester; Deusdedit, the first archbishop of Canterbury to be English, and others – may well not have been monks but rather priests belonging to the diocesan clergy continuing the original Frankish group at the cathedral. But we are told so little of anyone who was not a monk that it is hard to know. Effectively, such a diocesan clergy was supplementary to the monks instead of it being, as intended, the other way round. And this was still more the case for the Celts than for the Romans.

Furthermore, the latter were bringing with them a 'Mark II' type of monasticism, a more tightly communitarian type as reflected in the Rule of St Benedict, but a Benedictinism already modified by the urban needs and responsibilities of Gregory's own monastery of St Andrew's within the city of Rome. Here was a monasticism that had explicitly rejected much of the old Egyptian and Syrian ideal. There remained some room for the advanced to enter into a solitary life, but the Benedictine rule itself was one of a closely structured community with a singularly balanced timetable and decided disapproval of a too-intense ascetical discipline.

Benedict's was not, initially, an urban model and it was not a missionary one – and yet, in the circumstances of Gregory's pastoral and missionary strategy, a monasticism that owed much to Benedictine inspiration became to some extent both. Augustine and his companions were anything but enthusiastic missionaries. Only Gregory's severe insistence got them to England at all. And yet as a consequence of their mission and Gregory's complex instructions, an ideal of missionary Benedictine monasticism seems actually to have been passed across to subsequent generations of the English, to be taken up by Wilfrid, Boniface and others. Even a monk, living according to the Benedictine rule in as stable and unmissionary a way as Bede was at Jarrow, could find himself manifestly caught up in the excitement of the missionary enterprise. But Bede in doing so was, of course, recording an enterprise that he recognized was at least as much Irish as it was Roman. The interplay of the two in his own history is one of the book's most fascinating characteristics. In studying it we may, however, detect more divergences between the two than he himself laid stress upon, preoccupied as he was with the one particular issue of the dating of Easter.

Authority and organization

We have seen a divergence already in the matter of the priority of bishop and diocese. Basically the Romans were in this respect more traditional than the Irish, and in Gregory's greatest work, *The Pastoral Care,* they had a textbook account of just what episcopal responsibility was meant to include. Yet the way they had come to envisage the diocese was actually somewhat untraditional, because in the working Gregorian model a diocese was now clearly subordinate to the province and the metropolitan. The stress in the literature on the significance of the *pallium* sent by Rome to a metropolitan is crucial. Such a thing surely did not exist in the fourth century, but the insistence of Gregory, Theodore, Bede and Boniface on the *pallium* and its meaning cannot be missed. It was not just a matter of an additional vestment, but the symbolism of a new shaping of the church and its authority.

What the Roman missionary endeavour is here focused upon is a far more hierarchically, territorially and legally ordered church than anything the Irish or the Scots, who could hardly get even a map of dioceses straightened out for several more centuries, either wanted or experienced. Behind the *pallium* lay, of course, the authority of Rome. The Irish did not dream of questioning that authority, and it is clear, for example, how Cummian in southern Ireland appealed to it at need. But that was a different thing from organizing a church in which recourse to Rome, both by letter and in person, was something almost normal. For Wilfrid, Theodore or Boniface, that was most surely the case. This provides an impression of external control, largely lacking within the Irish experience. Control must, I suspect, inhibit inculturation. If one senses a particularly profound inculturation of Christianity with the Irish, that was probably a natural corollary of their rather high degree of ecclesiastical isolation, the absence of any systematic control from elsewhere.

In contrast, Augustine and his successors relished a measure of control, because they could experience in the see of Rome not only a vestige of the empire in which Jesus had been born, not only the 'Apostolic See', but also 'the universal church'. They could experience both the universality of the past – in its rich collections of books, documents and amazing buildings – and a universality of the present. If Augustine was himself an Italian, the next great bishop sent by a pope to England was the Greek Theodore, accompanied by the African monk Hadrian. Theodore, rather than Augustine, really shows the Roman system in operation, preoccupied with the establishment of territorial dioceses and the holding of regular synods but also concerned for the reconciliation of the divergent religious traditions within the country, as shown by his trust in the monks of the Irish tradition, such as Cuthbert and Chad.

It is to be remembered that Rome itself, through much of this period, was anything but narrowly Italian. In fact, for the greater part of a century, from the election of John V in 685 to the death of St Zacharias in 752, almost all the popes were either Greek or Syrian – and rather good popes they were, too. Thus when Willibrord went to Rome, it was the Syrian St

Sergius who ordained him archbishop of Frisia. Unless one realizes what 'Roman' actually meant at that time, one loses the moral and universalist context for the missionary preoccupation, from Augustine to Boniface, with establishing a pyramidal church organization of bishops and metropolitans across first Britain and then Germany, all drawing strength and guidance from the Roman see.

Location and kinship ties

No less important than an attitude towards diocesan organization was a divergence in the ethos of monasticism. The Irish looked for remote and wild locations – Iona, Lindisfarne, even the Skelligs – while the Benedictine-inspired monks looked for places far closer to people. Where Wilfrid picked on York, Ripon or Hexham, Aidan and Cuthbert preferred Lindisfarne, with a possibility of further escape to the Farne Islands.

With the place went the type of building. Few of the Irish monasteries had any very substantial building other than a church. Bede comments on the lack of solid buildings at Lindisfarne – how different from the stability of the buildings at his own Jarrow. The Irish were much given to *peregrinatio*, seen as a blessed state, but it was not much different from what Benedict denounced as 'gyrovagism'. Stability of lifestyle and building, undergirded by a steady increase in land ownership, on the one hand, can be contrasted with a spirituality of pilgrimage, a tendency to drift off in the summer months and a lack of concern for construction or land holding, on the other. The one stressed the communal life and the virtues of obedience and moderation, the other a more intense preoccupation with asceticism and an enthusiastic dependence upon providence. 'Let us cast our oars into the sea and give ourselves into God's hands,' declared three enthusiastic students setting off from Ireland on pilgrimage, as described in a story in the Book of Leinster. That sort of gesture would be unlikely to appear in a Roman tale of spiritual endeavour. Bede lived in the one tradition but showered most of his admiration on the other.

There is a further contrast that should not be overlooked. Characteristic of Irish monasticism, particularly clear in the Columban case, was the close link between monastery and kindred, and the preoccupation with a saint's genealogy. While this helped bind the monastic family together, providing great additional endurance, it could also pose a threat to catholicity. Almost all Columba's successors as abbot at Iona for a hundred years and more were close relatives.

In the Roman tradition this could not happen, or at least it could not be sanctioned by the example of the founding saints. Augustine, Paulinus and Theodore were far from their kin, and the ethos of the monastic communities they engendered was very different in consequence. Nevertheless, this contrast, powerful as it can appear, should not be overgeneralized. Even at Iona, Columba's third successor, Fergna, was a 'Brit'. In the case of Columbanus's continental monasteries, the bonding of the kindred must have mattered far less. In this, as in much else, the Columban case is far from being synonymous with 'Irish', let alone 'Celtic'.

Many people belonged in part to both the Columban and the Augustinian traditions. When Bishop Colman sadly departed from Lindisfarne after the Synod of Whitby, taking a considerable number of Irish and English monks with him, they established a monastery on the Irish coast on the island of Inishboffin. However, in summer the Irish went off on a wander while the English gathered in the harvest. Then the Irish returned and the English complained until Colman found a separate site on the mainland for the English to occupy. Here, even though the English had previously been in the essentially Irish community of Lindisfarne, they were now behaving more like Benedictines, while the Irish were clinging to their *peregrinatio.*

Or consider the two Englishmen, Egbert and Willibrord. Both spent years in Ireland, but Egbert finally went to Iona and persuaded the community there to accept the Roman Easter. Willibrord had been a pupil of Wilfrid at Ripon in his early post-Whitby days – the very incarnation, one may feel, of Romanism. But when Willibrord was 20, Wilfrid quarrelled both with King Egfrith of Northumbria and with Archbishop Theodore, and appealed to Rome against their division of his diocese into four. On the way to Rome, he spent a year preaching in Frisia. Willibrord, meanwhile, went to Ireland and stayed there for twelve years, after which it was the Anglo-Irish Egbert who encouraged him to set out for the European mainland as a missionary. Willibrord twice visited Rome, worked in Frisia and became the first archbishop of Utrecht, a church he seems to have modelled quite closely on Canterbury.

Willibrord was the first major English missionary to Europe, leading the way where Boniface and Willibald would follow. He founded the great monastery of Echternach (now in Luxembourg) just 101 years after Columba died and Augustine arrived in Canterbury. What a very great deal had happened in a hundred years! From Columba in Iona via Aidan and Cuthbert in Lindisfarne, from Augustine in Canterbury via Wilfrid and Theodore, to an English missionary establishing, no less decisively, the churches of the Rhineland. But who is to decide whether Willibrord was heir to the Irish missionary tradition or the Roman? He clearly belonged to both.

The English church of the seventh and eighth centuries benefited immeasurably from growing out of the confluence of two traditions, each enriching the other in a variety of ways. One cannot imagine that either movement alone could have done the job with the panache with which together they managed so well. If it would be wrong to say without qualification that the Irish subordinated bishops to abbots, it is unquestionable that for them what mattered most was the spread of monastic powerhouses, places of prayer and calligraphy, while the Romans were far more preoccupied with establishing a network of dioceses as a precondition for the development of pastoral care.[2] The Romans still thought in terms of roads, something the Irish cared little about, not having many at home. For them sea routes mattered a good deal more – and, in any case, they preferred remoteness to approachability. A choice between the call to 'get away from it all' and a sense of evangelical obligation to provide a focal point for larger Christian communities had formed part of the tension within the monastic experience well before the seventh century. The Irish preference was for the first choice but not so rigidly as to exclude the second. It would be a mistake to overstress the remoteness of the Irish monastery or the approachableness of the Roman. Iona, as many a story in Adomnán's *Life of Columba* makes clear, was far from unapproachable, while Comgall's Bangor was as easy to reach, by sea or land, as Canterbury.

An attitude towards road use may, all the same, signify more for the shaping of a spirituality than one might at first imagine. Do roads chiefly provide a locus for one's personal 'peregrination', the exile of 'white martyrdom' that replaced for the Irish the martyrdom of blood, which they never needed to experience? Or do they chiefly represent a tool whereby the pastor can keep in touch with his flock?

Pilgrims and missionaries

The contrast, such as it is, between the Irish and the Roman styles may well be caught through the matter of riding. Aidan represents the finest model of the Irish missionary, though somewhat unusual in his willingness to engage so much time in pastoral ministry. But he remained extremely reluctant to keep a horse. The Irish missionary went on foot; it fitted poverty and the sense of being a pilgrim. The Roman missionary preferred a horse; it was more efficient if you were to get around a vast diocese. There are few stories more gently telling of the contrast in attitudes than that of Archbishop Theodore, the great reconciler, ordering Chad, very much a man of the Irish tradition, whom he had appointed Bishop of Mercia, to ride a horse when he went on mission. Chad was 'most reluctant' to give up the pious exercise of walking, so Theodore, who admired Chad very much, insisted on actually helping him to mount his horse.

Finally, recitation of the psalms. The psalms were central to the lives of the monks of both traditions. Most of them probably knew the entire Psalter by heart, and yet no book was copied more frequently. Columba was himself transcribing it once more, as he had surely done many times before, on the last day of his life. Yet even here there were significant differences. The Irish ideal was, it would seem, to say all 150 psalms every day; the Benedictine rule divided them across a week. The modern breviary has redivided them across no fewer than four weeks! If one considers the implications of reciting the entire Psalter daily and the time it takes, the contrast between two kinds of monasticism, but also between two kinds of missionary endeavour, is usefully clarified. While this comparison is fascinating, it may still be misleading. The Benedictine rule was just that – a rule for a community. Daily recitation of the entire Psalter was more of an ideal – what one might manage on a good day, perhaps largely on one's own. A certain coenobitic restraint is here, too, in prayer to be contrasted with the more solitary Irish pursuit of monastic standards originally set by the fathers of the desert.

NOTES

1. The principal source for this chapter is, of course, Bede's *Historia Ecciesiastica Gentis Anglorum*. Next to it comes *Adomnán of Iona: Life of St Columba*, Penguin, 1995, translated and with notes by Richard Sharpe. These have been supplemented by Henry Mayr-Harting, *The Coming of Christianity to Anglo-Saxon England*, 3rd edn., B. T. Batsford, 1991; Patrick Wormald, 'The Venerable Bede and the "Church of the English", in Geoffrey Rowell (ed.), *The English Religious Tradition and the Genius of Anglicanism*, Ikon, 1992, pp. 13–32; James Campbell (ed.), *The Anglo-Saxons*, Phaidon, 1982; David Farmer, *The Oxford Dictionary of Saints*, 3rd edn., Oxford University Press, 1992; Robin Flower's little classic, *The Irish Tradition*, Clarendon, 1947; Máire Herbert, *lona, Kells, and Derry*, Clarendon, 1988; and Daíbhí Ó Cróinín, *Early Medieval Ireland 400–1200*, Longman, 1995.

2. It is ironic that the modern Irish church and its hierarchy should have been so excessively 'un-Irish' in this regard. By far the most spectacular missionary event in modern Irish history was the National Mission Week held at Dalgan Park, Navan, in September 1968 in honour of the 50th anniversary of the founding of the Columban Fathers, the National Missionary Society. It was striking how, while all the bishops of Ireland attended the formal dinner as guests, they sat in full regalia at a separate table, wholly isolated from the hundreds of missionary participants. In this they represented a bizarre caricature of the Roman model of missionary episcopacy at the celebration of a society whose patron saint – and Ireland's – had exercised great ecclesiastical authority but had never been a bishop.

The Legacy of Columba: Beyond the Celtic Myth

Micheal MacCraith

One August afternoon a few years ago, I was strolling down King's Parade in Cambridge when I noticed a bookshop window display on Celtic spirituality. It was a very interesting assortment of books, with the intellectual qualities of the works on offer in inverse proportion to the lavishness of their design, production and layout. The more bizarre and outlandish the content, the more attractive and artistic the dust jacket. The books that really had something to say on the subject, the scholarly and informed volumes, were conspicuous both by their drabness and by the absence of the word 'Celtic' from their titles. Marketing executives have found that this word is seductive. Place 'Celtic' before anything and it sells.

One of the big dangers of this recent upsurge in things Celtic is that the field is in danger of being taken over by the lunatic fringe, as scholars simply opt out of the contest. At a conference in Dublin in June 1995, Canon A. M. Allchin aptly described the field of Celtic spirituality as one divided between two camps, the scholars and the enthusiasts, with the scholars showing very little enthusiasm and the enthusiasts exhibiting precious little scholarship. Each side needs the other, and on balance it is the enthusiasts who are in most need of having their bizarre excesses curbed by the restraints of sound scholarship.

The making of the myth

Such scholarship tells us, first, that the image of the Celt is a construct. The Celts never called themselves Celts and were never conscious of a so-called Celtic unity. 'The Celts' (or ΚΕΛΤΟΙ) was a vague umbrella term used by the Greeks to categorize peoples who were non-Greek. The Celt is very much associated with the 'other', those who are different from 'us' because they do not speak our language, do not dress like us, have appalling table manners and so on.

Technically speaking, the term Celtic refers to a classification of Indo-European languages that are divided into two groups: Irish, Scottish Gaelic and Manx on the one hand, and Welsh, Breton, Cornish and Gaulish on the other. At a secondary level, the term applies to the material culture and peoples associated with these languages. Scientific interest in these languages came to the fore at the beginning of the eighteenth century and the image of the Celt was constructed during the reaction against the rationalism of the Enlightenment, with renewed emphasis being placed on feelings and the heart, and the cult of primitivism and the Noble Savage coming to the fore. The Celt was tailor-made to fit all these theories, and the development of this image was accelerated by three writers in particular: James Macpherson, Ernst Renan and Matthew Arnold.

James Macpherson (1736–96) was a native speaker of Scottish Gaelic who witnessed, as a young boy, the cruel suppression of the 1745 Jacobite Rising by the Duke of Cumberland's forces. He came to fame and controversy as a result of his so-called translations of the poems of Ossian. To his credit, it must be said that he tapped into a genuine vein of elegy and nostalgia associated with the Fiannaíocht literary tradition common to Gaelic Ireland and Gaelic Scotland, but he accentuated it in a manner more in keeping with the late eighteenth-century drawing room tastes of Edinburgh, London and Paris. While the bleak and gloomy *paysage* of his tales provided an ideal backdrop to the melancholy musings of the bard, Macpherson was doing little more than providing an accurate description of Highland landscape.

The works of Ossian became best-sellers. The Highlanders and their country became conveniently exotic, as fascinating to London tastes as the South Sea Islands but much more accessible, and the suppression of the 1745 insurrection ensured that the Highlanders were attractively different and no longer a threat to the stability of the United Kingdom. The association of the Scottish Celt with otherness and peripherality was already under way. The domestification of this quaint and innocuous Scottish exoticism into mainstream British culture received the highest seal of approval with the annual Balmoralization of the royal family, complete with tartan and kilts.

The image of the Celt received further impetus from a famous essay by Ernst Renan published in 1854, *La poésie des races celtiques.* Renan's essay begins with a journey from the centre to the periphery that is well worth quoting:

> Every one who travels through the Armorican peninsula experiences a change of the most abrupt description, as soon as he leaves behind the district most closely bordering upon the continent, in which the cheerful but commonplace type of face of Normandy and Maine is continually in evidence, and passes into the true Brittany, that which merits its name by language and race. A cold wind arises full of a vague sadness, and carries the soul to other thoughts; the tree-tops are bare and twisted; the heath with its monotony of tint stretches away into the distance; at every step the granite protrudes from a soil too scanty to cover it; a sea that is almost always sombre girdles the horizon with eternal moaning. The same contrast is manifest in the people: to Norman vulgarity, to a plump and prosperous population, happy to live, full of its own interests, egoistical as are all those who make a habit of enjoyment, succeeds a timid and reserved race living altogether within itself, heavy in appearance but capable of profound feeling, and of an adorable delicacy in its religious feeling.

In Renan's essay, we see the paradigm for the treatment of the Celt, the prototype of contemporary marketing that associates 'Celtic' with magical, mythical and misty. In typical nineteenth-century fashion, Renan places undue emphasis on race. He notes that the hatred of the foreigner formed an essential characteristic of the Celtic peoples and that just as they resisted foreign invasions in the past, they were still resisting the advance of modern civilization. Despite its constant defence of desperate causes, the Celtic race apparently had no aptitude for political life. If sex could be assigned to nations as to individuals, then the Celtic race would be an essentially feminine one. Gender scholars and feminists would have a field day with Renan. The Celts have worn themselves out in taking dreams for realities – even their tendency to drunkenness is due to their invincible need for illusion. And with a gem of a statement that would raise the hackles of most theologians, Renan asserts that 'this gentle little race was naturally Christian. Far from changing them, and taking away some of their qualities, Christianity finished and perfected them.' Somewhat paradoxically, however, he had previously described Joan of Arc as more Celtic than Christian.

What emerges from Renan's identikit of the Celts is a somewhat confused picture. On the one hand, they have the very positive traits of religious feeling and visionary qualities, while on the other, they are out of tune with modern civilization and incapable of governing themselves. Furthermore, these admirable qualities seem to be inextricably linked to their remoteness and ineptitude for modernity and political life. If the Celts modernized themselves, they would lose their spirituality. The Celts therefore cannot be allowed to modernize. Not only would the Celts make a disastrous shambles of governing themselves, but they would lose their spiritual qualities into the bargain. Hence they cannot be afforded the opportunity of self-determination and must be ruled by one of the great powers, be it France or Britain – all for their own good, of course. This feminine race needs Big Daddy, sugared or otherwise.

Renan's image of the Celt was taken a step further in a series of four lectures delivered by Matthew Arnold in the winter and spring of 1865–66 on the study of Celtic literature. Arnold was passionately concerned about the Irish question and felt that a more enlightened form of government by the British authorities would do much to cool Irish resentment. He believed that the comparative study of Celtic literature was a valuable academic discipline in itself, that an awareness of the beauties of this literature would do much to modify English opinion *vis-à-vis* Ireland, and thus he argued forcefully for the establishment of a chair in Celtic at Oxford. He singled out three elements as most characteristic of the Celtic literatures: style, melancholy and natural magic ('the gift of rendering with wonderful felicity the magical charm of nature').

Despite his insistence on the recognition of Celtic as part of the English cultural heritage, Arnold was nonetheless convinced that the Celtic tradition was dead and belonged solely to the past. While lauding the past achievements of Welsh literature, he argued that contemporary Welsh poets who had something important to say should say it in English. And as regards self-determination for the Celtic countries, simply perish the thought. 'What it [the Celt] has been, what it has done, let it ask us to attend to that as a matter of science and history; not to what it will be, or will do, as a matter of modern politics.' If the imaginative qualities of the Celts could soar untrammelled into the ethereal heights, they were also 'quick to react against the despotism of fact', and it was this negative corollary that rendered them unfit for modern civilization, political life and, most of all, home rule.

Developing the ideas of Renan, Arnold succeeded in setting up a stark dichotomy between the Celts and the Anglo-Saxons that became part and parcel of popular perception and has prevailed to our own day. If the Celts are spiritual, then the Anglo-Saxons are material. If the Celts are visionary and poetic, the Anglo-Saxons are rational and scientific. To the impracticality of the Celt one opposes the utilitarianism and philistinism of the Anglo-Saxon. In contrast to the rural and natural Celt, one has the urban, artificial Anglo-Saxon. And, of course, if the Celts are feminine, the Anglo-Saxons are masculine.

Altogether apart from the desirability or legitimacy of allocating traits such as these on a racial basis, one can see that the definitions come from the Anglo-Saxons themselves. The Anglo-Saxon is the norm, centre and colonizer, while the Celt becomes the 'other', the peripheral and the colonized. The Celts become a convenient receptacle for the nostalgia and the yearnings of the centre, while their subject status means they are no threat to the dominance of the norm, the centre and colonizer.

Celtic spirituality?

I submit that much of the current writing on Celtic spirituality is pervaded by the underlying assumptions of Renan and Arnold. If the Beatles started a trend in the Sixties in heading off to the East in search of gurus and an alternative culture and lifestyle, the peripheral Celts of the western European seaboard provided a much more readily accessible alternative in the Eighties and Nineties. And because many of the practitioners of Celtic spirituality are themselves blithely unshackled from the despotism of fact – be those facts theological, linguistic or historical – the Celt becomes the original pioneer of whatever happens to be flavour of the month. The Celts are the original ecologists, the original feminists, the original vegans, the original homeopaths, the original New Age movement.

'Celtic' is an elastic and user-friendly label that can be stretched and repackaged to mean exactly what one wants it to mean, and any yearnings and disillusionment in the normative centre find their solution in the Celtic periphery. As Donald Meek has said, Margaret Thatcher and her unfortunate legacy have, more than anything else, contributed to the upsurge of marketable Celtic spirituality. And because Celtic spirituality places great emphasis on its contemporary relevance and user-friendly status, it is highly selective: the gentle, cosmic elements are emphasized at the expense of awkward components such as prayer and asceticism and penance.

Many of the so-called experts on Celtic spirituality do not know any of the Celtic languages, in either their ancient or their modern forms. One recent anthologizer of Celtic prayers, Robert van de Weyer, lamented that many of his pieces 'were written in languages long since extinct'. That level of ignorance is just inexcusable and casts major doubts on the editor's ability to contextualize and analyse his sources. Most books on Celtic spirituality, with some honourable exceptions, should carry a government health warning. Some authors fail to realize, or at least fail to take into consideration, that many of the original texts were composed as poetry, and miss out on the very close links between poetry, praise and prayer in the literature of the Celtic languages. If one can argue for such a concept as Celtic spirituality, then this nexus of poetry, praise and prayer must be seen as one of its defining characteristics.

Numerous anthologies of Celtic religious texts and commentaries on Celtic spirituality have no sense of historicity. They blithely leap from Irish monastic poetry of the ninth century to domestic prayers of the Scottish Hebrides in the nineteenth century as if a thousand years of intervening history is completely irrelevant. There is also a tendency to idealize the rural at the expense of the urban. This is due in part to the legacy of Renan and Arnold, and in part to the romanticizing nature of the writings of Alexander Carmichael, in which the unremitting nature of the struggle to eke out an existence in the Western Isles is almost totally played down. (To his credit, however, it must be conceded that Carmichael himself was well aware of this relentless struggle, and that one of his reasons for producing this work was to force the authorities to take steps to improve the conditions of life for the poor cotters of the islands.) Extracts from *Carmina Gadelica*, Carmichael's collection of prayers and charms gathered in the Western Isles in the 1860s, figure prominently in anthologies of Celtic prayers.

A substantial number of works convey no idea whatever of the complexities involved in the establishment of Christianity in these islands. The impression is often given that the Celts had their own distinctive church. This view, of course, is not new and can be traced back to Matthew Parker, Archbishop of Canterbury, who argued in his *De antiquitate Britannicae ecclesiae* (1572) for a continuity between the British church of the Celtic period and the church of the Reformation, each being opposed to the Roman Catholic Church of the Counter-Reformation. This view we now know to be a gross oversimplification. We are now aware of different trends and traditions coexisting – sometimes in harmony, sometimes not – within one united Western church up to the time of the Reformation. We are also aware of different levels of church organization among the different Celtic peoples themselves. As Wendy Davies has said, 'There was no such thing as a Celtic church: the concept is unhelpful, if not positively harmful.'

Conclusions on the nature of Christianity in the Celtic-speaking countries must be based on a close and informed reading of the sources, sources that exist both in Latin and the vernacular. Evidence of such levels of scholarship, both wide-ranging and deep, are sadly lacking in many of the works that go under the heading of Celtic spirituality.

Nevertheless, despite the strictures of Wendy Davies and her older contemporary Kathleen Hughes regarding the existence of a Celtic church in the narrow organizational sense, Oliver Davies holds that there is a form of Christianity that is distinctively Celtic, and that the evidence for this is found primarily in works of hagiography and religious literature, a body of evidence not given adequate consideration by Kathleen Hughes and Wendy Davies. He submits that Celtic Christianity can be explained by the interaction between Christianity and forms of Celtic primal religion, and underlines three characteristics that distinguish Celtic primal religiosity from the classical Roman model:

1. The absence of the written word and the consequently oral character of Celtic learning led to an emphasis on poetry, imagery and mythology.
2. The tribal dimension of Celtic society entailed a strong emphasis on community.
3. The local nature of Celtic religion, with the cult of a deity being linked to a specific location, led to an interpenetration of religion and landscape. Consequently, God encountered humanity within the natural world and nature was taken up into the dialogue between God and humanity. Religious dialogue was not confined solely to the realm of the human spirit, as was the case in the late classical world. There are certain similarities between this Celtic attitude and the religious consciousness of the Hebrews.

The process of transformation resulting from the interaction between a major world religion and a primal religion is known as inculturation, a concept with which modern missionaries, of all people, will be quite familiar. In order to throw further light on the case of early medieval Ireland and Wales, Oliver Davies gives two modern examples of evangelization. In 1491 the kingdom of Kongo, now Angola, was evangelized by Portuguese missionaries. Christianity flourished and took on a strong local colour, relatively free of European influences. The Runa people of the Andes in modern Peru were evangelized by Spanish missionaries of the Counter-Reformation. They introduced a systematized form of Catholicism that stayed closely linked with European culture. In Kongo, where a high level of inculturation took place, Christianity put down deep roots, though moulded to a considerable extent by local beliefs and practices. Among the Runa, however, Christianity remained outside and alien to the people because it was associated with a culture that was in itself alien. The spread of Christianity in Wales and Ireland was closer to the experience of the kingdom of Kongo than to that of the Runa people, and the remoteness of the Celtic lands coupled with the lack of urban centres enabled Celtic Christianity to survive until the coming of the Normans in the twelfth century.

Davies stresses four distinguishing elements of Celtic Christianity:

1. Its *physicality*. This physicality is manifest mainly in an emphasis on asceticism and penance, and while this may not be popular at the current time, it has the advantage of drawing attention to our status as embodied beings. Davies feels that the desire to punish the body is, for the most part, subservient to the glory that will be received as a result of penance. Penance is largely seen as a spiritual opportunity and one way of including the body in our dialogue with God.

2. A persistent emphasis in early Irish and Welsh texts on *the place of nature* within the Christian revelation. In the classical model, nature is something to be controlled by the Christian saint. In the Celtic model, on the other hand, nature is something to be rejoiced in and for which one offers praise to God. This positive attitude to nature may well have been facilitated by the interpenetration of religion and landscape in pre-Christian Celtic primal religion.

3. The emphasis placed on the *creative imagination* of the individual. Davies notes, in particular, the art of the High Crosses, the illuminated manuscripts and the Christian bardic tradition. The place of the scribe in early Irish society and the belief of Welsh poets that they were directly inspired by the Holy Spirit indicate that the creative arts were at the very centre of church life. This emphasis on the creative imagination of the individual doubtless built on the role of poetry and imagery in the pre-Christian Celtic world.

4. The *spirit of community*. In this regard, it is well worth noting that the Irish word for community, *muintir,* derives from the Latin, *monasterium* (monastery). The communitarian nature of Irish society both facilitated the development of monasticism as the key institution in early Irish Christianity and contributed its own distinctive features to Irish monasticism. Equally important is the

prominence given to the Trinity, the source and model of community, in Celtic religious writings.

Whether the features mentioned by Davies are exclusive to the religious literature of the Celtic countries, rather than part of the common religious heritage of pre-Reformation medieval Europe, is a matter for further study, though I think that the function of vernacular eulogistic verse as a religious act is something distinctive to medieval Irish and Welsh literature.

Another commentator on Celtic Christianity is A. M. Allchin, who distinguishes three significant features:

1. The *goodness of creation* – which ties up with the second of the characteristics that Oliver Davies notes, the attitude to nature.
2. This positive attitude to the world, however, does not blind Celtic Christians to the *reality of evil* and the need for redemption. Evil, nevertheless, is ultimately defeated by the victory of the Cross.
3. The focus on the *closeness of the supernatural to the everyday world* in the religious writings in the Celtic languages. These texts make no clear-cut division between the religious and the secular domains. Even the most humdrum activity of the daily round, such as lighting a fire, offers an opportunity to encounter God. It must be emphasized, however, that the evidence for this attitude is to be found in the prayers collected by Carmichael in the Western Isles in the nineteenth century – and in the folk prayers collected by the likes of Douglas Hyde and Diarmuid Ó Laoghaire in the Irish language tradition – and not in the writings of the early Irish church.

Columba and his context

I have dwelt at some length on the question of Celtic Christianity and spirituality because of the upsurge of interest in this phenomenon in recent years. I have felt it important to point out the weaknesses and errors of much of the writings on this topic. I also felt it was important to start with a discussion of Celtic Christianity and its accompanying pitfalls, because it is within the context of this phenomenon that much of the discussion on Columba takes place. Yet despite all the caveats, I am convinced that the proper study of the history of Christianity in the Celtic lands is a valuable academic discipline, both for its own sake and for the practical and spiritual lessons that can be learned from it.

The recent 1400th anniversary of Columba's death, in 1997, witnessed a plethora of talks, articles and ecclesiastical services, all commemorating aspects of this great saint. I must confess to having been very disappointed by much of what was on offer. Even the sermons and talks of eminent ecclesiastics were shockingly superficial – little more, in fact, than unadulterated drivel. It was little consolation that this pious twaddle was equally balanced, in a most ecumenical way, across all the denominations, using a recipe of high legendary content with only the thinnest veneer of veracity.

No matter how attractive or edifying many of these tales may be, the fact remains that they are only tales, bereft of historical truth and conveying no insights at all into the mind of Columba himself. The tales seemed more often to be used to illustrate the particular hobbyhorse of the distinguished speaker than to enlighten us about the founder of Iona. If we are genuinely serious about the legacy of Columba, then the sources, such as they are, must be subject to the most thorough and rigorous analysis. Intellectual honesty, the search for truth and commitment to gospel values surely make that kind of scrutiny incumbent on us.

A document that cannot be omitted in any discussion of Columba is the *Amra Cholm Cille*, or 'Elegy of Columba', the earliest known document to mention him. This poem, one of the earliest written documents in the Irish language, was commissioned by Columba's cousin Aed mac Ainmirech, king of Cenél Conaill and later of Tara for twelve years before his death in 598.

Columba had a close relationship with his cousin and may well have been the moving spirit behind the Convention of Druim Cett, near Derry, in 575, which cemented the alliance between Cenél Conaill and the Antrim and Scottish kingdom of Dál Riata. The language of the poem is dated around 600, sustaining the assumption that it was composed in 597–8. The elegy, then, is an indication of the perception of the saint, at least in aristocratic circles, in the immediate aftermath of his death. The reference to his grave as 'good in its virtue' indicates that a cult of Columba grew up almost immediately after he died, and it is significant that the text shows no familiarity with the legendary material found in the *Life of St Columba* written by Adomnán.

The poem is ascribed to a poet called Dallán Forgaill, and while later tradition emphasizes his role as chief poet and a member of the aristocratic learned class, Thomas Owen Clancy and Gilbert Márkus are much more impressed by his easy familiarity with church learning and with Latin. He is well acquainted with the Bible and knows the contents of at least some patristic sources, such as John Cassian. He uses Latin words and numerous Irish borrowings from Latin. All this leads Clancy and Márkus to conclude that he must have had a monastic training – if, indeed, he was not actually a cleric.

Much of the information contained in the poem must have come from Iona itself, though we have no evidence to show that Dallán Forgaill ever visited that monastery. The poet focuses in particular on Columba's asceticism and on his learning, and while Máire Herbert comments that the poem is more revealing in its evidence of the commitment to Christian learning and to asceticism in the Irish church at the close of the sixth century than it is informative about the details of Columba's career, this judgement may err too much on the side of caution. If asceticism and learning are the areas most clearly singled out by the poet, perhaps this is simply because they are the qualities of Columba that most impressed his contemporaries. It may be equally significant that Columba's love of books is one of the striking features of Adomnán's *Life*. And while asceticism is not a very popular concept in the contemporary world, it is worth noting that Dallán Forgaill places equally great emphasis on Columba's sense of balance, stating that 'he would do no fast that was not the Lord's law'.

The poem is also significant as an indication of the integration of Christianity into Irish society by the end of the sixth century. Though it uses all the terminology associated with eulogistic verse, the value system of this society is transformed from secular glory and martial prowess to a Christian lifestyle. *Ollnia*, mighty champion, Columba may well be, but his battle is against the flesh and not against human foes.

Our chief source of information for the life of the saint, however, must be Adomnán's *Life of St Columba*. Adomnán was ninth abbot of Iona and died in 704. Internal evidence from the text suggests that Adomnán may have begun the book before 697 and that he was obviously writing after that date as well. He refers to the intercessory power of the saint changing a contrary wind to a favourable one, when Adomnán was hurrying back to Iona after a synod in Ireland in June 697. He wanted to be back in Iona in order to celebrate the 100th anniversary of Columba's death. The evidence suggests that Adomnán's writing of the biography was undertaken as part of the centenary celebrations, 'in response to the entreaties of the brethren'.

A further element is the context in which Adomnán wrote. Máire Herbert has drawn attention to the fact that at the time of writing Adomnán had accepted the Roman dating for Easter, while the monks of Iona were still clinging to the older Irish method, invoking Columba's practice as justification for their stance. Adomnán is at pains to point out that it is not a case of choosing between Rome and Columba. Accepting the Roman method is not a betrayal of their founder, whose memory may have been slighted when the Synod of Whitby, in 664, decided in favour of that method. The *Life* Adomnán has written is eloquent testimony that he reveres Columba as much as any of his monks do. Columba's sanctity is much more important for his followers than any particular ordinances regarding the dating of Easter or the precise nature of monasticism. It is all a matter of perspective, and Adomnán's ability to distinguish between what is essential and what is peripheral to a healthy tradition, revering it without at the same time being a slave to it, is a timely example for all of us who are concerned with reconciliation in Northern Ireland.

Another factor to be borne in mind is the possibility that Adomnán projected back on to Columba matters that pertained to his own day. A good case in point is the story of Columba's anointing of Aedán mac Gabráin, king of Dál Riata. This is the first instance of a fully developed royal anointing ritual to be recorded in European literature, and some have concluded that the first Christian ordination of a king anywhere in Europe took place on Iona in 574. Recent commentators have been more wary, however, and doubt whether Columba or even Adomnán himself was the inaugurator of this ritual. We do not actually know of any Irish king being anointed until the 'ordination' of the king of Munster in 793.

What is significant is Adomnán's use of biblical language and his Old Testament perception of kingship. The language used to describe Columba's choice of Aedán as king refers to Samuel's anointing of Saul, while his choice of Aedán's successor, Eochaid Buide, is based directly on the Old Testament narrative of Samuel choosing David to replace Saul. Adomnán's perception that kings, like abbots, hold office by divine providence is the real point at issue. And at a more local level, he is at pains to stress that Columba and his successors as abbot of Iona have a special role in mediating God's grace to kings in order to build up a Christian society.

Though writing 100 years after Columba's death, which is quite a long time lag, Adomnán insists that his account is reliable because he used only the best sources:

> No one should think that I would write anything false about this remarkable man, nor anything doubtful or uncertain. Let it be understood that I shall tell only what I learnt from the account handed down by our elders, men both reliable and informed, and that I shall write without equivocation what I have learnt by diligent enquiry either from what I could find already in writing or from what I heard recounted without a trace of doubt by informed and reliable old men.

It is significant that Adomnán mentions both written and oral sources; while he mentions his informant by name on a number of occasions, he does not specify his written sources. This may well spring from the fact that Irish law favoured the testimony of eye witnesses over that of documents. We are aware, however, of the existence of a document on the miraculous powers of St Columba written by Cumméne, seventh abbot of Iona from 657 to 669. There is good reason to believe that Cumméne compiled his work at the behest of his uncle Ségéne during the latter's term as fifth abbot, between 623 and 652, when he made an attempt to collect attested stories about St Columba. Only a passage from this document has survived, but as Adomnán makes no specific reference to it, it is impossible to ascertain to what extent he made use of Cumméne's work.

Herbert has cleverly subdivided the elements of the *Life of St Columba* into nine narrative types, most of which are based on the location of the particular event recorded. She notes a striking difference between the narratives associated with Iona and those associated with other locations. The background and even trivial details of monastic life are minutely detailed; the number of named eyewitnesses of the events recorded is quite high, mainly monks of the community; and the thaumaturgical element is considerably muted. The element of the marvellous, when it occurs, lies more in the interpretation of the event than in its nature.

It is the nature of oral storytelling that details are often subsumed into a timeless, idealized world, and the particular and irregular tend to be smoothed out. The opposite occurs in the Iona narratives, which are quite conscious of chronology and brimming with circumstantial detail. These indications have led Herbert to conclude that much in the Iona narratives stems from a written source, which is plausibly Cumméne's *Liber de virtutibus sancti Columbae.*

While according privileged status to the Iona stratum of the *Life of St Columba*, other issues have to be borne in mind. Hagiography is not biography but a particular mode of writing with its own conventions. It was not sufficient to be called a saint; a saint had to be seen to be a saint. And in the Middle Ages, prophecies, miracles and visions were the yardsticks by which sanctity was measured. Consequently, Adomnán divides his work into three sections: Book One dealing with prophetic revelations, Book Two dealing with Columba's miracles of power and Book Three dealing with his visions of angels.

In the early Middle Ages, lives of the saints were heavily influenced by two models in particular: The *Life of St Martin*, written by Sulpicius Severus in France at the end of the fourth century, and Evagrius' Latin translation of the *Life of St Anthony*, written in Greek by Athanasius. Adomnán was anxious to present Columba to his readers as the equal of Martin and Anthony, and these two lives influenced the structure and language of his work. The threefold division of the life and the use of two prefaces derive from the *Life of St Martin*, for example, and in some cases elements from both lives may have shaped the particular way in which Adomnán recounted a story. Adomnán's monastic readers would have been expected to pick up on the structural and verbal echoes in his work.

It has also to be kept in mind that Irish ecclesiastical literature was, to a certain extent, in competition with a highly developed oral tradition that placed special emphasis on the cult of the hero. The new Christian hero had at least to match the exploits of his pagan counterpart. This led to a certain amount of spiritual Rambo-ism in Irish hagiography, and while it is not as pronounced in Adomnán's *Life of St Columba* as it is in some of the lives of St Patrick, Columba does definitely take on the characteristics of the folk hero in some of the tales narrated. He routs pagan wizards in the land of the Picts and can perform wondrous feats – as when he increases the size of a poor man's herd from 5 cows to 105. The ecclesiastical box office demanded that Christian magic be bigger and better magic.

All these factors need to be considered before we are able to assess the historicity of a particular event in Adomnán's life of Columba. I have dwelt at length on these issues both to emphasize the pitfalls involved in reading Adomnán's *Life* at face value and to underscore the depth of meticulous and painstaking scholarship necessary for a proper interpretation of the text. Much fanciful speculation has taken place, for example, on the connection between the battle of Cúl Drebene in 561 and Columba's departure as an exile for Christ to Iona two years later. Modern commentators, in particular, like to portray the man of violence, churchman though he was, abandoning the sword for a life of peace and asceticism.

Attractive as this portrayal of Columba as a role model for paramilitaries in Northern Ireland must be, the evidence to warrant such a conclusion is simply not there. Herbert has suggested that what led Columba to Iona was the realization that his royal family connections would make it difficult for him to remain apart from the public arena and follow a life of asceticism. She quotes approvingly the words of T. M. Charles-Edwards that, by the end of the sixth century, choosing to be a pilgrim for Christ was 'the most intelligible form of asceticism available to an Irishman'. At the same time, it is unlikely that it was mere chance that led Columba to Iona, and it is most probable that he choose this site because of the good relationships between his royal kinsfolk and the leaders of Scottish Dál Riata. The real explanation for Columba's decision is, thus, much more mundane than the reasons given by the embroiderers of legend.

I would like to draw attention to two sources against which the veracity of Adomnán's historical information can be tested. One is the Irish annals, which ultimately depend on year-by-year notes begun in Iona no later than the 630s – if not during the time of Columba himself. The most important of these collections is the *Annals of Ulster*, which incorporates the records from Iona but continues down to the early sixteenth century. The other text is Bede's *Ecclesiastical History of the English People*, written in Jarrow in 731. This important source for Anglo-Saxon history contains chapters on both Columba and Adomnán, but Bede's lack of first-hand knowledge about Columba and Iona means that both his information and his interpretation are often questionable.

After all this work of deconstruction and the jettisoning of much attractive and exciting material relating to the saint, it may well be asked whether there is anything left. Yet despite this ruthless pruning, we can still salvage a hard core of facts that both give genuine insights into the saint himself and provide us with a precious legacy and guideline for Christian living in our own day. I will focus on three aspects: Columba's involvement in politics, his love of learning and his involvement in the creative arts.

Columba's involvement in politics

Columba was of royal stock belonging to Cenél Conaill, whose rulers – among the most powerful kings of Ireland at the time – were close cousins of the saint. It would never have occurred to Columba to abandon the political arena altogether, even for his preferred choice of a life of asceticism. The seclusion of Iona enabled him to combine both aspects of his life without detriment to the latter.

I have mentioned that he was most likely the moving spirit behind the Convention of Druim Cett in 575, which strengthened the alliance between Cenél Conaill and Dál Riata. Whether Columba, the third participant in this convention, was acting on his own initiative or at the request of others is a question that it is not possible to answer. He was on friendly terms with Rhydderon ap Tudwal, king of Dumbarton, and had dealings with Bridei, king of the Picts. It seems that his involvement with the latter had less to do with trying to win the king's conversion than with gaining safe conduct for his monks through Pictish territory.

Columba's biographer, Adomnán, was fully convinced of the role of the church in general, and of the abbots of Iona in particular, in emphasizing the sacred nature of kingship and in mediating God's grace to kings. The successors of Columba, in Adomnán's mind, had a vital role to play in helping kings build up a Christian society.

At a time when the attitude of the public in these islands regarding those who are unemployed, single parents, elderly or refugees is moving sharply towards the right, it is gratifying that the most radical stance on these issues is emanating from the Christian churches. In pointing out to governments their responsibilities towards the marginalized in our society, the churches are adopting a prophetic role and the subversive nature of the gospel message is becoming more apparent. It is significant that these very same causes are espoused by the modern Iona Community, founded by George MacLeod in 1938. Where peace, justice and human dignity are at stake, the churches must be politically involved. Columba and Adomnán would demand no less, not to mention Jesus Christ.

Columba's attitude to learning

I have already referred to the *Amra Cholm Cille* and its emphasis on asceticism and scholarship as the key elements in Columba's make-up. As well as calling him a sage and noting his study of Greek grammar, Dallán Forgaill devotes a whole section of his elegy to the saint's learning, which bears quoting in full:

> He ran the course which runs past hatred
> to right action.
> The teacher wove the word.
> By his wisdom he made glosses clear.
> He fixed the Psalms,

> he made known the books of Law,
> those books Cassian loved.
> He won battles with gluttony.
> The books of Solomon, he followed them.
> Seasons and calculations he set in motion.
> He separated the elements according to figures
> among the books of the Law.
> He read mysteries and distributed the Scriptures
> among the schools,
> and he put together the harmony concerning the
> course of the moon,
> the course which it ran with the rayed sun,
> and the course of the sea.
> He could number the stars of heaven, the one who
> could tell all the rest
> which we have heard from Colum Cille.

The poet emphasizes Columba's intellectual attainments as teacher and interpreter of the Scriptures, as one involved in establishing and distributing texts. In particular, he studied the Psalms, the books of Wisdom, Basil and Cassian. And in addition to exegetical studies, Dallán Forgaill tells us about Columba's interest in computistic skills, the astronomical calculations of sun, moon and tide necessary for establishing the dates for Easter.

The view of the saint's learning in the *Amra* needs to be complemented by that of Adomnán. At the end of the second preface, he tells us that Columba 'could not let even an hour pass without giving himself to praying or reading or writing or some other task'. This phrase is based on Sulpicius' *Life of St Martin*, but with the addition of writing as an approved activity. On four occasions, we find the saint disturbed as he was copying books. At the end of his life he was copying the Psalter:

> When he had come down from the hill and returned to the monastery, he sat in his hut writing out a copy of the psalms. As he reached that verse of the thirty-fourth psalm where it is

> written, 'They that seek the Lord shall not want for anything that is good,' he said:
>
> 'Here at the end of the page I must stop. Let Baithéne write what follows.'
>
> The last verse he wrote was very appropriate for our holy predecessor, who will never lack the good things of eternal life. The verse that follows is, 'Come, my sons, hear me; I shall teach you the fear of the Lord.' This is appropriate for Baithéne his successor, a father and teacher of spiritual sons, who, as his predecessor enjoined, followed him not only as a teacher but also as a scribe.

Books written in Columba's hand were known in Ireland and some were kept reverently in Iona. During a drought it was suggested that some of the elders of the monastery should walk round the fields that had been ploughed and sown, carrying with them the saint's white tunic and books which Columba himself had copied. Heavy rain fell, of course, and in due time there was a particularly good harvest. The text most often mentioned is the Psalter, but on one occasion it is a book of hymns.

Books believed to have been written by Columba were kept for centuries. Of particular interest is the *Cathach* or 'Battler' of St Columba. This manuscript consists of an incomplete Psalter on small parchment leaves, written in an Irish centre about 600. It was encased in a box and later in a reliquary, as it was believed to be a relic of the saint. The Psalter itself was only rediscovered when the reliquary was opened in 1813. We know that in the Middle Ages the *Cathach* used to be carried before the O'Donnell armies as they went into battle. The belief that this manuscript was one of the books copied by Columba himself is at least a thousand years old, and while it is impossible to be certain, the date of the handwriting – judged to belong to the very late sixth or very early seventh century – makes the tradition quite plausible.

While the evidence from Adomnán concentrates on Columba's scribal activities and the more mechanical side of learning, the reverence for books and for the psalms in particular is very telling, and to this extent, the evidence from the *Life* and that from the *Amra* complement each other. Columba was a man of learning and encouraged his monks to cultivate learning. The fact that the earliest Irish annalistic records date back to notes taken at a very early stage in Iona is further testimony to this interest in scholarship. Clancy and Márkus have put together a partial catalogue of the library of Iona at the beginning of the eighth century and it includes, among others, Jerome's biblical works, Augustine's *City of God*, the *Letters and Chronicon of Sulpicius Severus*, the *Conferences of John Cassian*, Cassiodorus' *Exposition of the Psalms*, the *Dialogues of Gregory the Great*, Isidore's *Etymologies* and his *De Natura Rerum*, Constantius' *Life of St Germanus*, and Cogitosus' *Life of Brigit*.

A love of learning has been long known to have been one of the distinguishing features of early Irish monasticism. The cultivation of learning is an essential element of the church's mission. Study is actually considered a form of prayer in the Hebrew tradition. In a world dominated by soundbites and mass entertainment aimed at the lowest common denominator, the late Bede Griffiths felt it was more incumbent than ever on the church to maintain its role in fostering learning and culture, the pillars of Christian civilization. It is sad to relate that the last 25 years have seen an insidious and virulent strain of anti-intellectualism gathering momentum in the Roman Catholic Church – all in the name of relevance and pastoral concern, of course. The growth of fundamentalism and rightwing groups in all the Christian denominations is further evidence of this anti-intellectual tendency. For it to prevail would be disastrous, both for the future of Christianity itself and for the future of Christian humanism. The legacy and challenge of Columba in this regard is most compelling. The Christian churches must not turn their back on two thousand years of learning and culture.

Columba's involvement with the creative arts

The medieval Irish vernacular tradition has always recognized Columba as a poet and a friend of the poetic class. Legend records that he intervened at the Convention of Druim Cett to prevent the suppression of the *filid*, or poets, altogether and that he came up with an acceptable compromise that resulted in a reorganization of the poetic order and a reduction of the privileges accruing to poets. Numerous poems in Irish have been ascribed to him that were not, in fact, composed until hundreds of years after his time. Is there more to this tradition than the normal custom of falsely ascribing poems and hymns to great saints in order to win them more importance and authority?

Passing from the world of legend to verifiable fact, it is interesting to note that the *Amra* states, 'He went with two songs to heaven after his cross.' This suggests that not only was the saint recognized as a poet at the time of his death, but two poems in particular were associated with him by that time. Clancy and Márkus think that this quotation refers to two Latin hymns, *Altus prosator* and *Adiutor laborantium*, which are ascribed to Columba both by ancient tradition and by the majority of modern scholars. The *Altus prosator* has an abecedarian shape, the first stanza beginning with A, the second with B, and so on right through the alphabet to Z. It is rather a gloomy work, heavily influenced by Scripture, and focusing on the Fall and the Day of Judgement. One verse will suffice to convey the tone of the poem:

> It seems doubtful to no one that there is a hell
> down below
> where there are held to be darkness, worms and
> dreadful animals;
> where there is sulphurous fire burning with
> voracious flames;
> where there is the screaming of men, weeping and
> gnashing of teeth;
> where there is the groaning of Gehenna, terrible
> and ancient;
> where there is the horrible fiery burning of thirst
> and hunger.

If the poem was intended to fill the Christian heart with godly fear, it definitely achieves its aim, but despite the powerful imagery and emotion, it is surprising that the mercy and tenderness of God are not mentioned even once.

The second poem, *Adiutor laborantium*, a 25-line work of praise and petition closing with a 2-line prayer formula, is much more attractive to the modern reader. Each line consists of eight syllables and ends in '-(i)um'. It creates a certain incantatory effect that may owe something both to the litanies of the medieval church and to the vernacular style of praise poetry. A short extract will convey some idea of the flavour of this poem, which stresses both our need for the mercy of Christ and its availability to us, an emphasis that is completely lacking in the *Altus prosator.* The image of the pilgrim rowing through the storm of life derives both from the gospel and from personal experience travelling to and from Iona.

Precor ut me homunculum	I beg that me, a little man
Quassatum ac miserrimum	trembling and most wretched,
Remigantem per tumultum	rowing through the infinite storm
Saeculi istius infinitum	of this age,
trahat post se ad supernum	Christ may draw after Him to the lofty
vitae portum pulcherrimum	most beautiful haven of life
Xristus	

Columba's verse is a happy combination of the ecclesiastical Latin tradition and the vernacular style of eulogistic verse. The fact that the saint chose poetry as a form of prayer and praise may well stem from the function and role of poetry in aristocratic Irish society. As eulogistic verse was a form of legitimization for the secular ruler, Columba's religious verse is an acceptance of the status and reality of the divine ruler. For the highborn ecclesiastic, the transition from secular eulogy to religious praise and petition must have been very easy. In this regard, it is interesting to note that a thirteenth-century Irish poet, writing in praise of poetry itself, says that praising anything created is ultimately praise of the creator.

In addition to Columba's personal contribution to poetry, some mention must be made of the role of Iona as a centre of the arts. If the copying of books was originally dictated by practical need as well by reverence for the word of God, the gradual development of more and more elaborate ornamental techniques bears witness to a growing awareness of the role of aesthetics in the search for God. One moves from the sparse and simple decoration of the *Cathach*, previously mentioned, to the large illuminated initials of the *Book of Durrow* and its carpet page designs of spiral and interlace patterns. Dating from the second half of the seventh century, most scholars suggest a place of origin for this manuscript in one of

Columba's monasteries, quite possibly Iona itself. The *Book of Kells* is, of course, the full flowering of this tradition of illuminated manuscripts. Most likely produced in Iona, it was taken to Kells sometime in the ninth century. Recent studies have shown that the wonderful illustrations in this manuscript are far more than mere decorations but contain an enormous wealth of theological insight, the interlace patterns of the illuminator overlapping and intertwining with his subtle interlacing of scriptural and liturgical themes – a most felicitous combination of visual art and creative theological imagination.

For Columba and his followers, the cultivation of the arts was inextricably linked with the praise and worship of God. The beauty and wonder and goodness of human creativity both reflected and indicated the beauty and wonder and goodness of God. Artistic talent, far from being denigrated, was a gift to be cherished and cultivated.

In an era that has witnessed the burgeoning of the creative arts in Ireland, from *Riverdance* to Seamus Heaney and Cathal Ó Searcaigh, from U2 to Brian Friel and Frank McGuinness, from Nuala Ní Dhomhnaill to Rita Ann Higgins and Liam Neeson – all these dynamic and creative impulses are more or less ignored by the churches. Are we going to abandon our time-honoured role as patron of the arts as well as our longstanding involvement with learning and scholarship? What sort of message does the drabness and philistinism and moribund state of so many of our churches and services – not to mention ecclesiastical personnel – send out to our young people? No wonder so many of our most creative and most talented artists are finding that the churches have nothing to say to them.

This is not an indictment of Christianity but an indictment of our betrayal of Christianity. A Christianity that excludes creative beauty and the cultivation of the artistic imagination is no longer Christianity. A Christianity that turns its back on the best strivings of the human spirit is a repudiation of the Incarnation. In an interview in *The Scotsman*, the novelist Bernard MacLaverty said that the great art of the centuries came from religion – stained-glass windows, paintings, music. 'I wonder what happens when you subtract God; are you left with the same art?' I think that the churches have to put that same question to themselves in reverse:

What happens when you subtract art; are you left with the same God? Are you left with any God at all?

The flowering of the arts in Iona and its filial monasteries is one of the highpoints not only of Irish but of European medieval civilization. For all his spartan asceticism, Columba could still raise his mind and heart and hands to the cultivation of art, beauty and truth. It is not sufficient for us simply to remember the glory that was Iona. As committed Christians, we must be willing to follow its example and foster and cherish the artistic talent in our midst.

I will conclude with the last recorded words of Columba, spoken to his trusted servant Diarmait:

> I commend to you, my little children, these my last words: Love one another unfeignedly. Peace. If you keep this course according to the example of the holy fathers, God, who strengthens the good, will help you, and I dwelling with him shall intercede for you. He will supply not only enough for the needs of this present life, but also the eternal good things that are prepared as a reward for those who keep the Lord's commandments.

These may be less the actual words of Columba than Adomnán's expression of his own views through Columba. Allan Orr Anderson and Marjorie Ogilvie Anderson have suggested that the controversy over the dating of Easter underlies these words, but that as far as Adomnán was concerned, 'dissension over the date of Easter was a sin greater than error over its date'.

Adomnán's preoccupation with peace was not confined to his own community, however. In 697 he travelled to Birr and promulgated his Law of the Innocents, *Cain Adomnáin,* to protect non-combatants – clerics, women and children – from violence. To ensure that this law was actually enforced, Adomnán prevailed on the leading men of church and state from all over Ireland and beyond, including the king of Scottish Dál Riata and the king of the Picts, to accept his law and act as guarantors for it. What we know of this law depends on an Irish ninth-century version of it that is more concerned with the rights of women than those of clergy and children.

Adomnán, with his concern for peace,
the protection of non-combatants and churches,
the rights of women and children;
Adomnán, with his ability to persuade the authorities that peace was not only desirable but achievable;
Adomnán with his uncanny knack of knowing when to bend and when to stand firm in matters of tradition;
seems to be the ideal model for Christian leadership today. If Columba's legacy of political action, cultivation of learning and the creative arts has much to recommend it, surely it is only in the context of a peace such as that envisaged and created by Adomnán that political and cultural life will flourish to its full potential. The challenge is ours.

BIBLIOGRAPHY

A. M. Allchin, *Praise Above All*, University of Wales Press, 1991.

——— and Esther de Waal, *Threshold of Light: Prayers and Praises from the Celtic Tradition*, Darton, Longman and Todd, 1988.

Allan Orr Anderson and Marjorie Ogilvie Anderson, *Adomnán's Life of St Columba*, Oxford University Press, 1991.

Matthew Arnold, *On the Study of Celtic Literature*, Kessinger, 1998.

Ian Bradley, *Columba: Pilgrim and Penitent*, Wild Goose Publications, 1996.

Alexander Carmichael, *Carmina Gadelica: Hymns and Incantations from the Gaelic*, ed. by John MacInnes, Floris, 1992.

Thomas Owen Clancy and Gilbert Márkus, *Iona: the Earliest Poetry of a Celtic Monastery*, Edinburgh University Press, 1995.

Oliver Davies, *Celtic Christianity in Early Medieval Wales*, University of Wales Press, 1996.

——— and Fiona Bowie, *Celtic Christian Spirituality: an Anthology of Medieval and Modern Sources*, SPCK, 1995.

Wendy Davies, 'The myth of the Celtic church', in N. Edwards and A. Lane (eds), *The Early Church in Wales and the West*, Oxford, 1992.

Máire Herbert, *Iona, Kells and Derry*, Four Courts Press, 1996.

Kathleen Hughes, 'The Celtic church: is this a valid concept?', *Cambridge Medieval Celtic Studies*, Summer 1981, pp. 1–20.

James Macpherson, *The Poems of Ossian and Related Works*, ed. by Howard Gaskell, Edinburgh University Press, 1996.

Donald E. Meek, 'Surveying the saints: reflections on recent writings in "Celtic Christianity"', *Scottish Bulletin of Evangelical Theology*, Spring 1997, pp. 50–60.

———, 'Modern Celtic Christianity', in Terence Brown (ed.), *Celticism* (Studia Imagologica: Amsterdam Studies on Cultural Identity 8), 1996, pp. 143–57.

———, 'Modern Celtic Christianity: the contemporary "revival" and its roots', *Scottish Bulletin of Evangelical Theology*, Spring 1992, pp. 6–31.

Ernest Renan, *The Poetry of the Celtic Races and Other Studies*, ed. and trans. by William G. Hutchinson, Walter Scott, n.d.

Richard Sharpe (trans.), *Adomnán of Iona: Life of St Columba*, Penguin Books, 1995.

Philip Sheldrake, *Living Between Worlds: Place and Journey in Celtic Spirituality*, Cowley, 1995.

'Maggots in the Luggage': Facing Contextuality

Lynne Price

Mission and maggots have been associated for me ever since I read Sylvia Townsend Warner's novel *Mr Fortune's Maggot* more than a decade ago. The book was published in 1927 and the story is set just prior to the 1914–18 war. It opens with a 'maggot', in the Oxford English Dictionary's second definition of that word – 'a whimsical or perverse fancy, a crochet'. A humble and earnest Church of England priest, the Revd Timothy Fortune, has a perverse fancy to leave the mission station and go alone to work on a more remote South Sea island.

He is informed by his superior that the islanders are like children, always singing and dancing, that their language has no words for chastity or gratitude, and he imagines how beautiful it will be 'to live among them and gather their souls as a child gathers daisies in a field'.[1] He arrives with his harmonium, teapot, some picture books and a sewing machine to make clothes for his converts.

After three years on the island, a boy called Lueli, Mr Fortune's one 'convert', saves the missionary's life at the risk of his own when volcanic fire grips their hut – demonstrating, Mr Fortune realizes, that greatest love which makes a man ready to lay down his life for his friend. But Lueli loses his own personal god: the statue that the missionary has instructed him to destroy is, as it happens, burnt in the fire. Lueli is lost without his god and tries to commit suicide. Mr Fortune, in turn risking his life, is instrumental in saving him.

After these events, Mr Fortune can no longer believe in his superior, invulnerable god, part of the European conspiracy that opposed gunboats to canoes and rounded up Negroes into an empire. He doubts whether God has ever been real to him. He has loved the boy for what he is, yet in a moment of stark self-awareness, sees that he has been unable to spend a day without trying to alter him, remarking to himself, 'How dreadful it is that because of our wills we can never love anything without messing it about.'[2] Disillusioned, the missionary leaves the island. We do not know what becomes of him.

Townsend Warner's biographer, Claire Harman, is of the opinion that it is, in fact, the first and more familiar dictionary definition of 'maggot' that dominates the tragedy – the fly larva, with its implications of infection and decay – rather than the whimsical fancy that prefaces Chapter 1.[3]

The novel, which was enthusiastically received – particularly in America – and was reissued by Virago, the feminist publishing company, fifty years later, was written by an English woman who disliked 'priests in their gowns, anti-semitism, the white man who is the black man's burden, warmongers' – and who never gave money to people collecting for missionary societies.[4] Encouraged by the enthusiasm of her lover for the cause, and dismayed by the rise of fascism in Europe, she joined the Communist Party in 1935 and was an active member, though her sympathies lay more truly with the anarchists.[5]

The two women, who lived together until death separated them, both retained a commitment to Christianity. Valentine Ackland, a lapsed Catholic, towards the end of her life became a Quaker, whilst Townsend Warner remained an Anglican until her death in 1978 at the age of 85, requesting that at her funeral the Thanksgiving for Rain should be read, regarding it as the nearest thing in the Prayer Book to a Thanksgiving for Death.[6]

The novel and its author raise many of the issues pertinent to the subject of mission and inculturation. The book reminds us of the fragility of the missionary process; outcomes cannot be known in advance and the propensity for conversion belongs with the purveyors as well as the recipients of Christianity. That a novelist should write in the 1920s with such perception of the complex interplay of personal relationships, cultures and religious beliefs – at a time when the Protestant missionary societies had barely begun to face these matters formally – is also instructive. The author herself serves as a reminder that Christianity is appropriated and acted upon in ways probably not envisaged by the institutional communicators. There is, in other words, an element of inherent ambiguity in missionary endeavour, whether it is inter-cultural or intra-cultural, just as there are a variety of perspectives from which it may be appraised.

The theologies that have been developing in the last thirty years or so – Asian, Black, process, interfaith, liberation and feminist – have as their hallmarks the validation of personal experience and responsibility, and the need for religion and everyday life to be held together. In general terms, their common processes are identification of one's own or the group's context and experience, dialogue with others or other groups, reassessment, and change in thinking and action. All could be viewed as attempts to confront reality that, in seeking to make Christianity meaningful to life, inevitably challenge the dominant traditional orthodox interpretations of faith and church institutions. It is this continual two-way process of mutual influence and critique reflected in the dialogical theologies that I feel to be important for mission in the West today.

I am reluctant to use the term 'inculturation' in the British context (and I confine myself to Britain in this chapter) because it currently carries different associations from those in non-Western countries. In Britain, prominent and vocal churchmen such as Lesslie Newbigin and Hugh Montefiore have attacked British culture and secular society, accusing them of not being 'Gospel-friendly' and blaming them for the relative failure of Christian mission.[7] Whilst not diminishing their Christian commitment and concern for those outside the institution, we could be tempted to paraphrase the Revd Fortune's superior in the mission field and say that their attitude to those outside is as to Enlightenment children who are hedonistic and have no sense of obligation to higher authority.

As Christopher Duraisingh, a former editor of the *International Review of Mission*, has pointed out, 'To a large number of Christians in the West, the very word syncretism is frightening.' He sees this as related to 'religion being reduced to a set of doctrinal beliefs and fixed liturgical practices' and therefore in contrast to the views of many theologians in the Third World, who see syncretism as a normal step in any creative encounter of the gospel in a local context and who understand both culture and religion as dynamic and changing.[8] This is certainly the view of several of my former research colleagues from overseas who contributed to *Mission Matters*.[9] I prefer, therefore, to use the term 'cultural relevance' to underline the interactive nature of faith and life and endorse a dialogical theological methodology.

I want to begin to look for some maggots that may have slipped into the missionary luggage, which have been brought back, as it were, with British overseas missionaries returning home. Do we have any alternative precedents for helping us move from a largely discredited colonial missionary approach to one that is relevant and effective? Despite their ambiguous associations, live maggots have been known for centuries to help heal infected wounds. Their use almost disappeared with the introduction of antibiotics, but they are now making a comeback in contemporary medicine, not only as a last resort when all else fails but as a positive treatment option.[10]

The second decade of the twentieth century seems a good place to start. We in the West are continuing to struggle with the dilemmas thrown up by a world which was at that time changing very rapidly in terms of ease of travel, speed of communication, the distribution of political-geographical-economic power, the juxtaposition of religions and ideologies. We still do not know whether we are modern, postmodern or incipiently post-postmodern. We are not sure even what these labels mean, for they relate – as David Harvey puts it in his book *The Condition of Postmodernity* – to 'the incredible confusions and oppositions across a spectrum of possible reactions to the growing sense of crisis in the experience of time and space' that came to a head just before World War I.[11] Under the heading of inculturation, we are perhaps addressing in Christian missionary ecumenical circles the same questions about universalism and particularity, about power and powerlessness, about domination and freedom, and about the way these polarities relate. These were just perceptibly evident at Edinburgh in 1910 from the point of view of Western Protestant mission.[12] The theme of the 1996 Conference on World Mission and Evangelism in Salvador, 'Called to One Hope: Gospel in Diverse Cultures', is in itself telling.

Adrian Hastings, in his *A History of English Christianity, 1920–1990*, describes the 1920s as 'the calm after the storm of the First World War, the calm before the quite unexpected storm of the 1930s'.[13] It seems appropriate, then, to start with this pregnant pause when, according to Harvey, divergent trends, still continuing today, appeared in response to the new, simultaneous perceptions of unity and fragmentation.[14]

With the Equal Franchise Act of 1928, women finally achieved the same voting rights as men. Lady Rhondda founded the feminist magazine *Time and Tide* in 1920; women such as Vera Brittain and Winifred Holtby used their journalistic skills to write not only on issues particularly affecting women, but on political ones. Holtby's visit to South Africa in 1926 to give lectures under the auspices of the League of Nations Union led to her passionate commitment, for the next nine years until her death aged 37, to the fight for the rights of the Black and Coloured population, particularly in her practical support of the Industrial and Commercial Workers' Union.[15] She noted, like Olive Schreiner before her, the parallels of the arguments against the enfranchisement of women and that of the 'natives'.[16] Vera Brittain's commitment was to pacifism, and she became a leading figure in the Peace Pledge Union; her *Testament of Youth* (1933) is something of a classic. Several of these two women's books and a collection of their journalistic writings have been republished, again by Virago, in the 1980s.[17]

Maude Royden, an Anglican, another woman active in the suffrage movement, had also gained a reputation as assistant preacher at the large London Congregational church, the City Temple, from 1917 to 1919, marking a breakthrough for the position of women in the churches, and was also an author, journalist and broadcaster. Sheila Fletcher published a biography of Royden in 1989, and Lavinia Byrne included Royden in her 1991 collection *The Hidden Tradition: Women's Spiritual Writings Rediscovered*.[18]

From just these three women – Brittain, Holtby and Royden – we get a glimpse of the breadth of women's concerns and of the interrelationship of the issues and groups with which they were very practically concerned, from what were, in fact, rather different perspectives in terms of their relationships to the church. We have an indication here of the way in which fragmentation stimulates networking and cooperation across boundaries. This is certainly a feature of the way women work in the interfaith field – an example can be found in *Speaking of Faith* (1986), edited by Diana L. Eck and Devaki Jain[19] – and is also my own experience of interfaith work in Birmingham, which was, in addition, markedly ecumenical.

According to Hastings, the 1920s was a decade in which the churches in England appeared to have not only lost the intellectual battle, in that the presupposition of intelligent people was unbelief, but their social and political role as well. Almost entirely excluded from ordained ministry, women church workers were kept firmly subordinate to male authority, says Hastings. He identifies the mission field as one of the few areas having room for female initiative.[20]

The 1994 publication *Mission Legacies*, edited by Gerald Anderson and others, offers 76 biographical studies of nineteenth- and twentieth-century 'leaders of the modern missionary movement', all of which appeared in the *International Bulletin of Missionary Research* from 1977 on.[21] Only six are of women. None are included in the sections 'Theologians and Historians', 'Theorists and Strategists' or 'Administrators'. It seems that we have met the same initial challenge as that faced by women working in biblical studies, hermeneutics, systematics and church history: the need for disclosure of the experiences and thinking of women. The six who are in the book include Ida Scuddor, who established Vellore Hospital and appears in the Southern Asia section, and Charlotte Moon in the China section. The other four are categorized as 'Promoters and Interpreters'. Two of them, Helen Montgomery and Lucy Peabody, were tireless promoters of and fund-raisers for American women's overseas missions. The other two are British: Ruth Rouse played an important role in the Student Christian Movement, and here 'promoter' seems appropriate; and finally, Florence Allshorn.

Allshorn is interesting and so is the fact that she made it into this collection, because she is not well known and wrote private letters rather than material for publication.[22] In 1920 she went to Uganda with the Church Missionary Society and stayed for four years, subsequently training women missionaries in England. J. H. Oldham, who knew her and wrote a short biography published in 1951, the year after her death, was of the opinion that 'she saw further than most into the meaning of the missionary task and the nature of its demands'. He wrote: 'The love of Christ was the ruling passion of her life, but the expression of it was in no way conventional. She had in her lifetime the art of making friends with all sorts of people professing a diversity of beliefs.'[23]

Allshorn was the eighth young woman to be sent to the mission station at Iganga and none had lasted more than two years, partly because of the climate and demanding work in difficult circumstances and partly because of the furious tempers of the senior missionary. She had reached a very low physical and spiritual ebb when, in her own words:

> One day the old African matron came to me when I was sitting on the verandah crying my eyes out. She sat at my feet and after a time she said, 'I have been on this station for fifteen years and I have seen you come out, all of you saying you have brought to us a Saviour, but I have never seen this situation saved yet'. It brought me to my senses with a bang. I was the problem for myself. I knew enough of Jesus Christ to know that the enemy was the one to be loved before you could call yourself a follower of Jesus Christ ... and I prayed, as I have never prayed in my life for that one thing.[24]

With this insight, continued prayer, the reading of 1 Corinthians 13 every day for a year and determination not to be beaten by the situation, gradually the relationship between the two women improved, and along with it the whole atmosphere of the school that they ran. Having seen that the problem lay with herself and realizing that the heart of the missionary enterprise was human relationships, Allshorn put this insight into practice in her subsequent training of missionaries and then in the founding of the St Julian's Community. Put quite simply, she looked on the Great Commandments as foundational. She wrote in a letter:

> There is all the difference in the world between religious people and Christ-like people. You can be religious and yet somehow keep self as the largest thing. ... But to be able to delight in God and

> others to such an extent that 'I want' goes right out
> *is* the heart of it.[25]

Her biblical model of mission was that of the salt, light and mustard seed. She was fond of quoting: 'Those who possess truth because they live it, are sought by others; whereas those who are chiefly concerned with the propagation of doctrine have to seek an audience.'[26]

It is interesting, isn't it, that Oldham, architect of the ecumenical movement, secretary of the International Missionary Council, editor of the *International Review of Mission*, an organizer of the 1937 Oxford Conference, should be the one to perceive the missionary significance and implications of Allshorn's emphasis on the importance of the individual's love of God and relations between persons. Florence Allshorn, he considered, saw the danger of the missionary movement and the church organized to the point where everything was subordinated to keeping the machine running and providing welfare services. If the church put the job before right human relations, it would cease to be the manifestation of love and an example of community.[27]

Our second returning missionary at first glance appears very different from Allshorn. He was a Methodist minister who returned in 1922 from a few years in Madras with the Wesleyan Missionary Society, punctuated with time as an officer in the Indian Army Reserve and then as chaplain to British Army forces near Baghdad during World War I. Leslie Weatherhead became one of the few Methodists well known outside his denomination.[28] There was a popular saying that Sangster loved Jesus, Soper loved an argument, and Weatherhead loved people. He was a prolific writer, lecturer on psychology, frequent broadcaster and famous evangelist. Formally accused of 14 points of heresy for his book *After Death*, published just after his return to England, he was a few years later refused the pulpit of Wesley's Chapel in London because he had published a book on sex. He accepted the invitation to ministry at the Congregational City Temple in 1936, where before it was destroyed by an incendiary bomb in 1941, people queued to attend Sunday services in the church – which held 2,000.

Weatherhead was a pioneer in relating psychology, religion and healing, and worked for cooperation between doctors, psychologists and clergy.

Already in the 1920s, as part of his pastoral ministry, he was practising hypnosis, dream interpretation and suggestion with patients – referred by medical doctors – who could be helped by what he then termed 'psycho-religious healing'. His book *Psychology in Service of the Soul*, published in 1929, was written deliberately in 'popular style', which seemed to be effective – the 28th impression was made in 1960, so was still in demand with the public nine years after the publication of his scholarly magnum opus, *Psychology, Religion and Healing*, which was also highly acclaimed in Britain and the United States, within and outside church circles.

His most popular book, however, was *The Transforming Friendship*, published in 1928. It sold 100,000 copies in ten languages. In this book he defined Christianity as 'the acceptance of the gift of the friendship of Jesus'.[29] Theology to Weatherhead was a secondary activity. It was an understanding of Christianity that Weatherhead still held in *The Christian Agnostic*, his last major work, published in retirement in 1965.

He believed passionately that Christianity is a way of life, not a set of propositions with which one must be in intellectual agreement. 'The Gospel According to You', 'The Gospel According to Billy Graham' and 'According to My Gospel' were titles of sermons preached over the years. Nothing was more important than the individual getting in 'right relationship' with God/Christ/the Holy Spirit (he thought that *in experience* these were all the same) and living out the insight from that personal relationship in relationships with other people and in joining with others to combat evil and injustice. 'My opinion is that in Britain in the twentieth century', he wrote in 1940, 'one of the greatest enemies of Christianity is a religion *called* Christianity which is a pale imitation of the real thing. ... It is too smug, too complacent, too compromising, too comfortable, too unadventurous, too pedestrian for the real thing.'[30]

His creative methodology of evangelism, which I have called 'faithful uncertainty' and gives my book on the subject its title, was dialogical. His *modus operandi* was essentially to address questions people were asking – whether about contemporary movements such as Christian Science and spiritualism, or about suffering, or attitudes to war. Whilst sharing his own knowledge and thinking, he invited his listeners and readers to engage for themselves in the experience/reflection process and to take responsibility for their lives.

His tireless research and experimentation into the complex relationship between spiritual, psychical, physical and mental functioning and disfunctioning led him into controversial areas, but at every step he shared his findings with the lay public. His approach was discursive rather than apologetic, and he made lesser-known and more unconventional aspects of the Christian theological tradition available to a wide audience, as well as the fruits of critical biblical scholarship and imaginative approaches to Bible reading akin to the Ignatian spiritual exercises.

Christians, he considered, should be open to truth wherever it came from, and Christianity needed the insights not only of Christians from non-Western cultures but also of other religions in order to evolve. His theology, which he did not attempt to systematize, was influenced by his own mystical experiences (though he did not claim to be a mystic) combined with the extensive pastoral experience that gave him intimate knowledge of the hopes, fears, joys and sufferings of ordinary people. It led, for example, to a stress on divine immanence and passibility that is now more fully explored in process theology.

'To make God real, to change men's lives' was his own formulation of his mission and was reflected in the attempt to open up before people all the possible ways the former might be achieved, knowing that it would result in a plurality of theological and Christological interpretations and a variety of actions in response to life's circumstances. Nobody knows all the truth, he declared. 'All say with St Paul, "we know in part".'[31] Ongoing and deepening personal relationship with God as revealed by Jesus Christ, honesty and integrity were, in his view, the most important requisites for mission and evangelism.

Allshorn and Weatherhead both recall Christians to the need for critical self-reflection in mission – a dimension given only minimal attention in the Gospel and Culture movement and Decade of Evangelism literature. They both regard the Great Commandments rather than Great Commission as the foundation, means of enabling and goal of Christianity. They were both innovators in their respective vocations and open to change.

Weatherhead demonstrates in his dialogical methodology that it is possible to communicate Christian faith in a way that is contextually relevant and that vitalizes theological reflection. He engaged with the realities of his time and worked not only ecumenically but with individuals and groups outside the churches. As it happens, he referred in his writings to Florence Allshorn, Vera Brittain, Winifred Holtby, Maude Royden and Ida Scudder. He changed his own theology in the light of experience and worked throughout his long ministry to bring healing of body, mind and spirit to suffering individuals. I have met, or come to know of, many people who continue to be profoundly grateful for his preaching, psychological counselling, broadcasts, prayers or books at important turning points of their lives. Weatherhead demonstrated that to be faithful *and* uncertain is not detrimental to Christian witness.

We find that we are very close to Antonie Wessels' position in the last chapter of *Europe: Was It Ever Really Christian?* It is the integrity of Christians' lives, the way words and actions hold together, that is decisive for mission.[32] Wessels begins his last chapter with the Venerable Bede's account of the beginning of the Christianization of Northumbria, when the question was asked, 'Where do we come from before this life and where do we go after it?' Weatherhead began his 1923 book, *After Death*, with the same narrative – a cautionary reminder that whatever the historical context, human beings have the same questions, which do not lend themselves to definitive and final answers in this life. As a character in one of Winifred Holtby's novels puts it, 'The dilemmas recur, and the decisions have to be remade again and again.'[33]

To summarize, I have chosen to focus on dialogue as both a method of evangelism and as a theological methodology. It seems to me to offer an alternative to an authoritarian, institutional view of mission, and to underline this I have used the term 'contextual relevance' instead of 'inculturation'. I have drawn material from early twentieth-century Britons, mostly women, representing a range of commitment to organized religion, to underline the categorical fuzziness of what constitutes Christian thought and practice. In choosing to focus on individuals rather than conceptual categories, I have attempted to hold in relation life as it is experienced with intellectual reflection.

The newer theologies respond to the challenges confronting human beings in concrete situations and attempt to articulate the good news of what God, as revealed by Jesus, is in those situations. As Edward Schillebeeckx observed in 1981, the theologian is always the latecomer in respect of Christian practice. Practice is preceded by faith but not by theology.[34] I do not view feminist theology as an example of the process of inculturation but rather as an intellectual response to concrete contextual realities that involves mutual influence and critique. I was unable to find any precedents for the application of feminist theology to reflection on mission. A survey of recently published collections of missiological papers revealed few women, let alone feminist, contributors. There is work to be done here on how the articulation of feminist insights is enabling Christians in Britain today to witness to their faith. How are new readings of texts, the disclosure of 'the hidden tradition', new metaphors of God, new liturgies, affecting people's faith and the way they live their lives?

Finally, a word about our maggot carriers, Florence Allshorn and Leslie Weatherhead. Both declared the indispensable heart of life and mission to be love of God and neighbour. Neither dogma and creeds, nor claims to superiority and institutional authority, are adequate substitutes. As Paul pointed out in 1 Corinthians 13, without love and the costly discipleship it demands, there is just a lot of noise!

NOTES

1. Sylvia Townsend Warner, *Mr Fortune's Maggot*, Virago, 1978, p. 3.
2. Townsend Warner, p. 3.
3. Claire Harman, *Sylvia Townsend Warner: A Biography*, Chatto and Windus, 1989, pp. 70–71.
4. Harman, p. 140.

5. Harman, pp. 140ff.
6. Harman, pp. 292–3; 320–21. 'O God our heavenly Father, who by thy gracious providence dost cause the former and the latter rain to descend upon the earth, that it may bring forth fruit for the use of man; We give thee humble thanks that it hath pleased thee, in our great necessity, to send us at the last a joyful rain upon thine inheritance, and to refresh it when it was dry, to the great comfort of us thy unworthy servants, and to the glory of thy holy Name; through thy mercies in Jesus Christ our Lord. Amen.'
7. Hugh Montefiore (ed.), *The Gospel and Contemporary Culture*, Mowbray, 1992, 'Introduction'. Lesslie Newbigin, *The Other Side of 1984*, WCC, 1984; *Truth to Tell: The Gospel as Public Truth*, SPCK, 1991.
8. Christopher Duraisingh, 'Editorial', *International Review of Mission*, April 1996, pp. 165–6.
9. Lynne Price, Juan Sepúlveda and Graeme Smith (eds), *Mission Matters*, Peter Lang, 1997.
10. Maggot Therapy Project, Ronald A. Sherman, MD, M.Sc., DTMH, Department of Pathology, University of California. Information from the Internet, March 1997.
11. David Harvey, *The Condition of Postmodernity*, Blackwell, 1990, p. 266.
12. The tensions were revealed at Edinburgh in the issues of missions/local churches, Christianity/non-Christian religions, nationalism/individualism.
13. Adrian Hastings, *A History of English Christianity 1920–1990*, SCM, 1991, p. 181.
14. Harvey, pp. 270ff.
15. Vera Brittain, *Testament of Friendship*, Virago, 1980 (first published 1940), Chapters 13–15.
16. Brittain, p. 214.
17. Paul Berry and Alan Bishop (eds), *Testament of a Generation: The Journalism of Vera Brittain and Winifred Holtby*, Virago, 1985.
18. Albert Clare, *The City Temple 1640–1940*, Independent Press, Chapter 31; Kenneth Slack, *The City Temple – A Hundred Years*, The Elders Meeting of the City Temple, 1974. Referring to her last book, *A Threefold Cord*, Slack says: 'It was a book which revealed perhaps more than anything could have

done the source of the deep sensitivity to the mystery of pain and the questionings of faith which enabled Maude Royden to minister so effectively in this century' (p. 27). Lavinia Byrne (ed.), *The Hidden Tradition: Women's Spiritual Writings Rediscovered*, SPCK, 1991.

19. Diana l. Eck and Devaki Jain (eds), *Speaking of Faith: Cross-Cultural Perspectives on Women, Religion and Social Change*, The Women's Press, 1986.
20. Hastings, pp. 48–9.
21. Gerald H. Anderson, Robert T. Cooke, Norman A. Horner and James M. Phillips (eds), *Mission Legacies: Biographical Studies of Leaders of the Modern Missionary Movement*, Orbis, 1994.
22. There is a brief biography by J. H. Oldham, *Florence Allshorn and the Story of St Julian's*, SCM, 1951; *The Notebooks of Florence Allshorn Selected and Arranged by Members of St Julian's Community*, SCM, 1957; and an address she gave, subsequently published in the *International Review of Mission*, October 1934, called 'Corporate Life on a Mission Station'.
23. Oldham, pp. 7–8.
24. Oldham, p. 28.
25. Oldham, pp. 51–2.
26. Oldham, pp. 152–3.
27. Oldham, pp. 164ff.
28. The material relating to Leslie Weatherhead is drawn from my book *Faithful Uncertainty: Leslie D. Weatherhead's Methodology of Creative Evangelism*, Peter Lang, 1996. Only direct quotations from Weatherhead's books are footnoted here.
29. Leslie D. Weatherhead, *The Transforming Friendship*, Epworth Press, 1928, p. 25.
30. Leslie D. Weatherhead, *This Is the Victory*, Hodder & Stoughton, 1940, pp. 286–7.
31. Weatherhead, *Victory*, p. 126.
32. Antonie Wessels, *Europe: Was It Ever Really Christian?*, SCM, 1994, p. 194.
33. Winifred Holtby, *Mandoa, Mandoa!* quoted in Brittain, p. 333.
34. Edward Schillebeeckx, *Ministry: A Case for Change*, SCM, 1981, pp. 101–2.

Perspectives ~ Mission Theology

Christian Political Discourse as Public Confession

Duncan B. Forrester

The story of shattered life can only be told in bits and pieces.
– Rainer Maria Rilke

I intend to argue in this chapter that Christian contributions to public debate are, or ought to be, a way of confessing the faith, a part of the mission of the church, a form of evangelism. Public debate, in other words, presents an opportunity and, indeed, an obligation to witness to the truth of the gospel; it is not simply a place where wisdom derived from the Christian tradition is offered to help resolve tricky issues on the public agenda. Christian ethics at its heart is gospel, precisely because it is *Christian.*

In order to develop this theme, I start with some history – looking at Augustine, the Christendom project and the legacy of the Enlightenment – before exploring some aspects of the current situation and looking in more detail at a particularly revealing and tricky contemporary case: the question of justice. My assumption – which I do not have the space to defend here – is that modern political culture has become highly fragmented, and that this fragmentation leads to both difficulties and opportunities in theory and practice; it provides the context within which a 'challenging and constructive inculturation' of the gospel is possible today.

Augustine and pagan political theology

In the twilight of the ancient world, confronted with the charge that Christianity – the 'new religion' – was in some sense responsible for the collapse of the Roman *imperium* in the face of barbarian onslaughts, Augustine developed a political theology that was also a theology of history, or at least a set of guidelines for interpreting the signs of the times, and an emphatic repudiation of the pagan political theology of the empire. Augustine's *City of God* was both, in Peter Brown's words, 'a deliberate confrontation with paganism'[1] and a major effort of theological construction that amounted to a specific confession of the faith in a particular historical context. Pagan political theologies and their Christian reflections saw the development of the Roman Empire as being the subject of history; they could not accommodate the possibility that the empire might degenerate and collapse, and that such an event might be in any sense a judgement of God.

Augustine, in contrast, affirmed that the Roman Empire was, and always had been, corrupt. It had been founded by a gang of robbers led by Romulus, demonstrating the general truth that earthly states without justice are bands of robbers, and robber bands are states in miniature.[2] It is not legitimate, Augustine suggested, to sacralize the empire – or any other political system, for that matter. Even the best of existing systems are provisional, partial and defective. The earthly city has no claim on our ultimate allegiance; only God and the heavenly city deserve unconditional loyalty. The gospel is not the good news of the *Pax Romana*.

Augustine's political theology refuses to deify any temporal order, even that of the church visible, as it strives to interpret the signs of the times in the light of God's purpose to bring the heavenly city into which the elect will be gathered, and in which people are bound together by sharing the highest love, the love of God. Only in the heavenly city, the city of God, are true justice, peace and fellowship to be found. Thus Augustine affirms in the strongest terms the spiritual significance of the temporal order, while excluding it from the sphere of the sacred. Politics in the temporal city needs to be challenged, illumined and nourished by the gospel. Only in relation to the heavenly city can the earthly city be understood aright as either a gang of robbers held together by their love of power and riches, or as a band of pilgrims lovingly seeking the city whose builder and maker is God. Challenging the adequacy, justice and finality of the earthly city is, in fact, a way of proclaiming the gospel.

Augustine unhesitatingly rejects the three kinds of theology presented by the Stoic Varro – mythical, natural (or philosophical) and political. He contends that classical mythical and political theologies made no serious claim to truth, but were regarded as indispensable forms of social control, ways of legitimating the established order and ensuring loyalty and obedience. Natural or philosophical theology made an attempt to reach beyond the limits of the city to seek a more general truth, but it was commonly regarded as inherently seditious, something to be kept from the ears of the common people. Because it did not attend to revelation and confused nature with nature's God, philosophical theology, despite its pretensions, was doomed to futility.

In rejecting classical political theology, Augustine was not rejecting political theology as such. Indeed, his own project in *City of God* was the inauguration of a new style of political theology that related to the political order in a more subtle and complex way than classical political theology *because it saw its task as speaking truth to power rather than explaining and justifying the existing order, and as interpreting history in the light of the gospel.* And the truth that is spoken to power can be nothing other than the gospel, which is, for Augustine, inescapably in the public square even when it concerns itself with the soul and with subjectivity. Augustine saw speaking truth to power as public confession of the faith, an essential aspect of the mission of the church.

The Christendom project

Whether Christendom was the establishment or the subversion of Christian faith is an issue that is still much debated.[3] Oliver O'Donovan has sought, in a powerful book, to rehabilitate 'that centuries-long engagement with government which we call "Christendom"'.[4] Christendom involved an enlargement of the theological agenda. No longer was it possible to avoid the dilemmas facing those who exercised power. There was now a sustained and serious effort to shape society by the gospel, for 'Those who ruled in Christendom and those who thought and argued about government believed that the gospel was true. They intended their institutions to reflect Christ's coming reign.'[5] O'Donovan is right in suggesting that in the Christendom era, when the truth of Christianity was taken for granted as the truth of politics, both church and political order were seen as witnesses to the kingdom of God.

The conscious intention of Christendom was mission, the proclamation and manifestation of the truth of the gospel. But the reality was often very different. Often Christian political theology came to perform the same functions in the same way as the old pagan political theologies. Old practices of sacralizing politics were revived, and the political and ecclesiastical orders (regarded as interdependent) were absolutized. Old ways of thought about politics were reintroduced and often sat very uneasily alongside the worship of a crucified God:

> In both its forms, Byzantine and Western, Christendom meant the definitive entry of Christianity into the public realm, there to fulfil functions unthought of in the early days of the church. These went far beyond prayer for, and obedience to, the authorities, the demystification of power and the claim that the great central images of the Christian faith – the Kingdom, the Lord, the City, and so on – have a public bearing on earth. Now the church itself was a powerful institution and was looked to for support and guidance by the rulers, who repeatedly saw it as the ideological wing of government, and little more. Church leaders had to learn how to be chaplains to the powerful, not merely pastors of little flocks of the weak.[6]

If the intention of Christendom was mission, the reality was often ambiguous and contradictory. But this has been characteristic of mission down the ages. And it ill becomes us, in the wake of two world wars and the Holocaust, to despise the Christendom project.

And yet, in recognizing that Christendom was never a monolithic uniformity but comprehended a diversity of often conflicting impulses, it becomes difficult either to endorse O'Donovan's attempt to rehabilitate Christendom or to denounce Christendom as unqualified apostasy after the style of Alasdair Kee. Christendom, in fact, was both a project noble in its conception, something that was almost inevitable as Christianity became the majority faith, and a drastic adulteration of the gospel. We must not forget that under Charlemagne whole tribes were forced to convert at the point of the sword and were baptized by hosepipe, as it were; that the history of Christendom was punctuated with pogroms against the Jews, bloodthirsty crusades against the Muslims and massacres of Albigensians.

When Christendom began to expand across the Atlantic, the record was even more ambiguous. The year 1492 represents, in a sense, the apogee of Christendom. Columbus sailed the ocean blue in order to conquer and convert the New World, absorbing it into Christendom. In 1992, while some people celebrated 'the evangelization of the Americas', others denounced the genocide of native American peoples and the prolonged plunder of the Americas for the sake of Europe. The conquistadors, in extending the bounds of Christendom, read this royal *Requerimiento* to the chieftains of the tribes they encountered:

> I ask and require of you ... that you recognize the Church as sovereign over the entire universe, in her name the Supreme Pontiff called Pope, and the King and Queen ... as your superior lords ... to consent and permit the priests to preach to you. If you do this, you do well and their Royal Highnesses and I will receive you with all love and charity. But, if you do not do this ... with the help of God I will enter powerfully against you and will war against you everywhere and in every way that I can. And I will subjugate you in obedience to the Church and their Royal Highnesses. I will take you, your women and children, will enslave you and as such will sell you ... and I will take your belongings and will do unto you all the harm and evil that it is in my power to do.[7]

Also in 1492, it was finally decreed that all Jews and Moors must leave the territory of Spain. Ethic cleansing is not an invention of the twentieth century. Internally the Inquisition maintained the semblance of orthodoxy. Many saw Christendom as a glorious vision, but with hindsight its awful ambiguity is only too obvious.

At the heart of the ambiguity of the Christendom project regarded as an expression of the mission of the church lay the question of the relationship between the gospel and power, an issue that is still omnipresent in the practice and the discussion of mission. If mission is very centrally concerned with speaking truth *to* power and announcing the good news that the powers have been subjected to Christ, what happens when mission is subtly transformed into speaking truth *from* power? With the collapse of Christendom, in the sense of a social and political order that claims to be founded on Christian truth and recognizes to some extent Christian constraints on the use of power, Christian mission faces new problems and fresh opportunities.

In his attack on Christendom, the Danish thinker Søren Kierkegaard saw the need to recognize that Christendom was dead and act on this recognition, particularly in the life of the church. This provided the condition for faithful witness to the truth, for effective mission.[8] For 'Christendom has done away with Christianity, without being quite aware of it,' he wrote. 'The consequence is that, if anything is to be done, one must try again to introduce Christianity into Christendom.'[9] We have still to assimilate in our understanding and practice of mission that Christendom is dead, and that this is not to be regarded wistfully as a tragedy or as a challenge to resuscitate it, but as an opportunity for a recovery of integrity in mission, for the reintroduction of Christianity in a more modest and authentic form into the nations that once formed Christendom.

Universalizing modernity

The disintegration of Christendom in the sixteenth and seventeenth centuries – although the Western world remains full of potent remnants and relics – laid the foundations for a new scheme of order. The Enlightenment project of building a tolerant, liberal and rational world was on every count impressive both in its conception and in its achievements. The West has been deeply marked by the Enlightenment in a way many other parts of the world have not.

A fundamental assumption of the Enlightenment universalizing intellect was that society can get along perfectly well – indeed far better than in unenlightened times – without particularistic religion in the public realm, or with religion firmly relegated to the private and domestic sphere. Kant, for instance, argued in his *Perpetual Peace* (1795) that the peace of the social and political order must be established on ahistorical and universal rational moral principles. These may be 'affirmed and ennobled' by religious beliefs, but the beliefs themselves have a marginal role and in the last analysis are dispensable.

In the Enlightenment, political theology for the most part became an embellished form of political philosophy – capable, for instance, of accommodating Adam Smith's economics as a department of natural theology. Despite the avowedly secular nature of the discourse, the tendency increasingly was to sacralize existing orders. A note of prophetic challenge and critique was rarely heard. Christianity became, in Metz's words,

> an extremely privatized religion that has been, as it were, specially prepared for the domestic use of the propertied middle class citizen. It is above all a religion of inner feeling. It does not protest against or oppose in any way the definitions of reality, meaning and truth, for example, that are accepted by the middle class society of exchange and success. It gives greater height and depth to what already applies even without it.[10]

There is not here a gospel to be proclaimed, a challenging truth to be witnessed to.

Enlightenment political theology had other problems, too. A universal disembodied rationality showed itself impotent against the primordial loyalties that are so central to all of us. The tendency of Enlightenment rationality to disregard or deplore all particularist tendencies limits its ability to relate effectively to a world in which particularism is always powerfully present. It seems powerless to curb or channel nationalist fervour in the Balkans today. It deplores ethnic cleansing with the rest of us, but it finds patriotism barely comprehensible. It is incapable of understanding and affirming what is good in particularism, and it has repeatedly shown itself impotent in the face of upsurges of nationalistic fervour. The inability of the German universities to resist Hitler effectively is another case in point.

The critique of Enlightenment modernity, of course, goes much further. The desire to recognize, create and celebrate an orderly, systematic world finds its ultimate denouement, it has been argued, in the Holocaust. Universalizing abstract systems of thought are inherently oppressive, according to the postmodernist critics. And by ironing out difference they end up strangely unreal and unrelated to concrete experiences.

Kierkegaard again makes the point effectively: he was a resolute opponent of the grand theorists and systematizers of his day, of whom Hegel was the chief. Hegel had distanced himself from the Aristotelian tradition, which saw philosophy's task as unveiling the order and rationality of the universe so that human life could conform to reality. Both Hegel and Marx developed systems based on a conviction that the world is full of defects that must be put right if it is to be intelligible. Marx differed from Hegel in rejecting the notion that thought had the power to transform; for him, a material radical transformation was required in which human agency played a major part.[11] But both, in their varying ways, were grand theorists, subject to Kierkegaard's strictures. 'In relation to their systems', Kierkegaard wrote, 'most systematisers are like a man who builds an enormous castle and lives in a shack close by; they do not live in their own enormous systematic buildings. But spiritually that is a decisive objection. Spiritually speaking a man's thought must be the building in which he lives – otherwise everything is topsy-turvy.'[12]

Kierkegaard's suspicion of systems and grand theories was well grounded. He knew that the castle of theory often serves in its magnificence to conceal what is actually going on, to disguise an often unpalatable reality and even to legitimate awful practices. He understood thought, and above all thought about God, as something that must be *dwelt* in, must relate to experience, and must expose untruth and injustice wherever they are found. The castle of theory needs to be cut down to size, demystified as it were, so that humans can live and flourish there.

Accordingly, Kierkegaard saw his role as a theologian as being like that of Socrates, asking questions, exposing falsehood and, gadfly-like, stinging people into awareness of the truth. He wrote in parables and epigrams and meditations that were deliberately unsystematic. He wrote *Philosophical Fragments*, followed by an immense volume, playfully entitled *Concluding Unscientific Postscript.* And in communicating so, Kierkegaard perhaps gives us clues as to effective theological communication in the modern, or postmodern, age at a time of moral fragmentation. Truth is not something to be comprehended, controlled, used or appropriated. It is rather to be indwelt, lived out in action and witnessed to. And that is the Christian mission.

A fragmented world

The modern missionary movement, with its Christocentric universalism, is in fact a typical Enlightenment/modernist project. But Kierkegaard in a real sense anticipated a world that is as postmodern as it is post-Christian. The condition of postmodernity is a pluralist society in which not only are many theories and world views allowed and tolerated, but there is a profound suspicion of grand theories and theologies, of systems that make claim to truth. These are essentially seen as coercive and inadequate to reality. Society, *pace* Rawls and others, does not need a consensus to survive, according to the postmodernists. Indeed, consensus can only be achieved by force or manipulation. It inherently involves a limitation of freedom, which in a fairly straightforward sense becomes the great central value of postmodernity. There is, in Lyotard's words, a profound 'incredulity towards metanarratives'.[13] The postmodern mind knows itself to be homeless, but it also recognizes that no home exists. The mindset is melancholy and anxious, but it is also willing to come to terms with the fragmentation of reality and refuses to impose an artificial and fragile order upon it.

Postmodernists typically see the eastern European communist dictatorships that collapsed more than a decade ago as both an exemplification of the Enlightenment project and its nemesis. Vaclav Havel would probably decline to call himself a postmodernist, but his analysis of Czechoslovakia under the communists has a postmodernist flavour. Havel saw the death throes of the old communist regimes as indicative of a far more extensive and profound crisis that could perhaps be called the collapse of modernity, the Enlightenment project having run its course. The sad communist systems were 'a kind of warning to the West, revealing its own latent tendencies'.[14] The East holds up a mirror to the West; both are modernist societies in deep crisis.

The system – and Havel clearly means both the old Marxist systems, in which decay, decadence and demoralization were easy to discern, and the societies of the West, in which decline is more concealed – depends on *ideology*, whose function 'is to provide people ... with the illusion that the system is in harmony with the human order and the order of the universe'. Ideology legitimates power and oppressive dictatorship, for it pervasively suggests that 'the centre of power is identical with the centre of truth'.[15] Ideology – overtly in the old Marxist regimes, more covertly in other modernist societies – is thus the main pillar of the system that effectively creates and internalizes a false reality: 'It is built upon lies. It works only as long as people are willing to live within the lie.'[16]

Havel's diagnosis may be, at least superficially, postmodernist, but his response is not. He does not despair of knowing and living in truth, of witnessing to truth, either in unitary ideological despotisms or in conditions of pluralism and thoroughgoing relativism. He comprehensively rejects the modernist project of rebuilding the world according to some great rational scheme, especially a scheme that promises the overcoming of the human condition and a future contrived perfection. But Havel affirms the primary importance of 'togetherness', particularly that form which is 'being for' others.[17] And in this he reminds us of the unavoidable centrality of the church in the Christian mission.

Postmodernists characteristically celebrate the fragmentation and pluralism of postmodern societies as a condition in which, for the first time, true freedom is possible. In postmodernity there is a new delight in feelings and emotion. Mystery and wonder are again in fashion, for the Enlightenment project of demystifying the world has been replaced with the re-enchantment of the world.[18] There is a new quality of concern with action and with morals, with a realistic acceptance of the ambiguities and uncertainties with which action is surrounded, and a new respect for the concrete and the particular. Action does not necessarily call for justification or need to be fitted into some great scheme if it is to be authentic. 'Saints are saints', writes Bauman, 'because they do not hide behind the law's broad shoulders. They know, or act as if they felt, that no law, however generous and humane, may exhaust the moral duty, trace the consequences of "being for" to their radical end, to the ultimate choice of life or death.'[19] Indeed, commitment to great moral or political systems and ideals can sometimes conflict directly with an ethical attitude to the concrete other, as in Dostoevsky's doctor, who said:

> I love humanity ... but I wonder at myself. The more I love humanity in general, the less I love man in particular. In my dreams ... I have often come to making enthusiastic schemes for the service of humanity, and perhaps I might actually have faced crucifixion if it had been suddenly necessary; and yet I am incapable of living in the same room with anyone for two days together, as I know by experience. ... In twenty-four hours I begin to hate the best of men. ... But it has always happened that the more I detest men individually the more ardent becomes my love for humanity.[20]

In its concern with the concrete, with action and existence, with freedom, and in its suspicion of grandiose and impersonal schemes and systems, postmodernity presents opportunities and challenges to the mission of the church. Indeed, the recognition of fragmentation opens a whole range of evangelistic opportunities.

Others, such as Alasdair MacIntyre, see the postmodern condition as a *predicament*. Modern society, for MacIntyre, is morally fragmented, since there are no generally accepted criteria for the resolution of moral disputes and conflicts.[21] No widely recognized moral framework exists; the situation is volatile, for behaviour lacks a rationale or a place in a larger scheme that makes some claim to truth. The moral fragments that survive today were embedded and embodied in various traditions and practices that are, for the most part, dismissed as discredited and irrelevant survivals among deviant minorities. We cannot understand moral standards properly, MacIntyre believes, without situating these fragments in the context of the traditions of moral enquiry from which they originally came and from which they have become detached. Only if we take seriously the traditions of moral enquiry, he believes, may we be able to make progress towards resolving key issues of today.

Both MacIntyre and the postmodernists recognize that fragmentation is characteristic of the contemporary world. The postmodernists celebrate this fact; MacIntyre laments it as a grave predicament. I would argue that, from the angle of the Christian mission, we should recognize that fragmentation presents opportunities and challenges that are at the same time fresh and strikingly similar to the situation in the ancient world when the Christian faith was born. We can learn from the early church how to witness to the truth in a fragmented age. Whether fragmentation is a predicament or an emancipation, the gospel can be proclaimed in a fragmented age. That is the immediate task. Whether MacIntyre is right in suggesting that we should work towards a new Christian consensus on Aristotelian and Thomist foundations is a question we may leave aside for the while. My own inclination is that the establishment or restoration of some general consensus based on Christian foundations is inconceivable for the foreseeable future, and probably in the light of historical experience undesirable. Today we have to witness to the truth in a world in fragments.

The case of justice

Disputes that appear to be irresolvable about justice and goodness represent not only academic difficulties but also major problems of practice for people 'on the ground', as it were. Hence they become pressing issues for Christian mission and political theology. Politics and policy-making easily degenerate into, in MacIntyre's telling phrase, 'civil war carried on by other means',[22] an arena in which interest groups compete for control, using ideas as weapons rather than constraints and as justifications for volatile policy changes that in fact are little influenced by overarching moral considerations. Or the ideological pendulum swings from one extreme to the other without the reasons for the change being clear or generally acceptable.

The situation is exacerbated by the pervasive uncertainty about the grounding of justice. Increasingly, secular theorists see justice as based on a consensus. But this is a fragile foundation for an account of justice, because if such a consensus exists (and that is by no means certain), opinions change and ultimately people need a surer conviction than that their opinion is shared by many others.

Practitioners often feel that they are making do with fragments of moral insight, and fragments that are frequently in unacknowledged conflict with other fragments, or are not recognized in the way the system or institution is run. And practitioners sometimes recognize that the fragments that are most important for them as insights into reality, as in some sense *true*, and that are central to the sense of vocation which sustains them in their practice, are derived from a tradition that was and is nurtured in a community of shared faith to which they may or may not belong, and which is now a minority view in society. There is a widespread awareness that the foundations of practice have been shaken.

Let me give an example of what I am talking about. In a working group on criminal justice, an experienced woman prison governor, a committed Christian with a strong sense of vocation, sat silent through long discussions of the standard theories of criminal justice and punishment. None of them seemed to fit reality or give adequate guidance for practice. Then she said, quite quietly, that she had two rather different primary concerns. The first was that in the prison system today so few people were willing to face up to guilt, or respond to it in any serious way. Her second concern was with forgiveness and reconciliation. Few people, she said, regard the criminal justice system and prisons in particular as having anything much to do with forgiveness – indeed they tend to assume that forgiveness and mercy are the contrary of justice.

But the members of the group, as we discussed the prison governor's concern with forgiveness, reconciliation, reception back into fellowship, felt compelled collectively to affirm that forgiveness and reconciliation are the goal, the end, of punishment, and that unless this is held in view as a guiding principle, a system of criminal justice is in danger of losing moral credibility. We recognized that this was in some sense *public truth*, which was accepted as such by those in the group who made no profession of faith as well as by Christians who discerned the roots of the priority of forgiveness and reconciliation in their faith, and found there resources for its clarification. The gospel was being proclaimed, and received, as true.

A theologian should not, I think, be ashamed of offering initially in public debate in the conditions of postmodernity no more than 'fragments' of insight. Postmodernists (and sociologists of knowledge) are, after all, right in affirming that systematic, carefully developed theories can sometimes conceal practices that are inhumane and brutalizing; ideologies can serve as the emperor's new clothes, so that the theologian's task, as a little child, is to cry out, 'But the emperor's got no clothes on!' A fragment of truth reveals that to which most people have allowed themselves to be blinded. Truth-telling in a fragmentary way becomes even more important when the scheme to conceal the emperor's nakedness is something that is hurting people and destroying community.[23]

Such a fragmentary theology assumes that in this life we never see save 'in a mirror, dimly', and only at the end 'face to face' (1 Corinthians 13.12). This might make us more generally cautious about regarding theology as some grand, coherent modernist theory rather than a series of illuminating fragments that sustain the life of the community of faith that nurtures them and claim also to be, in some sense, 'public truth'. After all, the Gospels and even the Epistles do not present a 'system'. Rather they are full of parables, stories, epigrams, injunctions, songs; fragments, in short. The system-building came far later, and it is still not easy to coordinate the material into a coherent, consistent system. Perhaps theologians should sympathize with the postmodernists' suspicion of systems and system-building! Is it perhaps enough, with the man born blind, to know one thing with assurance: 'I was blind, now I see' (John 9.25)?

Kierkegaard was well aware that fragments often fit together or are derived from larger systematic wholes. Moral and theological fragments come from specific quarries. He knew that theological fragments by which Christians live and which shape their practice have their home in a community of shared faith – the church – which, if it is true to its calling and its mission, does not look back wistfully to an unrecoverable past but looks forward with expectation to God's future, and meanwhile offers its fragments as a contribution to the common store and seeks to embody its insights in its life. Only at the end will the fragments, the 'puzzling reflections in a mirror', give way to a face-to-face encounter with the Truth.

When a fragment is recognized as in some sense true, one should expect an interest in its provenance, in its embeddedness in a broader truth. Is it perhaps a compelling task and opportunity for us to bring together 'theological fragments' that have been illuminating, instructive or provocative in grappling with issues of practice 'on the ground', reflect on them and on their embeddedness in the structure of Christian faith, and enquire whether this gives clues as to a constructive contribution in the public realm today?

Are there theological fragments that might be recognized as public truth and serve to give some coherence and integrity, even in 'the desolation of reality that overtakes human beings in a post-religious age that has grown too wise to swallow the shallow illusions of the Enlightenment' (John Gray)? And might these fragments perhaps be the aptest way of confessing the faith in the public realm today?

NOTES

1. Peter Brown, *Augustine of Hippo: A Biography*, Faber, 1967, p. 312.
2. *De civitate Dei* III:4.
3. See, for example, Alasdair Kee, *Constantine or Christ?*, SCM, 1982.
4. Oliver O'Donovan, *The Desire of the Nations: Rediscovering the Roots of Political Theology*, Cambridge University Press, 1996, p. 193.
5. O'Donovan, p. 194.
6. Duncan Forrester, *Theology and Politics*, Blackwell, 1988, pp. 28–9.
7. Quoted in two sixteenth-century documents: Fernandez de Oviedo, *Historia natural y general de las Indias*, and Fr Las Casas, *Teoria y leves de la conquista*. See

Luis N. Rivera Pagan, *Evangelizacion y Violencia: La Conquista de America*, Ediciones SEMI, 1991, p. 53. Translation by Guillermo Cook.

8. Søren Kierkegaard, *Attack on Christendom*, Princeton University Press, 1968, and *Training in Christianity*, Princeton University Press, 1944.

9. Kierkegaard, *Training in Christianity*, p. 39.

10. J. B. Metz, *Faith in History and Society*, Burns and Oates, 1980, p. 45.

11. N. Lobkowitz, *Theory and Practice: History of a Concept from Aristotle to Marx*, University of Notre Dame Press, 1967, pp. 340–41.

12. Alexander Dru (ed.), *The Journals of Søren Kierkegaard*, Oxford University Press, 1938, 583. Cf. 582.

13. Cited in Stephen K. White, *Political Theory and Postmodernism*, Cambridge University Press, 1991, pp. 4–5.

14. Vaclav Havel, *Living in Truth*, Faber, 1987, p. 54.

15. Havel, p. 39.

16. Havel, p. 50.

17. See Zygmunt Bauman, *Life in Fragments: Essays in Post-Modern Morality*, Blackwell, 1995, pp. 44–55.

18. Zygmunt Bauman, *Post-Modern Ethics*, Blackwell, 1993, p. 33.

19. Bauman, *Post-Modern Ethics*, p. 81.

20. Fyodor Dostoevsky, *The Brothers Karamazov*, Heinemann, 1912, pp. 52–3.

21. Alasdair MacIntyre, *After Virtue: A Study in Moral Theory*, University of Notre Dame Press, 1981, pp. 104–5.

22. MacIntyre, p. 236.

23. Notice that Bauman characterizes 'the post-modern perspective' as 'above all the tearing off of the mask of illusions; the recognition of certain pretences as false and certain objectives as neither attainable or, for that matter, desirable' (*Post-Modern Ethics*, p. 3).

Fragments and Links in an Unjust World

Hong Jung Lee

My response to Duncan Forrester's proposals in 'Christian Political Discourse as Public Confession' is a complementary suggestion rather than a critical assessment, for I am not a Christian social ethicist but a Korean missiologist. I will suggest three complementary perspectives that, I believe, are irresistible when doing Christian political discourse at the present time.[1]

A new context

At the present juncture in world history, we are experiencing, at an unprecedented rate, the major developments of the globalization of markets and capital in alliance with the nation states, transnationalization, and the domination and control of information technology. At the same time, many parts of the world are experiencing the ill effects of uneven development and deep imbalances and injustices in their economic and ecological life. It seems to me that the present world has been brought under the dominion or hegemony of cultural forces such as CNN, the Internet and Hollywood, which dictate values, symbols, lifestyles, aspirations, morals and identities.

In the process of globalization, liberalized economic activity becomes the central organizing principle of world operation, and the corporate bureaucrats, the technocrats and the capitalists are the major players in world activity. In spite of some promise from such developments, we cannot ignore their inherent dangers. For one thing, the globalization of markets and capital lends moral legitimacy to the methods and impositions of corporate entities, given the dominant commercial and consumerist values that they have so strongly upheld. Human life is defined more and more in terms of economic principles and market realities.

On the other hand, alongside such developments is the seeming reassertion of a new *kairos* in our time, that is, there are signs of the ending of modernity and the beginning of a postmodern era:

1. A wide dispersal of power, contrasted with the North Atlantic-centric hegemony, leading to the affirmation of a genuine pluralism of traditions, cultures and religions, and a dialogue among them;
2. 'Earthism', in contrast to nationalism and economism, a refocusing of human activity on the healing of the earth;
3. Holistic thinking, in contrast to Enlightenment rationalism and the fragmentation of academic disciplines, the quest for a new way of thinking that is more organic, ecological, relational, communal, non-dualistic, non-substantial, non-anthropocentric;
4. Liberation from sexual repression combined with an awareness of new forms of sexual exploitation and the ambiguities of sexual practices; and
5. New conceptions of power that are not patriarchal or hierarchical but embody empowerment, reciprocity and participation.

These contrasting developments are very much in sight, even outside the West. In Asia, while globalization has overtaken much of the economic and political agenda, organic communities have also made important breakthroughs in popularizing the agenda of the marginalized peoples as reflected in multicultural movements, gender-justice groups, dirty-footed theologies and so on. Clearly, our time calls for a restatement of the task of social ethics in a post-Cold War era, a post-Christendom world, the condition of late modernity and the dawn of a postmodern period.

The present situation in Christian political discourse may no longer be a call to an analysis of a distinctly local context but a context we share with the rest of the world. Christian social ethicists should be enabled to see a local context from a global perspective, and a global context from a local perspective. The comprehensive analysis of the local–global and global–local interaction becomes one of the essential elements in doing Christian political discourse. In this sense, one sure implication of this situation is the need to re-examine the discourses of ideology and politics today. The recent decline of long-established parties of the left and the so-called victory of the West over communism seem to me a clear sign that all ideological positions of progressive ethicists must now be reappraised. At a time when the various camps of the left are consolidating their ranks for a more effective role, we need to assess from our ethical perspective what ideological visions can be pursued and what kind of political participation is required in our given historical milieu.

In face of this quest, we should take into consideration our distinctive calling as theologians, ethicists and even missiologists. A problem of our time seems to be the fragmentary and dualistic ways of thinking and doing among ideologues, political practitioners, corporate bureaucrats, even theological circles. Current conversations in politics, economy and ideology seem to have relegated moral and theological discourses to the sidelines, as if the latter belong only to otherworldly concerns. Ideology, for instance, tends to pay nothing more than lip service to religious ideas and always speaks with contempt against matters of spirituality. If Christian political discourse wants to demonstrate its emancipatory role in this whole project, it must begin to reassert itself and resist the hegemonic methods of other disciplines, setting out new rules of the game.

Stories of the people: the main resource

Christian political discourses should see, in particular, the significance of the fragmentary and subversive stories of the people, that is, the religio-political and socio-cultural biographies of the people, beyond any particular religious tradition. As seen in the central shifts in science, the shift from objects to relationships, from analysis that looks for fragmentation and specialization to synthesis that looks for patterns behind patterns and processes beneath structures, relationship should be the basis of all definition. In this light, metaphor is more adequate than logic for describing the whole fabric of mental interconnections; metaphor is right at the bottom of being alive. For the structural analysis of living creatures, stories, parables and metaphors are considered essential expressions of human thinking, of the human mind. The role of stories is intimately connected with the importance of relationships as the essence of the living world. What is important and true in a story is not the plot, the things or the people, but the relationships between them. A story is an aggregate of formal relations scattered in time and develops a web of formal relations through a collection of stories. The matrix of the collection of stories is a coherent and precise pattern of relationships.

Christian political discourses should see, from a missiological perspective, the possibility that the 'infrastructure of God's historical revelation'[2] can perhaps be reconstructed through the religio-political and socio-cultural biographies of the Minjung. The stories are media of transmission of Minjung events that take place in the concrete socio-economic and political context in which the Minjung exist in their conflict with the religio-political ruling power and its ideology. The stories contain messages or wisdom that can be theologized as a part of God's mission in which the Minjung suffer and struggle for their own dignity, subjecthood, and liberated and sanctified life. The stories that have been transmitted as the language of the Minjung – very often depoliticized stories – have the dynamism to stimulate the eschatological hope of the Minjung toward messianic politics instead of political messianism and to create a new Minjung-centred religion that liberates both the oppressive religions and the oppressed people. The stories of the people, in a sense, reveal the ultimate purpose of God's mission in history and show the way in which all realities can participate in God's mission.

In the stories of the people, the world is very often perceived as a whole, universal, organic, living community. From bottom to top, all realities are universally and organically related to each other. They exist in an interrelated order, on a just and mutually living principle. The identity of each reality is determined by its relationship with others. The stories show how the identity of the Minjung has been crucially defined by the religious and political superstructure. They illustrate the Minjung's awareness not only of their loss of power, but also of a messianic hope. The stories also show the hermeneutical process of the people's subjective historical consciousness and their subsequent awakening, that is, the process of 'conscientization', praxis and reflection of the Minjung – a gradual but total conversion. The stories manifest the fact that through their messianic suffering and death, the Minjung heuristically achieve their messianic wisdom and vision – the Minjung consciousness – and they actualize both passively and actively a paradigm shift from politico-religious messianism to messianic politics and religion.

An ecumenical political discourse beyond Christocentric universalism

In Christian political discourses, the concept of the *oikoumene* as a household (*oikos*), an interrelated whole, requires an ecological perspective that understands creation as the living space of all living things, a space created and protected by God. The *oikoumene* as the 'one household of life' should therefore extend beyond the world of humankind, of the one human race, to creation as a whole. In this sense, history can no longer be regarded as the central category of interpretation, because human history can be bound up only with the history of all living things. The human household is incapable of surviving without being related to the other households, that is, its natural environment.

The *oikoumene* is a matter of dynamic, real relationships – the actual yet endangered connections and relationships between churches, between cultures, between people and human societies in their infinite variety, and between the world of humankind and creation as a whole. 'Being-in-relationship is as much a part of our nature as being-in-oneself.'[3] Autonomy and interchange, selfhood and relationships condition each other: human knowledge is accompanied by the 'quest for connections', ever more comprehensively by the 'original interconnectedness'.[4]

The biblical image of the 'house of living stones', the 'house of Israel' and the 'house of God' includes the whole range of meanings of the root *oikos* (house/household), such as ecology, economy, ecumenism. The premise is always that Jesus Christ is the cornerstone and that the Christian community as a living house, as a sign of God's plan for salvation (*oikonomia*), will unite all peoples in justice and peace in one human family.[5] In these images, church-centred ecumenism is inextricably bound up with the struggle for the unity of humankind, because the whole inhabited earth of human beings is thought to struggle to become what (the exclusively Christian) God intended them to be. This ecumenism needs a diverse understanding of the divine reality and of the relationship between God, the world and humankind, which would make it possible to overcome the tendency to Christo-monism and give a coherent understanding of the dynamism of history and the relative autonomy of the created world. The concentration on a Christology from the top does not give the humanity of Jesus Christ its full force.

This Christocentric universalism can easily be degraded to, or make a compromise with, a closed system of domination and dependency, which can be oppressive and paralysing in its effects. It can be said to parallel a critical perception of the imperial *oikoumene* of the *Pax Romana* as a threatening reality.[6] In the light of the power structure of the 'transnational *oikoumene*', today's enigmatic ambiguity of the *oikoumene* can be characterized as militarily secured, politically administered, economically organized and scientifically planned. This closed system obeys a logic of power aiming at total control and increasingly stifles life, threatening to make the earth uninhabitable.

On the contrary, the biblically based perception of the *oikoumene* proves to be a 'liberating impulse' that is founded on the 'totality of relationships' rather than structures.[7] It can be characterized as a living interaction rather than death-dealing autonomous laws. With faith in God who has established the covenant for the whole of creation, and by the hope that God will dwell with humankind, with God's people, it is convinced that the earth is habitable, that is, that the whole inhabited earth is the household of life. In this concept of the *oikoumene*, its ecological, social, political and ecclesiological dimensions are linked in the closest possible way.[8]

The *oikos* as space for living not only draws a boundary around itself, but also enables relationships to be formed. The space of the living person is, on the one hand, enclosed space and, on the other, the 'possibility of communication with neighbouring beings and their environments' that evokes neighbourliness. In this possibility, every frontier enclosing the living space of a living thing can be regarded as an open frontier, and in this situation, the 'ownership of any given space' and the 'community of the living in the universal cohesion of communication' are not mutually exclusive but the very conditions that make one another possible.[9] It seems that in the ecological structure of the household of the *oikoumene*, there is always a harmonious duality between 'boundary and openness, independence and relationship, rest and movement, the familiar and the alien, continuity and discontinuity'.[10]

Doing Christian political discourse in the plurality of the *oikoumene*, we Christians need to find a more inclusive and modest way of understanding the reality. Christian political discourse as a way of God's mission should proceed in a dialogical way, aiming at mutual transformation rather than a dominating moral hegemony. Christian political discourse as public confession should therefore be regarded as a mutual invitation towards the liberation of life, the *oikoumene*. In my view, only the people as the centre of the web of mission can provide the criterion for this public Christian engagement.

NOTES

1. For a fuller discussion, see Hong Jung Lee, *Reconstructing a Korean-Ecumenical Theology of Mission in the Plurality of the Oikoumene*, unpublished Ph.D. dissertation, University of Birmingham, 1995.
2. Suh Namdong, *Minjung shinhak ui tamgu*, Hangil-sa, 1983, pp. 155–61, 356–7.
3. Konrad Raiser, *Ecumenism in Transition: A Paradigm Shift in the Ecumenical Movement*, WCC, 1991, p. 86.
4. Raiser, p. 86.
5. Raiser, pp. 83–4.
6. Klaus Wengst, *Pax Romana and the Peace of Jesus Christ*, SCM, 1987.
7. Raiser, p. 86.
8. Raiser, p. 90.
9. Jurgen Moltmann, *God in Creation: An Ecological Doctrine of Creation*, SCM, 1985, pp. 142–4.
10. Raiser, p. 88.

Farewell To Missionary Innocence

Werner Ustorf

It is commonplace today among churches all over the world to call for the return of mission to the West. I think this call is justified, and I have myself participated in an ecumenical study process aimed at developing one of the tools for this mission, namely formulating a missiology of Western culture.[1] Some questions still need asking: What kind of West, or Western culture, are we talking about? What are the contours of Christ in this culture, and how do people there recognize the face of Christ? Will the churches in the West, too, need to be an object of mission? Who are the missionaries? Are we to see culture in the light of the gospel or the gospel in the light of culture, and what does it mean when we say 'the gospel'? And finally, does 'return' mean that old, or perhaps somebody else's, answers are given to questions that are not, or are no longer, asked in the West? In this chapter, I will attempt to explore some of these questions from and within a European context.

The coming and return of mission

Part of this context is Europe's long Christian history. It is therefore important to distinguish the question of the *coming of mission* from that of the *return of mission*. I will give a well-known example to illustrate the distinction. In his *Ecclesiastical History of the English People*, which was written in the eighth century, Bede mentions the baptism of King Edwin in York and the conversion of the people in Northumbria in 627. Visions, trade and international relations played an equally important part here, but there was also an argument of critical discernment. One of the king's chief men expressed this in the story of a sparrow that flew through a comfortably heated hall one winter's day. The sparrow was only safe and warm in the hall, outside it was cold all around – the cold out of which the sparrow came and to which it would have to return. That was the analogy to human life, the terrible ignorance of what precedes this life and what comes after it. The argument was clever, for this non-Christian went on to say that if this new teaching, Christianity, really offered more certain knowledge, then it might be justifiable to accept it.[2]

'Certain' knowledge is a strong criterion, even when it is anything but absolute. At that time it concerned a Celtic cosmos of meaning, partly even a Celtic Christian, a Germanic and a Latin Christian one, which had to be linked together in York in one way or another. This required escaping from the narrow space of tribal culture and connecting with the treasures of the Latin world culture. However, space in every respect – religious, cultural, intellectual – on the British Isles at the time could only be provided by what was then regarded as the centre of the world, Rome. How would King Edwin's people react to the present situation? I suppose the reaction would not greatly differ from what is happening in post-Christian England today. People have often, as it were, become sparrows again, wishing to know what precedes life and what follows it. Where, today, is the new centre that opens for them the entrance to the 'free space' of the world, the key to the secret of God and the passage through death? In such situations people look again for new – and, if possible, better – offers. Just as in York more than a thousand years ago, the old altars are being destroyed and new ones experimented with, perhaps resulting in disillusionment when these experiments fail. The difference today is that Christianity is often seen as belonging to the 'old altars'. Considering mission and conversion in relation to contemporary European culture requires us to address the people's quest for 'certain knowledge' and the question of why Christianity is no longer expected to fulfil this.

Inside and outside Christianity

Two processes are currently influencing European Christianity, one coming more from the outside, the other more from within. This distinction between *outside* and *inside* is bound to be questionable, and I use these terms in a geographical sense only. The process from the outside is well known. Since the Columbus project of 1492 and the Vasco da Gama epoch starting in 1498, Christianity has experienced its largest increase – or advance – for more than a millennium, mainly in the Americas, Africa, Asia and the Pacific. Missiology is currently taking on board what we could call the 'non-Western paradigm shift' in the history of Christianity. Local theologies are mushrooming in the world's cultures, and one thing has become clear: navigation on the sea of faith is possible by using Western and a lot of other maps and charts. New Christian territories have been discovered, new maps are around, and the overall cartography of Christianity has changed substantially. That is affecting Western Christianity deeply. In a global context and given the search for a common humanity, the question arises of whether the church in the West sees the new cartography as a problem or as a chance for new liberation towards the fullness and the inclusiveness of God's philanthropy in Jesus Christ. I am very sure that European theology is in need of tools and models of how to learn from these new sources of wealth.

However wide the implications of the new cartography of Christianity may be for the European context, I would like to focus here on the second process, the one pressing from the inside. At the beginning of the twenty-first century, and in continuation of a longer trend, European Christianity is facing its biggest recession since the rise of Islam. Recessions in Christian substance are by no means new phenomena in church history. Kenneth Scott Latourette, the grand master of mission history, has taught us to see the movement of Christianity precisely as an oscillation between advance and recession.[3] It is certainly up for discussion what a recession actually is and how it can be quantified, but there are some undeniable sociological trends.

In Britain, for example, church membership and attendance have been increasingly shrinking over the past decades. Several churches outside the mainline denominations, such as the Orthodox churches or some evangelical–charismatic groups, fare better, partly due to immigration, but they do not reverse the overall trend. It may be a matter of dispute whether Britain was *ever* a 'Christian' country, but it is certain that today it is not.

Neither have Islam, Hinduism and Sikhism, the most important religious newcomers to Britain, managed to make significant inroads into the Anglo-Saxon population. The great majority of the population does not participate regularly in institutionalized religion. Britain is not just post-Christian, but post-religious: established religion has ceased to be the unifying basis of national culture.[4] The paradox, which is common elsewhere as well, is that around 70 per cent of the British people declare themselves to be 'religious'; a significant number believe 'somehow' in God.

In fact, the wealthy Western cultures are bubbling religious markets; they have become a kaleidoscope of diverse spiritual movements and groups. The confrontational exclusiveness of terms such as 'Christian' and 'secular' is seen increasingly as a language fossil or as a terminological survival of the power games of previously dominant groups, namely the churches on the one hand and the culture of agnostic liberalism on the other – both currently losing their ability to control the minds of the West. The question of the 'biography' and 'identity' of 'God', another term that has lost its established contours, is no longer a matter for theological specialists only; it has become a subject of public debate. There is even, some suggest, 'an epidemic' of tracking and chasing God.[5] This certainly is a new contextual feature of the West: there is a desire to recapture the proper subject matter of the search for that to which we usually refer as 'God'.

Many Europeans, it seems, are now turning inward or to non-orthodox and non-institutionalized free spaces, at any rate places where religious control and initiative are in the hands of the people. This coincides with the fact that religious communities which make demands that are authoritarian in doctrine and lifestyle, or go strongly against the cultural climate – among which are Christian charismatic groups – remain, all in all, a minority phenomenon. Religious institutions no longer succeed in representing the totality of modern socio-cultural life.

I should not like to interpret these perceptions with a mood of doom but rather positively, as the emancipation of religious symbols from the control of religious institutions. A reappropriation of religious initiative by the people, even when this takes place in a non-church context, can certainly not be a matter of indifference to Christians, who refer to Jesus of Nazareth and the God of, particularly, the common people.

However, the situation is not without its dangers. The religious transformation of Europe, which some might say is taking place in an uncontrolled manner, is threatened and marginalized because, as a result of the secularist taboo, it is not given a recognized place in modern culture.[6] Nonetheless, it is still a place where the common question of reconciliation and redemption is raised in a new way. This is a place where the gospel may be understood in a new fashion. The Good News as the message of salvation only works when this message is embedded in the immediate reality of people, the very places where they experience either the proximity or the remoteness of God.[7]

Europe's religious landscape transformed

I am presenting a tentative sketch of how I see the religious topography of Western Europe. I am not discussing the value, say, of the secularization hypothesis, or of pluralism and postmodernist paradigms, and I am not commenting on the presence of other religions. I have touched upon these questions, but they are far too large to cover in a sketch. My aim is simply to summarize my encounters with people – 'religious' ones and self-declared 'non-religious' people – over the past few years, and that means that I can speak with no authority other than my own.

The important feature of Europe's religious landscape, in my perception, is its transformation. This transformation concerns less the religious side of the human longing for the infinite, as such, than the way the religious quest is expressed. The modes of expression are so various that old terminological habits of classifying them, such as 'secular' and 'religious', have become less and less helpful. The religious dimension is present in nearly all spheres of so-called secular life, and vice versa. That, however, has created a somewhat ambiguous situation: on the one hand, people are now free to regain their religious initiative and live it out in places that are not controlled by religious institutions; on the other, we have the crusaders of acquisitiveness, wealth and domination, who are only too keen to exploit the religious longing and take over the place that church and liberalism have vacated.

In this context, I have repeatedly heard the following issues raised:

- People usually expect the church to give competent guidance in matters of daily life. They expect solidarity, and they hold Jesus in high regard. However, the Christian tradition is no longer felt to be 'true' in the sense of propositional sentences about 'what is the case'. The dogmatic package is seen more as an illegitimate attempt to 'circumcise' the contemporary world. The 'truth' of Christianity is not expected to emerge in sentences and words, but in the testimony of one's life. The questions we are facing could read: 'What does theology do and say if Christianity can no longer be construed as true in the traditional sense? What is to be said and done when Christianity continues to be important long after it has ceased to be true?'[8] Truth in terms of a propositional statement is no longer an accepted criterion.

- The texts of the Bible are losing their privileged position in Europe's cultural and religious life. Other texts have come in and have found a home. All texts, however, religious or not, tend to be seen as products of culture and history: in short, as fiction. Why should the fiction of a certain period of history and a particular culture be of more importance than today's fiction? What is the right of the present over against the past?

- There is a sort of popular revolt against an image of a god who is detached from the world and from life. There is a remarkable desire to become an active counterpart of God, not a spectator or a passive object that has to be ransomed. With this goes a further desire, namely to search right in the centre of one's being for the wholly ineffable place, where there is unity of life and death, reunification with the source. The examples of experiences qualified as numinous are countless. What is their message? I think it is, formally at least, a double message: the kingdom of God is within us, and people do not wish to believe if that means to *force* their own souls into believing. They want to feel the presence of God, so to speak, and to be able to love God in every single movement of their heart.

- The counter move is, however, a methodology of permanent suspicion in relation to one's own motivations, constructions and even experiences. The verdict of this methodology is self-defeating. It says, 'How can we believe that the human being is made in the image of God, if there is evidence that God is made in the image of the human being?' On whatever side the conflict is resolved – feeling God in one's heart or being rigorously agnostic – great psychic energy will be required to keep the respective dangerous opponent out.

Experience alone is ambivalent. It can transform the selfish individual (the form of human survival fitted to a capitalist economy) into a person who is truly for others, but it can also increase the scope of narcissistic delusion. The experience of transcendence is not 'safe' unless explored in a community *and* in a much wider contextual and, finally, inter-contextual debate. My interpretation of these few impressions is that one certainly can find clear indications of religious narcissism in people's desires, perhaps even forms of religious masturbation. This, however, would be nothing new, and it would surely apply to a wide range of *Christian* religiosity as well. The basic problem of the current period of religious transformation in Europe is much more profound and located somewhere else, in the field of mediation – or, more accurately, non-mediation. For a sizeable group, perhaps the majority, the tension between human insatiability – religious and nonreligious – and God's inexhaustibility does not find an acceptable resolution.

If these observations have general validity, then one would indeed be allowed to speak of changes in the religious topography of Europe. There, people have silently freed the history or the story of Jesus of Nazareth from protection by theology and church, and have set it freely in the cultural context, right among the offers of other religions and world views. The church tradition is increasingly regarded as a vehicle that, alongside others, may be used on the way to truth without itself being the final point of truth. For some people the gospel seems to be like a burst pod of flower seeds, whose contents are scattering in order to continue their existence in another, different form. The memory of Jesus Christ survives not only in the churches but also outside, albeit in quite a different mode. Beyond the linguistic confines of the church there are people searching for love without any claim to possession. There, justice and reconciliation are also made themes of discussion and struggle, to which the church cannot possibly remain indifferent.

Towards a new understanding

But how ought the church to understand this new post-Christian situation? How should Christianity regain the initiative, and what is the missionary task in this context? I should like to give a brief sketch of two theological assessments of Europe that I think are significant. The first is essentially concerned with the practical question of mission in Western culture. The second, in my view, applies the concept of purity to theology, assuming that the 'holy' can be separated from the 'unholy' – a concept derived from ritual behaviour. This has immediate and profound implications for mission.

Following the line of discussion started by Lesslie Newbigin in Britain,[9] the former Anglican bishop of Birmingham, Hugh Montefiore, summarized its outcome in the proposition that European cultures (in contrast, for example, to non-Western ones) had taken a course that was 'not Gospel-friendly'[10]. That is the first position. It claims that in the Europe of modernism, a fundamental shift of cultural presuppositions or paradigms has taken place, to the effect that in modern culture the human ratio has been made absolute, leading to a secularized and at best pluralistic perspective, and at worst to relativism or even to nihilism. In this hostile context, which does not offer any point of contact, the Christian tradition cannot be inculturated[11]. Cultural hostility, therefore, is regarded as responsible for the failure of all efforts to re-evangelize Europe so far. The conclusion drawn from this is that modern cultures need to be restructured so that there will be new points of contact which will allow the Christian truth to be made relevant again.[12]

This is an extremely demanding programme, and it has a certain tradition in the missionary movement. The most articulate expression of this attitude is found in *Christianity and Reality*, a confidential document that the Swiss theologian Emil Brunner wrote for the International Missionary Council in 1930. Brunner contended that the proclamation of the church in the context of the modern paradigms of freedom and 'I-loneliness' had lost every point of contact with culture and had become 'unreal'. The church no longer presented the gospel but mere 'surrogates' – having either submitted to modern culture in modernizing adaptation, whereby she doubled and repeated the modern consciousness of autonomy by disguising it in religious terms, or succumbed to the allegedly orthodox sacralism of the past, thereby offering only a 'mummified truth'.

How could a point of contact be regained? According to Brunner, faith would grow as little on the soil of modern culture as a new forest after a process of clearing, because the humus had been washed away. Christian proclamation could succeed only after the formation of, as he put it, new 'culture humus'.[13]

To summarize, this first position, despite all its criticism of culture, makes culture – that is to say, the 'right' one – the *precondition* for evangelization. This was a major missiological issue during the time of colonialism. The question of accepting local culture as a vehicle for the gospel, usually in relation to the native populations of the Americas, Africa and Asia, was hotly debated. Western missions in many cases expected non-Western Christians to enter the gospel through the 'safe' door of a foreign, namely Western, civilization. Now it seems that Western missions are suggesting the use of the same methodology in the West, expecting the native population of Europe to enter the gospel through a culture that is not their own.

The second position is no less resolute. Here the idea of a point of contact is generally rejected, because the gospel is believed to be fundamentally insusceptible to inculturation, to any fusion of religion and culture, whether in a premodern, modern or postmodern world. The gospel always remains foreign and defies all attempts to understand or appropriate it. In 1932 Karl Barth expressed this line of thought in radical one-sidedness: the Christian message neither linked up with pre- or non-Christian traditions nor entered into negotiations with them, but made its appearance simply as a *dictator*, in the sense of a creation from nothing.[14] In 1946 he pointed out that none of the Christian denominations, including the growing ecumenical movement, had succeeded in arresting the 'error, the decline and fall of Europe', especially not the barbarism of Nazism. None of the churches found a prophetic word that would really have been capable of preventing the catastrophe.[15] The cause of the darkness in Europe, from the Crusades to imperialism and fascism, was not to be found in the lack of a proper point of contact or in insufficient inculturation, but rather in the fact that the church gave in to the temptation to 'beg' for people's interest and play up to them.

According to Barth, God's free grace in Christ for the sinful and the miserable should be proclaimed freely and independently: there is no other way. The gap assumed by the first position to exist between gospel and *modern* culture is here affirmed but extended to being a gap between gospel and culture *in principle*. Indeed, Barth does not offer any suggestion of how we might bridge this gap. Humanity cannot reach God on its own account, it can only be reached by God. Barth's standpoint is unequivocally missionary, and it can claim to be in line with a minority tradition within the missionary movement.[16] Even to the 'savages' of the modern age, the gospel should be preached straight out. And this means, indeed, without any doubtful help towards understanding, without desperate attempts at inculturation, but confident of the fact that humans wherever they rebel against God will find a hearing with God.

New inhabitants of the tradition

Yet things cannot be separated so clearly, and these are not mutually exclusive standpoints. It will become evident that they are complementary, or at least must be kept in balance. An illustration of the difficulty is provided by the French Revolution, which not only introduced a new calendar, the beginning of a new epoch in human history, but also a declaration of human rights (in August 1789). Both the content and the iconography of the posters and placards officially announcing the declaration referred to Moses' reception of the tablets of the Law on Mount Sinai. The point here is not only the clear assertion of a new epiphany of God, an interpretation of the new event of God working in history that takes the place of the older tradition, that of the church. Also important is that the French Revolution handles the semantic potential of the biblical tradition in exactly the same way that the Christians of the early church used the Hebrew Bible. Islam, in turn, reformulates the Jewish and Christian tradition and owns it in a specific way.[17] The promise of salvation is always borrowed from its old owners and appropriated by the new inhabitants of the tradition, and it does not take long before the various groups start upgrading themselves to being the 'actual' People of God, howsoever this god may be understood.

In the European cultures of the last two centuries, we have four exclusive traditions alongside one another – Judaism, Christianity, Islam and Secularism, especially when secularism[18] is understood as non-religious rather than 'neutral'. All four are much closer to each other than they usually think, because they all go back historically to the same root. The fact that the Christian version of this root is increasingly on the decline is new. This is, of course, by no means to say that the other versions are in good condition; they all share the dilemma in one way or another, but they are not the subject of discussion here.

Mission as translation and appropriation

The appropriation and transformation of a religious tradition is legitimate in principle. This is the first decisive assumption. Of fundamental significance for us is the transformation as documented in the New Testament. It occurs in the transmission of the tidings of Jesus Christ to the non-Jewish, and especially Hellenistic, culture. The claim of the equality of Jews and Gentiles before God bases itself on the Easter experience. With the inclusion of the Gentile world in the salvation of the God of Israel, a double dynamic, which has been active so far and will be so in the future, has been put into effect: on the one hand, the cultural root of the message of salvation is brought into a wider perspective as a result of its universalization; on the other, the cultures of the Gentile world are destigmatized and accepted as giving valid expression to the message of God's universal love for humankind – no culture is privileged, none is sacrosanct.

Since all are included in the election, the criterion for membership of the faith is not the cultural requirement of *circumcision*, whether this be understood literally or in the sense of some other pre-wrapped dogmatic–ecclesiological parcel. The 'translatability' of the gospel, linguistic as well as cultural, becomes the task and the condition for Christian mission. Mission, in turn, leads to a pluralism of the languages of faith. New languages produce their own, sometimes surprising, formulations. This cultural pluralism has been expressly affirmed in the New Testament, it has theological quality, because neither any individual language nor all languages taken together exhaust the Christ reality in its directness and wholeness, and because all concrete historical expressions of faith are equally non-absolute.[19]

That is the reason why, on the one hand, Christian faith can only feel at home in a living and specific culture. We, and all the Gentiles, can only express fully our gratitude for God's grace and our homage to God in our own cultural environment and language (Romans 15.9). On the other hand, in relation to the principalities and powers in all forms of culture, the gospel must always remain fragile and alien.[20]

The necessary but dangerous principle of inculturation, and with it of innovation and change, has seemed to gain ground rapidly since the end of Western colonialism. At the same time, all efforts towards a re-Christianization of Europe have so far been incapable of arresting the tendency towards marginalization. Both processes taken together certainly require a reaction, an attempt to agree on the common principles of faith. What, however, is the 'middle course' or the centre of the gospel? The New Testament scholar James V. Brownson, presenting a 'missional hermeneutics', concluded that the 'announcement of the story of Jesus' identity, death and resurrection as a story of salvation' (for the whole of humankind), in this abstraction, constitutes the central statement of the New Testament – everything else is already subject to controversy.[21] In my view, this shows most impressively the necessity as well as the risky freedom of the process of inculturation. It means, in fact, that for us what Brownson calls the 'naked structure of the Gospel', as such, does not exist.

The history of mission shows that the sometimes considerable efforts of missionaries, Western or other, to control the direction of the spiritual transformation taking place in a target culture often, in a dialectic reversal, makes it easier for people to run off and away with the gospel. One of the reasons for this is that missionaries often implicitly work with the model of 'circumcision', that is, with the idea of a *repetition*, giving their culturally coloured answers to questions that are not even raised in the local culture. As a rule, it is the indigenous Christians, men and women who in the midst of their environment inquire into the presence of God, who find the answers that are decisive for them. 'For people to feel secure in their new faith', the Scottish historian of mission Andrew F. Walls writes, 'they must have satisfactory answers to the questions left by the old.'[22]

Learning anew the mysteries of God

Looking back over the history of the church in Europe, it would be hard to conclude that the problem of European Christianity can be explained in terms of a failure of inculturation. The opposite may, in fact, be closer to the truth: the church inculturated too well. The job was done so thoroughly that Christianity exhausted itself, so to speak. It spilt over into nearly all areas, from agriculture to education and philosophy, giving so much of its life that the different segments of culture were able to appropriate it, reformulate it and continue perfectly well without it.

In a way, the church could have recognized in European culture, from revolutionary to scientific thinking, a transformed image of herself, but usually did not. Brunner was right when he criticized the church for reacting in two equally wrong ways: either to repeat in religious or pious language what European culture could easily say itself (it did not need a pious monkey) or to escape into the prison of pseudo-orthodoxy, which in reality was yesterday's combination of Christianity and culture (modern Europe did not want second-hand information).

But Brunner was wrong when he called for a new *gospel-friendly* culture, which does not exist in reality. Here, the systematic theologian behaved like the proverbial king who is rejected by his people and so asks his advisers to provide him with a new population. I prefer to keep the tension between the need for inculturation and the rejection of inculturation. That, however, makes it nearly impossible to define mission in terms of a sharp statement or a 'sound bite', and perhaps one should not give way to the temptation to produce such. Without exhausting the scope of mission, the New Testament uses approximately one hundred different terms to describe it. It is unwise to add one's own terminology.

However, something can be done: I can give an account of reflections that the quest for mission has generated for me. They relate to three areas of concern – ecclesiology, dogmatics, and spirituality:

- First, the church as an established tradition has now become a minority in Europe and is thus freed to rediscover its place on the side of the common people. The God of Jesus is one-sidedly with the people, suffering with, for and in humankind, and participating in the search for the restoration of broken lives, in all cultures and traditions, inside and outside of Christianity. The church takes part in God's mission, it does not own it; the church works towards salvation, but she herself does not save anyone. Therefore, all the forces and traditions in European culture that are, in their own fashion, influenced by Christ's way – extra-church and non-church though they may be – must be acknowledged as associates and equals in their attempts to liberate our life from the powers and principalities, and their competence needs to be recognized. This means, for example, that the history of Christianity in modern Europe can no longer be understood as *church history* but precisely as the *history of Christianity*, or the history of the movements triggered off by the Jesus tradition, inside and outside the church.

- Second, the plurality of answers to the question of what it means to be human has become a basic reality of European life. These other answers do not call for guidance from a Christian perspective. However, the new pluralist encounter calls for a missionary initiative, namely a reinterpretation of the way in which church, theology and the common faithful understand the Christian tradition in this new context. God, the source of life, is also in places where the church is not yet or no longer. Western Christianity, therefore, needs a theological approach that allows reflection on the coming and going of the church and the trans-historical presence of God. A new dogmatic Christian symbol is required for the trustworthiness and the uniqueness of God throughout human experience.

- Third, Christianity does not mean selling a product that is better, nicer or more powerful than other products. In fact, in Europe other offers seem to be more powerful at the moment, and the record of the church in Europe is far from being nice. What Christianity has to offer is a *space* where people get the chance to reconstruct and re-create themselves before God. Taking Christ as the exemplar of the divine–human encounter means to accept thankfully the wide space of God's liberating mediation. This is an open space in which the absence and the suffering, the love and the otherness of God is experienced, generating the space for genuine history, for human freedom and for various ways of interpreting Christ. It is also a space where Europeans, Christians and other, can learn how to enjoy, and be taught, the mysteries of God.

NOTES

1. This process started in 1992 in Paris, when some twenty missiologists, mainly from the United States and western and northern Europe, under the guidance of Wilbert Shenk, now at Fuller Theological Seminary, decided to set in motion an international process of study and exploration of the question. Seven workgroups were established and presented their results at a culminating conference in Washington five years later. Alan Neely, H. Wayne Pipkin and Wilbert Shenk edit the Christian Mission and Modern Culture series, published by Trinity Press International, which is already extensive.
2. Bede, II.13, quoted from the English version, D.H. Farmer (ed.), *Ecclesiastical History of the English People*, Penguin, pp. 129f.
3. K. S. Latourette, *A History of the Expansion of Christianity* (7 volumes), Harper & Brothers, 1937–47; *A History of Christianity* (2 volumes), Harper & Row, 1953, paperback edition, 1975.
4. John Gray (Fellow of Jesus College, Oxford), 'The shadow of the state cross', *The Guardian*, 28 August 1994.
5. See Peter Lennon, 'Science's new God squad', *The Guardian*, 3 May 1995. Lennon refers to the following books, published since the mid-Eighties, particularly by scientists: Jack Miles, *God – A Biography*; Paul Davies, *God and the New Physics* and *The Mind of God*; Stephen Hawking, *A Brief History of Time*; Leon Lederman, *The God Particle*; Frank J. Tipler, *The Physics of Mortality: Modern Cosmology, God and the Resurrection of the Dead.* The Theology Department of the University of Birmingham has published a volume entitled *Dare We Speak of God in Public?*, Frances Young (ed.), Mowbray, 1995.
6. D. Hay and G. Heald, 'Religion is good for you', *New Society*, 17 April 1987 (report on the Gallup National Survey of religious experience in Great Britain, 1985). See also Geoffrey Ahern, *Spiritual/Religious Experience in Modern Society: A Pilot Study*, Alister Hardy Research Centre, Oxford, 1987, 1990; Edward

Robinson and Michael Jackson, *Religion and Values at Sixteen Plus*, Alister Hardy Research Centre, Oxford, 1987. The most recent research is D. Hay and K. Hunt, *Understanding the Spirituality of People Who Don't Go to Church*, University of Nottingham, 2000.

7. See W. Hollenweger (ed.), *The Church for Others*, WCC, 1967, p. 32.
8. William Hamilton, *A Quest for the Post-Historical Jesus*, SCM, 1993, p. 8.
9. The easiest access to Newbigin's position is by way of his work *Truth to Tell: The Gospel as Public Truth*, WCC, 1991.
10. Concept employed by Hugh Montefiore in the study, edited by him (and following in the footsteps of Lesslie Newbigin's works), *The Gospel and Contemporary Culture*, Mowbray, 1992, 'Introduction'. This position has been radicalized by Wilbert Shenk in *Write the Vision: The Church Renewed* (Christian Mission and Modern Culture series), Trinity Press International/Gracewing, 1995.
11. See with respect to this concept K. Müller and Th. Sundermeier (eds), *Lexikon Missionscheologischer Grundegriffe*, Reimer, 1987, pp. 176–80 and 181–5; H. Krüger et al. (eds), *Oekumene Lexikon*, Lembeck, 1983, pp. 726–32.
12. H. Richard Niebuhr has discussed the questions arising from the concepts of Christ as the enemy and the transformer of Western culture in his *Christ and Culture*, Harper, 1951.
13. Emil Brunner, *Christentum und Wirklichkeit*, manuscript, presumably December 1930; German version (24 pages) in the archives of Evangelisches Missionswerk Hamburg, 155; English version (26 pages) in the archives of the Ecumenical Council of Churches, Geneva, 26 11 34/20. The main concept was already developed in outline by Friedrich Fabri, director of Rhenisch Mission, about the middle of the nineteenth century, with an eye to German liberal culture.
14. 'Die Theologie und die Mission in der Gegenwart', *Zeichen der Zeit* 10, 1932, pp. 189–215, especially 208.
15. 'Heaven only really comes to earth where everyday relationships between people within and outside the community are healed.' Karl Barth, *Die christliche Verkündigang im heutigen Europa*, Kaiser, 1946.
16. In the nineteenth century, for example, mission theologians such as Franz Michael Zahn and Gustav Warneck fought against those groups which held

that the so-called 'savages' in the newly gained colonies should first be 'civilized' before mission could be thought of. Since the publication of *In Darkest England* (1895) by William Booth, the founder of the Salvation Army, it has become good manners to speak of the secular 'savages' of the industrialized world. Here as well, there was and is a tendency to de-culturize the 'savages' as a precondition for Christianization.

17. The question really is whether a 'Christian Europe' ever existed. One has to realize that Judaism and Islam may be called historically old, partly even older, 'European' religions than Christianity (compare, for example, southern European Islam and Scandinavian Christianity).
18. See Charles C. West, 'Secularisation', in N. Lossky et. al. (eds), *Dictionary of the Ecumenical Movement*, WCC, 1991, pp. 914–18.
19. Lamin Sanneh in *Translating the Message*, Orbis, 1989 – which attracted much attention – speaks in this respect of a 'Gentile breakthrough'.
20. The culturally iconoclastic aspect of Christian self-assurance, however, can also be exaggerated, especially if it is applied not to one's own culture but to that of other people. Since any transfer of the gospel implies at the same time the handing down – and therefore the possible jeopardizing (handing over) – of the gospel, Christian missionaries from the cultures of the West in the continents outside Europe, as well as in the so-called urban jungle of European working-class neighbourhoods, often acted according to the motto, 'When you leave the gospel to the people, take care that they do not run off with it!'
21. 'Speaking the truth in love: elements of a missional hermeneutic', *International Review of Mission*, July 1994, pp. 479–504, especially 499.
22. 'On the origins of Old Modern and New Southern Christianity', in Hans Kasdorf and Klaus Mueller (eds), *Bilanz und Plan: Mission an der Schwelle zum Dritten Jahrtausend (Festschrift George Peters)*, Bad Liebenzell, 1988, pp. 243–52.

Mission in Itinerant and Narrative Mode

William Eggen

An Englishman's home is his castle.
An Irishman's story is his master.

It is surely presumptuous to try to describe in those terms the difference between Columba's missionary approach and Augustine's. Still, at the turn of a century marked by the perturbing *Shoah* experience and the crumbling of Western empires, we are invited to consider the missionary task in terms of the narrative model underneath the peregrinating practice of Celtic monks. At a time when mission is less about proclaiming a victorious Cross than about making sense of daily crucifixions, it tells us that our calling is in listening and ministering to the wayfaring word that precedes and attracts us. Prior to any *kerygma,* the bringing of that word, mission is to encounter it: hear it and help it find its 'wording' and actualization.

As the great metanarratives are petering out, and the thirst for life stories engulfs our cyberspace, a postmodern awareness tells us that the incarnated Word is not to be found in sterile schemes of textbook theology. As a creative flux, rather, it pre-exists any definition or structure. The itinerant searchers for God whom we commonly refer to as the Celtic monks were driven by a yearning for the traces of that creative flux, to witness and name it, and to discover its unfathomably inspiring workings. Theirs was not a romantic mystique of nature's eternal reflux, but a conviction that salvation history makes us see the contorted realities of human life as harbouring God's creative and saving Spirit, incarnated in human words and actions.

Many a liberation theologian, looking with deep suspicion at theories about inculturation and dialogue with non-Christian religions – as mere gimmicks to camouflage hidden proselytizing intents or as an abdication of social involvement – scorns the flourish of narrative witnesses in the

Latin American heartland and elsewhere. The focus on Jesus stories in EATWOT [Ecumenical Association of Third-World Theologians] circles and its preference for so-called cultural, rather than social and economic, issues have caused them alarm. The concept of a narrative approach to mission is therefore in dire need of clarification. Is Jesus the hero of storytelling?

The narrative approach emphasizes a 'poetic' and 'hermeneutic' understanding, which precedes rather than precludes action. To grasp this, we must first realize how this narrative mode contrasts with the metanarrative ones that, for so long, have tended to squeeze the human reception of God's revelatory action into some unilinear vision of history. In his *Small Apology for the Narrative*, J. B. Metz spoke of the 'dangerous memory' that should pass on underneath the doctrinal overlay of salvation history. What God said in those thousands of short stories that eventually came to be welded into the canonical Bible and its official reading came to us summarized in a coded rendition of the Christ event (a metanarrative). But how much was chipped off in the process? Anthropologists have noted that Africans often grasp much deeper evangelic meanings than those which imperialist, White-dominated preachers choose to tell them. Undoubtedly, they may draw some heretical conclusions; but should we not believe that the Spirit will help them find an equally salutary and valid view of God and God's holy family, the church?

We know that Jesus wandered around the country. Rather than staying among the ascetics at Qumran, at the baptismal site on the Jordan or in some Medina-type ideal community, he joined the wayfarers to help them shape their life stories, to share their meals in Bethany or Emmaus, and then go on. His word drove out people's sickening spirits, precisely because he got involved in their stories – at the well, on the mount, at Zachariah's or Simon's table. His miracles and parables follow a similar narrative and 'poetic' model. This meaning-creating action of healing, this participation in people's struggle to make sense of humanity, this descending with each one of us into the hell that besets us, is what we refer to when we call him the Incarnated Word. As a prophet he does not specialize in revealing immutable essences, but shows how God's word is in the revitalizing of people and in the outmanoeuvring of evil spirits: not by preaching some transcendent eternal, but by harnessing the creative forces of life. Paul may have been converted by a bolt of lightning, but all the others learned to be missionaries by following the itinerant prophet – and Paul, of course, to comply.

As factual and fictional stories become ever more popular, and as the science of narratology makes great strides, missiology is well advised to reconsider the methods of the pilgrim monks. But we must first establish the conceptual links between 'pilgrimage', 'word' and 'tale'. Let us note that – as Heidegger has reminded us – the Greek word *logos*, which has so much dominated our missionary approach, derives from a root *legein*, meaning primarily 'gather' rather than 'proclaim'. Like the Latin *legere*, it means to discover the items that make sense when put together. So we are engaged in a 'poetic' search for God's traces (and this is the most likely root of religion). It tells us how Jesus saw the missionary task of the Son, when he explained he had come to 'gather', like a shepherd, the lost ones of Israel. The *logos* is primarily what goes out to where the creative forces are at work and await 'gathering' and 'wording'.

Surely, to free these forces from stifling and distorting powers requires an 'educative', sometimes even surgical, intervention by well-trained hands (shaped by fasting and prayer, as Mark 9.29 tells us). But this is different from the teaching of abstracts or the administration of sacramental structures. For it consists primarily of encountering God's presence in the individual life story of the people – and by 'people' we definitely do not mean the 'anonymous mass' that constitutes the political opponent of the oligarchy. However valid and crucial the political struggle for liberation remains, preachers who tell believers that Jesus is primarily interested in their personal life stories have a point. The narrative is more important than the metanarrative, when it comes to liberation as well, provided 'personal' means more than just 'individual', as Ricoeur's hermeneutics tells us.

The missiological link between peregrination and narration must, therefore, be found in a correct understanding of liberation, as the core concept of the biblical tradition. A pilgrim search for the face of God is characteristic of the Semitic traditions. The Exodus symbol and the yearning for the Temple in Jerusalem embody a deep longing of the human soul. Islam has ritualized this longing in the laws of the pilgrimage *(hajj)* and the turning to Mecca (the *qibla)* during prayer. But this search for God's liberating presence can materialize only through a permanent struggle against what binds us to fixed stakes and interests. That is the experience of all religious search, as the tradition of the Celtic monks shows. Their mission was not so much one of preaching as of joining creation's search for God's creative presence.

Opening up to a neighbour's story, therefore, is more than a heuristic device. Our own and our neighbours' stories are not just inspiring illustrations of the road to take. They are the only places where God can be found, in both the cognitive and the practical sense. In fact, the famous saying in Matthew 25.40 that 'what you do to the least of these, you do to me' has been enervated missiologically by identifying 'me' with Jesus (or worse, with sweet baby Jesus). For this 'me' is the object case of the 'I am', which is God's name. This means that anyone going out to hear and attend to a neighbour's life story is truly on a pilgrimage towards the God whose name is no other than the 'I am' (and not 'there was, once upon a time' or 'there shall be'). In other words, to listen to people crying out 'I am, I am, I want to be, to live and to contribute to life,' and to help them come into their own, is the prime act of missionary faith.

The statement that God's Word became flesh and sojourned among us has improperly been taken to mean that the man Jesus contained all truths, to be spread across the globe. In fact, Jesus was the Word in his pilgrimage towards the Father (that is, God's creative presence in the world) and in his complying with that remarkable mission: proclaiming release to the captives (Luke 4.18). In this we have the coming home of the Word, when it gives voice to the voiceless – doing to God, as his Father, what he does to the least of his neighbours, and honouring the Father in the oppressed, the disowned, whose stories tend to be banned and nullified. By honouring their story as his Father's voice and by ministering to their worrisome longing – not just for a hearing, but more precisely for a purification – he was returning to the one who sent him. So his missionary pilgrimage was in search of the narrative presence of the 'I am', who spoke to him (in multifarious ways) at the well, at table, on the mount, near the grave. He is the Word because he allows the 'I am' to tell his/her narrative and because he rebuilds his/her temple in full splendour by helping to thwart the evil forces.

In our postmodern times, mission is not just about indulging in cultural niceties or emotional witnesses, but rather in the hard labour of purifying the listening ear and seeking eye that search for God's face and for the miraculous narrative of creative presence in people with their daily ecological, social and communicative struggles. Postmodern humanity may have rediscovered the narrative and linked it to Nietzschean ideals of mastering the flux of life in the peak performances of a TV appearance or lottery jackpot. But our mission in a Christian sense – while acknowledging that the flux of life rather than the eternal essences harbour God's true presence – will focus its searching eyes and ears not so much on the self and its performances, but rather on the 'appealing' other, the wholly other, in search of a healing and liberating presence. The pilgrim monks, like the African diviners or healers, teach us that only a common search and struggle will allow us collectively to find the divine face.

The Christian communities that, perhaps, understand this radical calling best, both in their countries of origin and abroad, are the rapidly growing African (and Caribbean) congregations. They seem often to grasp quite profoundly how mission has turned from *bearing witness to* an eternal order into *witness of* the workings of God's Spirit, in what can be called the condition of 'nomadism' (G. Deleuze). This is the condition of 'flux' in which each individual's narrative counts as a creative force and believers have a calling to highlight and bolster the three concerns of true *ecumenicity* (care for humankind's *oikos*, in both the ecological and economic sense), *catholicity* (openness to the whole of humanity) and *Christocentrism* (the search for the healing force in each other to be salvaged, uplifted and enlivened). Joining the other in the depths of his or her struggle is what the Christian itinerant witness is all about, envisaging 'witness' in its double sense. Missionaries involved in this task as professionals need an applied anthropology, teaching them the skills of an engaged encounter and sensitive 'witness'.

Prospects ~
Redefining Mission Practice

Celtic Spirituality Goes Inner-city and Interfaith

Jay Kothare

At the very outset, let me concede that I am not a scholar. I am just a parish priest. And I am Black and have been working in Britain's inner city for more than twelve years. So what on earth is a Black, Third World, inner-city parish priest doing examining the relevance of St Columba and St Augustine to the contemporary church? I have been a student of Celtic spirituality for some time, and during that time I have attended a number of seminars, workshops, retreats and lectures on the subject where, embarrassingly enough, I invariably seemed to be the only Black person. The audiences were exclusively White, middle class, college educated and mostly clerical. It was obvious that Celtic spirituality, at least as it was being represented in our times, was not of interest to the members of the working class or to the kind of people who live in our urban priority areas.

If I had not continued to work in the inner city, I would have concluded that Celtic spirituality was an elitist, middle-class affair without much reference to the lives of the common, ordinary people. Soon, two things became clear to me. First, I realized that far from being a profane and God-forsaken place, the inner city is the very place to encounter and wrestle with the spirit of the true God. Vilified as a deprived, derelict and depressing zone, the inner city is a place of profound spiritual quest. In other words, the inner-city folk who are normally conspicuously absent from workshops or seminars on spirituality staged by middle-class people are themselves very much interested in spiritual matters at a very deep, down-to-earth level. Second, the more closely I scrutinized Celtic spirituality, the more clearly I perceived parallels between the spirituality of the ancient Celts and the spirituality of contemporary inner-city people.

The purpose of this chapter is to initiate a dialogue between the two. Both spiritualities are alive and in the process of being discovered and applied in the quest to recapture a sense of holiness in our overly secularized world. In my own ministry in urban priority areas, I saw Celtic spirituality as an aid in identifying and articulating the treasures of inner-city spirituality. And, in turn, the inner city helped me realize how relevant Celtic spirituality is to the struggle in the inner city. I have been to Iona, to Lindisfarne, Durham, Whitby, Jarrow and to many an ancient Celtic scene in Wales, Scotland and Ireland. But strangely enough, nowhere have I seen the presence of Celtic spirituality more strongly than in the multifaith, multicultural and multiracial inner-city enclaves of Britain. This is what I am trying to demonstrate here. Yes, the spirituality of Aidan, Columba and Cuthbert is alive in our inner cities. It need not be confined in time to the pre-medieval era nor in space to the windswept Hebrides and mist-wrapped Wales. The best way to study the spirit of the Celts is to rediscover it where normally one would scarcely dream of finding it, namely, in the inner cities.

As I noted earlier, Celtic spirituality is increasingly in danger of being hijacked by a White, middle-class, suburban, college-educated clientele and distorted into an academic, yuppified parlour spirituality or of becoming fashionable among the growing bands of New Age fanatics and taking on the aura of a pseudo-mystical hippy philosophy of life. A similar fate has befallen the spirituality of the aborigines of America and Australia. I do not want Celtic spirituality to be represented and interpreted as a bland, sweet, asocial, apolitical tradition. I want it to be taken seriously as the spirituality of a people involved in the grim struggle for spiritual and social liberation. That is why I propose that we should study Celtic spirituality with reference to the contemporary struggle for social renewal in the inner city.

If Celtic spirituality is at home in the inner city, then the Celtic model of mission and ministry is bound to be relevant to the contemporary inner-city context. The many challenges that the early Celts faced in the task of mission are in our days being heroically tackled in the inner city. I believe the Celtic masters were much more sensitive to the whole issue of missionary inculturation than Augustine ever was. Inculturation, interfaith dialogue, ecumenism, empowerment of the poor, spiritual direction, ecology, contemplative prayer, basic faith communities – these are some of the burning issues that concern us today. But these issues are not as contemporary as we may believe. The Celtic church was far ahead of its time in coming to grips with them, and the modern church has important lessons to learn from its example. Ninian, Aidan, Patrick, Columba, Cuthbert and Hilda were not just holy hermits confined to their isolated monastic cells. Besides being masters of prayer and ascetic practices, they were missionaries and pastors to their respective communities. Hence, the Celtic, Columban model of mission and parochial ministry should be examined in terms of its relevance for the contemporary church, particularly in her inner-city enclaves.

The Cross

The first impression one gets of the inner city is of a crucified landscape full of alienation, pain and forsakenness. The spirituality of the inner city stems directly from the Cross and so does the spirituality of the Celtic peoples, who themselves have had a long, gory history of conquest, occupation, marginalization, forced emigration and ethnic cleansing. In many ways, the Celtic story of suffering continues into our times – as is evident in a divided Ireland, partly colonized and scarred by fear and violence. The Highland Clearances and the Irish famine of the 1840s are still freshly etched in folk memory. The experience of a hardworking crofting and fishing people in the barren, windswept terrain of the Hebrides is not far different from that of inner-city people, who live in a spiritual desert of their own. Both are condemned to eking out a living in an inhospitable setting.

Both have suffered the indignity of being second-rated by the dominant people with whom they live. When St Augustine landed in Ebbsfleet in 597, the Celtic bishops – most of whom were Irish – rose to welcome him, but he remained seated. This incident set the precedent for the Roman practice of rubbishing the Celtic heritage. The Synod of Whitby was its climax. Everything Celtic, whether it was the style of tonsure or the Easter date, was deemed inferior to the Saxon or the Roman way and got thrown out. In the course of time, Celtic tongues were driven out of use and even Celtic music and musical instruments, such as the bagpipes and the harp, were proscribed!

The Celts continue to be demeaned in our inner cities. The Irish are mocked as 'Paddies' or 'Mickeys' or other abusive names in an endless string of ethnic jokes. The phrase 'taking the mickey' is an instance of contemporary Celt-bashing not much different from the Paki-bashing that manifests verbally or physically in our inner cities where ethnic peoples are robbed of their humanity by being labelled 'Pakis', 'Coons', 'Niggers' and the like.

The Cymry people were pushed westward by the invading Saxon hordes, who not only occupied their land but branded them 'Welsh', meaning the foreigner! (It is interesting that the verb 'to welsh' has a pejorative meaning in the English language.) The Blacks in the inner city, like the Celts in the past, are in many ways displaced people thanks to the colonial history and the internecine wars in Third World countries fomented by neo-colonial foreign policies pursued by European nations. The end result has often been the break-up of entire families and clans and a total breakdown of the social fabric, creating an exodus of refugees with nowhere to go. Many of them, desperate for a foothold, are lured to the shores of developed nations and end up doing jobs too dirty for the host population.

Forced removal from their ancestral lands was the common experience of all Celts. First, they suffered colonization by the Romans under whom, however, they did manage to enjoy a fair measure of stability, being left alone to consolidate their Christian heritage. After the Roman legions withdrew in 410, the Picts and Anglo-Saxons destroyed the old order of the Romano-British community. Their Celtic Christian culture gave way to a new barbarism. Celtic place names disappeared. Patrick Thomas quotes the Celtic historian Gildas from *The Ruin of Britain*, written in 540:

> All the major towns were laid low by the repeated battery of enemy rams; laid low, too, all the inhabitants – church leaders, priests and people alike. ... Others, their spirit broken by hunger,

> went to surrender to the enemy; they were fated to
> be slaves for ever.[1]

This experience of pillage, rape and slavery burnt itself into the psyche of the Celtic people. Their corporate experience of woundedness spawned a spirituality that honoured the reality of the earth, flesh, community and suffering.

The Celts listed three distinct kinds of holy suffering or martyrdom: red, white and green. Red martyrdom, signifying blood and death, stood for the physical, social and political oppression they faced. It was mostly ordinary people who were at the receiving end of this red martyrdom – in the shape of slavery, slaughter, rape, pillage and torture.

White martyrdom was the bloodless alternative open to the hermits, who left behind a corrupting and persecuting system and took refuge in remote hideaways. They built cells and hermitages on islands, in deserts, in forests, in barren valleys, on hilltops and in deserted shrines, there to devote themselves to a life of prayer and penance. They would periodically return to the world to serve, teach and heal the suffering masses. Cuthbert, Columba, Aidan and Henry, the hermit of Coquet Island, were great practitioners of white martyrdom, embracing poverty, hardship and isolation as a gesture of solidarity with the poor. They deliberately chose inaccessible and inhospitable places, rendering themselves vulnerable to starvation, Viking raids, wild beasts, storms, droughts, wintry conditions and attacks by brigands. White martyrdom was a way of emulating Christ in holy emptiness and vulnerability on the Cross, sharing in forsakenness, becoming defenceless, and depending only upon divine guidance and succour. It was, in Patrick Thomas's words, 'an imitation of God's deliberate self-limitation in Christ, the supreme risk taken in love which led to the agony of Calvary'.[2] However, white martyrdom was not the prerogative only of the hermit. People sometimes chose to become exiles from their homes and lands in fear of an invasion; sometimes the exile was forced upon them. In the latter case, they proved themselves worthy candidates for both red and white martyrdom.

The inner-city poor suffer their full measure of red martyrdom, with police brutality directed towards Blacks, street violence, vandalism, break-ins, drugs, crime, disease, death, starvation and racist attacks. The urban priority areas could match the Celts' white martyrdom with their own grey martyrdom, symbolized by the grey cement jungle of housing estates and tower blocks riddled with unemployment, social deprivation, squalor, graffiti, boarded-up shops and overcrowded schools. The dominant mood of grey martyrdom is not being in control of one's own life, being powerless and forgotten, being reduced to anonymity.

The green variety of Celtic martyrdom consisted in emulating the simplicity and penitence of the early Christian communities of Antioch and Jerusalem. It was a martyrdom played out in the inner and interior life through the taming of lust and greed. The crofters, shepherds and fishermen who eked out a bare subsistence on the windswept, craggy terrain of the Hebrides and Northumbria were the unsung and unseen practitioners of this green martyrdom. Their legacy continues today in the witness of people living in Gaelic parts of Britain who still struggle against all the odds, yet not without retaining their dignity, integrity and loyalty to their spiritual roots. Equally, in the inner city today, the awesome discipline of green martyrdom is observed by the folk who do without. In a society addicted to consumerism, most inner-city people make do with what little is available. This is, of course, not poverty one chooses but poverty into which one is forced.

The threefold martyrdom – red, white and green – links the early Celts with the people of the inner city. The reality of the Cross is at the heart of the spirituality of both. The burden of the spiritual 'Were you there when they crucified my Lord?' mirrors the intimacy of the Cross in the lives of Blacks in the inner city as much as on the cotton plantations of old. The Celts carried in their bosoms a similar sense of the Cross as an ever-present reality. Esther de Waal refers to Blathmac, a Celtic bard, describing crucifixion 'with a sense of vivid immediacy, as though telling of what he himself had witnessed'. [3] This is typical of Celtic imagery. The here and now of the Cross links the suffering of Christ with the suffering of every subsequent generation, including those of the inner city.

People admire the High Crosses dotting the Celts' landscape but seldom understand that for the Celts a cross was not just a theological symbol referring back to an event two millenniums ago. Rather, their crosses celebrated God's solidarity with those out in the crofts, at sea, in valleys, on islands. The symbolism of the Celtic wheel cross is missed when we stress the wheel and ignore the cross, giving Celtic spirituality its notorious New Age image. We need to underline the cross within the wheel and recover the proper balance between the two. The solar wheel cross of the Celts points to the brokenness of our human situation and the promise of wholeness.

However, popular impressions of Celtic spirituality dwell all too eagerly on the wholeness, giving the Celts a rather romantic, poetic and exotic aura. An equally naive treatment has been meted out to the Native American peoples. Admirers of aboriginal spirituality are so caught up in the mystique of the aborigines that they lose sight of the Cross and suffering in their lives. So, if we want to understand the realism ingrained in Celtic spirituality, we need to study it along with the contemporary spirituality of the inner city. Celtic spirituality is not about fairies, angels and cherubim. It is about making whole what is broken and crucified.

A people on the move

The Celts and the inner-city dwellers are God's people on the move, whether by choice or without choice. Columbanus, also known as Columba the Younger, used to say, 'I am always moving from the day of my birth to the day of my death.' This sums up his Celtic passion for journeying, wandering and being on the way for Christ's sake, *peregrinatio pro Christo*. The early Irish saints braved the reef-ridden coastal seas in their frail skin coracles in order to reach out to the farthest corners of the continent. They jokingly called it 'crucifying oneself on the blue waves'. It was a manner of trusting the feet, guided by intuition, rather than making plans in the head for one's way forward. According to an ancient Gaelic maxim, 'Your feet will bring you to where your heart is.' To be trapped in the status quo was akin to death and atrophy, and one was enjoined to move on to find one's 'place of resurrection'.

This perpetual pilgrimage was to be undertaken as a penance, to put oneself in the position of the Patriarchs, the Prophets and Christ himself – who all had to flee their place of birth and seek refuge as exiles in an alien land. Among the Celts, this penitential *peregrinatio* required one to live abroad, away from one's country of origin, one's roots, one's home, family and friends. The destination of this holy wandering would be what the Celts called a 'disert', a desert, a desolate space that one sought not to escape from life's problems but to examine the state of one's inner life in solitude and poverty. The objective was to make oneself so transparent and vulnerable that problems would become more clear and intense rather than be hidden under a flurry of worldly activities.

Another objective in leaving one's country was actively to court the hardship of living in a country not one's own, either in pursuit of truth or mission or as an adventure, as in the case of St Brendan. Columbanus aptly described this as 'living on the world's edge', *ultimi habitatores mundi*. The contemporary Irish poet John Irvine, in his poem 'Saint Colm-Cille and the cairn of farewell' commemorating St Columba's farewell to his native Ireland before sailing to Iona, has managed to honour the painful memories of the exile of so many Irish people in our times:

> The oaks are green in Derry now,
> The waves break on the Irish shore
> My grief that I must say farewell –
> Farewell for ever more.[4]

A maxim popular among immigrants cites Glasgow as the capital of the Highlands and Islands of Scotland; similarly, London and Liverpool may, with a touch of irony, be considered capitals of south and north Wales, respectively, since it is to those cities that modern Celts have had to exile themselves in order to find a livelihood. The inner-city folk of other ethnic minorities (I say other because I do consider the Gaels living in English inner cities an ethnic minority) have had their share of this perpetual wandering for truth, security and livelihood. Many have been economic migrants looking, like Abraham, for the Promised Land. Many more have left their countries of origin for fear of persecution and, in the process, forfeited their families, friends and possessions. They had little choice but to settle in the heart of the grim and grimy inner cities of Western nations whose colonial and neo-colonial foreign policies contributed, in the first place, to the political and economic destabilization of their African and Asian homelands. Here, they live in a vacuum, totally vulnerable and naked, in a setting that is alien in language, creed, culture, customs and climate. Thousands of stateless refugees have been temporarily living in our inner cities (where else?) and are in constant terror of being deported. Their courage in the agony of their exile and their hope to wander forever until they find the magical island of truth makes all these new inner-city dwellers worthy allies of the ancient Celts in the pursuit of white martyrdom.

Community

Under the communitarian spirituality of the Celts, individuals derived and enjoyed their identity as unique members of the clan to which they swore allegiance and whose blessing and approval they sought for any personal initiatives. Equally tribal is the spirituality of the inner-city folk for whom a sense of belonging to the community is most imperative. The Celts believed in communal get-togethers and celebrations around a fire, sharing food and wine after a day spent out at sea fishing or on the croft farming or tending cattle. Inner-city folk, if they are employed, spend their day working hard in factories, shops or offices and get together, if not every evening, then on weekends, at least, on festive days to celebrate by feasting, singing, dancing and storytelling. The celebration may take place in a pub, a rented hall, a temple, a church, at a fair or in a family home. The joyful and rather noisy rite of communal celebration in our grimy inner-city enclaves could be regarded as a telling instance of the continuation of the ancient Celtic ethos into our times.

The Celtic community had a unique symbiotic relationship with place. The community hallowed the place and the place, in turn, moulded the community. Individual Celts not only related to one another but also to aspects of the locale, be it a tree, a boulder, a shrine, a stream, a hill, a knoll, a grove, a well, a cave. The community and its geographic space were attuned and integrated. Patrick Thomas writes about the Celtic Welsh:

> Because of the essentially tribal nature of Welsh society with its strong emphasis on the relationship between people and the place in which they live, this synthesis became enshrined in the patterns of

> daily life. The result was a spirituality which was domestic, communal.[5]

Inner-city folk are notorious for their uncritical fondness for their neighbourhood. (Pity the outsider who would even mildly poke fun at the dereliction of an inner-city enclave!) They love every bit of the neighbourhood, no matter how rundown, with littered streets, walls scrawled with graffiti, the old pub, the school, the corner shop, the old rectory. People love even locations with which they were least associated in the past. When, for instance, we closed down the storefront church in Thamesmead for lack of attendance, we heard complaints from residents who would never have dreamed of darkening a church door. The storefront church was an aspect of the community, and its closure was felt as an infringement of their territory.

The Celtic model of community, like the inner-city one, was inclusive – accommodating the less fortunate, the poor, the hungry, the homeless and the alien. It was based on compassion and hospitality. The Irish understood the pain of the Black immigrants in the early 1960s who were not welcomed as tenants in White English homes, and so they opened their homes to the Blacks. This is a classic example of the inner-city sense of community. St Aidan is reputed to have redeemed slaves by paying out large sums of money. Once while he was attending a banquet at Bamburgh castle, King Oswald, on being told that there were hungry crowds begging at the gates, sent all the food from the tables and even had the large silver cups broken up to be shared among the destitute. St Aidan was so thrilled that he held up the king's hand, praying that it might never perish. The hand was still kept in Bamburgh church a hundred years later as a symbol of the Celtic ideal of openness to the marginalized. To quote from an old Celtic poem:

> The cows have grass to eat, the rabbits have burrows for shelter, the birds have warm nests But the poor have no food except what you feed them; no shelter except your house when you welcome them; no warmth except your glowing fire.[6]

All the Celtic saints – Cuthbert, Brigit, Aidan, Hilda, Columba – preached and practised hospitality to the poor, who received a ready welcome at the communities evangelized by these saints.

The saints

The Celts' fiercely proud sense of the self-sufficiency of their geographic setting becomes nowhere more obvious than in the veneration of their home-grown saints, whose presence and protection they invoked in their chants, runes, charms, blessings and prayers. According to Patrick Thomas:

> The tribal groups among whom these saints settled came to regard them as very much their own. They saw themselves as the 'people' of the local saint. Their priest was also the saint's priest – his or her successor – sometimes linked by ties of blood because of the hereditary nature of priesthood in many rural areas.[7]

Equally, inner-city folk – Rastas, Buddhists, Muslims, Hindus, Sikhs and Christians – have their territorial saints. The Rastas acclaim Haile Selassie, also called 'Ras Tafari', as the millennial Black Messiah who came to redeem Afro-Black pride and 'roots' spirituality. Sikhs venerate their ten gurus and *bhagats*; the Namdharis, a contemplative Sikh sect, follow their living master-saint, Jagjit Singhji. Muslims never tire of invoking peace on the Prophet and lesser saints such as Shah Jalal, the virtual patron saint of Banglatowns of Western inner cities. Gujerati-speaking Hindu exiles from East Africa pray to their own nineteenth-century Gujerati-speaking saint, Baba Jalaram. Buddhists revere, in addition to the Buddha, the contemporary Dr Ambedkar. St Martin de Porres, the Peruvian-born seventeenth-century saint of mixed Spanish, African and Native American ancestry, has been adopted by many inner-city Catholics. Indo-Pakistani Christians honour Sadhu Sundar Singh. The tens of thousands of Dalits from the Indian subcontinent who have settled in Britain and elsewhere in the West eschew the highborn saints, reserving their devotion only for Dalit saints. So the Ravidasis venerate Ravidas; the Walmikis, Walmik; and the Balaknathis, Balaknath. These

Dalit communities take pride in being identified by the name of their respective saint who, to them, is ancestor, prophet, patriarch, messiah and guru rolled into one.

The inner-city saints are household names among the inner-city folk with whom they have a kinship through caste, tongue, race or a shared experience of persecution and suffering. They are invoked daily, with votive lights and joss sticks lit in front of photos displayed in prominent nooks in homes. They are remembered at births, weddings and house-warmings; before, during and after journeys; on starting a new job or initiating any new project. They are petitioned for boons such as progeny, a suitable match, a job, a healing, an exorcism, success in an exam, a favourable outcome on an application for immigration and the like. Their feast days are observed in noisy communal celebrations that may go on for days.

The cult of local saints holds together inner-city communities, giving them a distinct identity and freedom to explore their indigenous spirituality without submitting to the centralizing dictates of institutionalized religion. The local saint's grace is freely accessible and people can dispense with the services of paid priests belonging to a distant hierarchy.

The family

The ancient Celts and inner-city folk share the heritage of a lay, non-ecclesiastical, communal, domestic and family-oriented spirituality. It is worth noting that Celtic prayers, as we know them, were not part of daily offices or yearly lectionaries to be used in sanctuaries. Rather, they were inspired around the family home to accompany routine chores of daily living and livelihood, such as milking, harvesting, planting, kindling a fire and cooking.

Both the early Celts and inner-city communities are made up of large, closely knit families and households. The locus of their homespun, earthbound spirituality is not the congregation that meets weekly in a public chapel but the extended family. The cottage, the yard, the farm, the cattle-shed, the tool-shed, the granary, the kitchen garden, the well – all of this living and working space was one holy sanctuary for the Celts. If there was a shrine, it was more an extension of the hallowed living space than anything else. In the inner city, people may attend a church, mosque or temple in addition to saying their prayers at home. But home is where God is most to be found. How often, I complain to non-churchgoers, I get the response: 'You don't have to go to church to worship God. You can say your prayers at home!' This is an expression as much of a growing disenchantment with institutional religion as of an awareness of the sanctity of the people's ordinary living space.

Celtic priests and bishops, in contrast to the Roman model, were married men with families and supported themselves by plying secular trades. Even the so-called hermits did not sever family ties but would emerge periodically from long retreats to be with their kith and kin. St Brendan, before he set sail westward to discover the legendary island, is said to have consulted his extended family about his adventure. Again, as an old man, he returned from his hermitage to die in the arms of his sister. This closeness to the home, the family and the clan is an essential feature common to Celtic as well as inner-city spirituality.

Ecumenism

The inner-city ethos is made up of a motley assortment of faiths, philosophies, cults, cultures, creeds, ideologies, '-isms' and schisms. Obliged to share their congested space, members of this multinational, multilingual, multiracial community have managed to evolve a truly ecumenical spirituality. The Celts would have approved of it, as they themselves left behind an ecumenical, pan-European, multiethnic genre of spirituality. Although they were originally of a homogenous ethnic stock, their spirituality came to be owned by peoples of diverse ethnic strains – Saxon, Roman, Irish, Pictish, Welsh, Norse, Norman, Germanic, Iberian and the rest.

Celtic Northumbria was the northernmost frontier of the Roman Empire, often referred to as 'Britannia Inferior' in contrast to the southern part of Britain, 'Britannia Superior'. Northumbria, being a border region, was fortified with Hadrian's Wall, suitably garrisoned by Roman legions composed of mercenaries from such different parts of the empire as North Africa, Italy, Germany, Britanny and Spain. Long before Anglo-

Saxons came to live in England, there were legions of Black North African soldiers settled in Northumbria. The Celtic north, then, like our inner-city enclaves, boasted a multiracial and multinational population.

Even among the Celts, there was a wholesome intertribal spirit of ecumenical exchange. St Patrick, a British Celt, converted the Irish, who crowned him their patron saint. St Columba, an Irish Celt, set up monastic cells on the west coast of Scotland and Christianized the Picts. St Ninian, a Scottish Celt, went out to convert the Britons. St Aidan, another Irishman, built cells on Iona and Lindisfarne from which the Saxon Cuthbert blazed the trail of Celtic spirituality across Northumbria. Columbanus, an Irish Celt, trained in Rome and took the torch of Northumbrian Celtic spirituality as far away as France, the Swiss Alps and northern Italy. Wilfrid, a Saxon educated in Rome, became a missionary to Friesland. The Venerable Bede, a Saxon product of Northumbrian monasticism, became a model of scholarship throughout Europe. St Henry of Coquet Island, noted for its link with Cuthbert, was a Dane.

This pan-European, cross-tribal and multilingual character of the Celtic movement is comparable to the inner-city ambience. The Celts were as quick to share their knowledge with other peoples as they were to imbibe new impulses from them. For example, they modelled their eremitical tradition after the spirituality of the Desert Fathers. The main figures that are universally found chiselled on the High Crosses are those of SS Paul of Thebes and Anthony of Egypt, the twin North African pioneers in Christian monasticism. The Celts also owed to the Copts and the Syrians the graphic techniques they employed in embellishing their manuscripts. The Celtic dialects, music and chants are known for their uncanny affinity with the Indian.

The Celts travelled and evangelized throughout the North African and Continental lands, shedding as well as receiving the light of Christian spirituality. They managed to transform the many cultures they encountered, but they did so with a sensitivity all their own. At home as much as abroad, they infused the new Christian faith with their pre-Christian Celtic spirit. Alwyn Marriage observes:

> Celtic Christianity *integrated*, rather than *subjugated*, other traditions such as pre-Christian folk religion

> and Eastern Christianity. The fact that the Celtic Church flourished before the Great Schism might add to its potential as an ecumenical force. But even today, it demonstrates a respect for the revelations others have received. If tolerance is a British virtue, perhaps it is one we learned from Celts. It is certainly worth developing as our national identity continues to evolve in an exciting pluralist society.[8]

Common creation

An abiding sense of the unity and connectedness of things, persons and events constituting the created order is a feature of Celtic spirituality symbolized by the warp-and-woof plaiting knot pattern (which is, incidentally, also prevalent in Native American art). In the Celtic universe, nothing is isolated, incidental or accidental. Everything fits into a pattern. All things are connected, affecting one another for better or worse.

The Celts believed that creation is not as it appears to the naked, untrained eye. One needs to look at it through 'washed' eyes. Then, to use another Celtic phrase, one would begin to perceive 'the mountain behind the mountain'. And creation would manifest the glory, the joy, the wisdom and the power of the creator. This perspective comes very close to the inner-city attitude of wonder, reverence and awe towards creation as the handiwork of God. This is not pantheism but a way of tracing the wonder of created things back to the creator, of offering things up to God, seeing the transcendent God immanent and manifesting in things around us.

This is very much part of the faith of millions of African, Afro-Caribbean and Asian people living in the inner city. Even in their drab and gloomy setting, they are alive to the sacred mystery of the stars, the sun, the moon, the earth, the rains, the trees. They are thankful for and aware of being connected with the wider universe. A Hindu once said to me, 'Each morning on my way to work, when my train crosses over the Thames at Charing Cross, I mutter a silent prayer – for the Thames, to me, is like our holy Mother Ganges.' Even from her dingy council house window, an

Asian would look up and hum a chant of praise to the sun, the moon, the polestar and the homing birds. Muslims, during the fast of Ramadan, would wait for the crescent moon to rise before breaking the holy fast.

Even bare space is never empty but filled with the energy of which we are all a part. Esther de Waal uses the phrase 'common creation' to describe this uncanny sense of participation in the world of energy, made up of animate and inanimate things as though it were one single web of life gifted by the creator.[9] The ancient Celts had this sense, which is mirrored in a poem aptly titled 'The presence' by R. S. Thomas, a modern Celtic poet:

> I feel the power
> that, invisible, catches me
> by the sleeve. ...
>
> I know its ways with me;
> how it enters my life,
>
> is present rather
> before I perceive it, sunlight quivering
> on a bare wall.[10]

We need to remember that the Celts saw the presence of God in the world around them not because their world was pleasant. Far from it. In reality, barren deserts, windswept shores, dusty fields, stony crags, dense forests infested by ferocious beasts and brigands made up much of the Celtic landscape which, in its lack of appeal, might easily bear comparison with the stark inner-city enclaves. In either case, the setting is inhospitable. But even through this harshness, God's prompting word is ever waiting to be heard. This ever-present voice of God sounding through creation is symbolized in Celtic music by the ceaseless background drone of the bagpipes. In inner-city classical Asian music, we are reminded of it by the constant bass note of the tanpura. Among the Afro-Caribbeans and the Rastas, we hear it in the haunting beat, a hallmark of the sacred soul music of Bob Marley.

Hearing and seeing God in all things means encountering the divine presence even in small, ordinary, insignificant things. Nay, it is precisely the so-called ordinary and common things that hold in their bosom the mystery of the crucified God. David, the Welsh bishop-saint, would enjoin his disciples to 'be diligent in small things'. Indeed, God shines through the weak, the small, the common. The Celtic genius lies in looking for the extraordinary in the ordinary. The most profound mysteries of God are waiting to be discovered in the wreckage of the inner city, whose unglamorous and unglitzy residents are the ones chosen to incarnate the grace of God. A favourite motto of the Celtic saints was to 'do useless acts'. Setting out to do useless acts means acknowledging that there are no useless acts as such; all acts are important, holy and integral to the seamless fabric of life. No one act or gesture or person is more important than another. This is a manifesto of the inviolable dignity and equality of us all. It is a charter of the sheer goodness of the people of the inner city.

The God of the Celts and of the inner city is revealed in the material and the earthly. The tangible world of flesh and matter is God's blessed sacrament. We catch a glimpse of this ancient Celtic vision in a poem called 'Reredoes' by the contemporary Celtic poet Euros Bowen:

> The reredoes was not
> an ecclesiastical adornment
> of symbols,
> but plain glass,
> with the danger of distracting the celebrant
> from
> the properties of the communion table.
> for in the translucence
> the green earth
> budded in the morning view
> the river was in bloom,
> the air a joyous flight,
> and the sunshine
> set the clouds ablaze.
> and I noticed
> the priest's eyes
> as it were unconsciously
> placing his hand
> on these gifts,

as though these
were
the bread and the wine.[11]

Every thing is touched, sanctified and transformed by God, for whom there is no curtain between sacred and secular, spiritual and political, natural and supernatural. Alwyn Marriage writes that Celtic spirituality 'recognises the whole of life as sacred, shot through with God. This attitude does not concentrate on immanence to the neglect of transcendence, for the God who is revealed in ordinary tasks and relationships is utterly other. To worship God in daily life is not cosy but awe-inspiring.'[12]

The wheel of prayer

The omnipresent Celtic and inner-city God is nowhere more palpable than in the face of every human being. How touching is the Hindu gesture of *namaste*, with joined palms acknowledging the divine in the people one meets. This discovery of God within us is at the heart of the multifaith contemplative spirituality – whether Hindu, Muslim, Buddhist, Sikh or Rasta – blossoming in the inner city. Finding God within may smack of old-fashioned apolitical mysticism. But to people in the inner city, it is a way of nurturing self-esteem, self-worth, self-confidence and self-awareness, gaining independence from outside influences and trapping the inner resources to transform the outer social structures.

The inner city is the prayer zone of our post-Christian society. Here, Hindus, Buddhists, Muslims and others in their millions pray regularly, day and night, at home, at work, on the bus, in the street, in shops – at every available time and place. I was once showing a White English ordinand round my inner-city parish. He boasted of his aspirations to bring to God the alien heathens living in our midst. Imagine his shock when right in front of us at the street corner a Somali Muslim woman unrolled her prayer mat and proceeded to do one of her five daily rounds of obligatory prayer! On the bus we sat opposite an elderly Hindu who quietly caressed a half-hidden rosary in the front pocket of his jacket as he muttered a mantra. Later, we visited the humble bed-sit of an Irishwoman who, as she brewed tea for us, hummed a rune that she had learned from her grandmother during her childhood in County Cork. To round off our day, we visited a Sikh home where the family was celebrating an *akhanda-path*, a continuous recitation of the Sikh scripture.

At the end of the day, when my guest and I sat down for the evening office, we felt it was only a mild flicker in the powerful stream of prayer that we had witnessed in a normal day of an inner-city parish. Prayer in the inner city is, as St Paul enjoins, a ceaseless activity (1 Thessalonians 5.17). Here, people believe literally in prayer as a full-time occupation.

The inner-city wheel of prayer keeps turning round the clock. There are prayers to rise, prayers to go to bed, prayers for dressing, prayers for slaughtering, prayers for leaving home, prayers for coming home, prayers for bathing, for eating, for cooking, morning prayers, afternoon prayers, night prayers. The Celts would feel very much at home in the inner city's seamless prayer-armour. They, too, intoned prayers round the clock – prayers for kindling a fire, for 'smooring' (smothering) it and again for lifting it, for milking cows, herding cattle, grinding corn, spinning yarn, planting trees, for ploughing and harvesting and so on.

The Imam of a house mosque in Sparkbrook once said to me, 'Sometimes my prayer is my work, and sometimes my work becomes my prayer.' Prayer and work become closely intertwined in Celtic spirituality also. Ester de Waal writes, '"Bless the handling of my hands" is the summation of prayers by which from dawn to dusk, from rising to sleeping, men offer themselves and their work to God Who will consecrate them, body and soul, and all their labours.'[13]

Prayer is not an excuse to cease work. Instead, prayer flows in tandem with work. When prayer becomes second nature, it prospers rather than hinders work. This daily, hourly, rhythm of work and prayer was observed among the Celts not only by hermits in their prayer cells and monasteries but also by the common run of men and women in their homes, in fields, on fishing boats and elsewhere. Leslie Hardinge describes the Celtic scene:

> The days were filled with prayer, study and manual labour ... in dairy, granary, or in the fields, each worshipped God in his appointed task, and made his toil a sacramental thing. ... The secret of the

> early Celts lay in this, that they linked sacrament with service, altar with hearth, worship with work.[14]

The supernatural

All nature, being the handiwork of God, was perceived by the Celts as pregnant with infinite possibilities of transformation and healing. They trusted in the Spirit's power to sway the course of so-called natural processes. Even such a level-headed scholar as the Venerable Bede, in his biography of Cuthbert, recounts one miracle after another supposedly performed by the saint. Miracles of healing diseases and deformities, tracing lost cattle, taming wild beasts, calming a storm, communicating with birds and animals are integral to the life of a typical Celtic saint.

Modern biographers, not knowing how to cope with the supernatural component in Celtic spirituality, sheepishly write it off as hagiography or put a metaphorical gloss on it. To the ancient Celts, there was no dividing line between the natural and the supernatural; the one is only a logical extension of the other.

The inner cities with their large populations of Third World minorities practising ancient faiths and spiritualities are a fitting context in which to question the cold rationalism of a secularized Western Christianity drained of mystery, wonder and magic. The Protestant Reformation, aided by the Enlightenment and a runaway technological revolution, allegedly led to the disenchantment of the world around us. Now we need Celtic and inner-city spiritualities to re-enchant it so that we can perceive it once again with the 'washed' eyes of the ordinary householder who could see mystical presences all around her humble home:

> Who are they on the lawn without?
> Michael the sun-radiant of my trust.
> Who are they on the middle of the floor?
> John and Peter and Paul.
> Who are they by the front of my bed?
> Sun-bright Mary and her son.[15]

The guru

Inner-city spirituality revolves around the personality of the guru or the spiritual master – a living example of truth and wisdom, teaching by word as well as by example. The guru is mentor, guide, friend and fellow pilgrim. The Celts had a similar figure whom they called an *anamchara*, a soul friend – which is akin to the Buddhist term *kalyana-mitra*, meaning a spiritual friend. The *anamchara* lived a life of holy poverty and guided people in prayer, helping them through sickness, bereavement and other crises. Inner-city folk, like the Celts, strongly believe that spirituality is not something one can imbibe from a mere book. Only a living teacher, who has been tested and tried by suffering, is in a position to transmit spiritual insights. So the guru or *anamchara* is a very down-to-earth person, deriving wisdom from a practical engagement with the world. Both are mystics with their feet firmly planted on the ground; teachers who never cease to learn from their disciples; masters who are dear friends. And most important, they are not professionals who charge a fee for their services!

Scour the inner city and you will get to hear stories of the inner-city *anamchara*, Hindu *sant*, Muslim *pir*, Catholic saint, Buddhist *bhikku* and Sikh guru. The stories are perfectly interchangeable, for each offers a spirituality that transcends all sectarian boundaries, an ecumenical spirituality for people of all faiths and none.

Celtic spirituality has resurfaced in our urban priority areas in a new garb and under a new name. Anyone wishing to minister to the people living there could benefit from an engagement with the way the ancient Celts felt, thought and prayed. Through this partnership, we can at long last begin the experiment of translating the perennial insights of the Celts to the slums of the inner cities of the world.

NOTES

1. Patrick Thomas, *Candle in the Darkness: Celtic Spirituality from Wales*, Gomer Press, 1993, p. 27.

2 Thomas, p. 25.

3. Esther de Waal, *A World Made Whole: Discovering the Celtic Tradition*, Fount, 1991, p. 122.

4. Oliver Davies and Fiona Bowie (eds), *Celtic Christian Spirituality: An Anthology of Medieval and Modern Sources*, SPCK, 1995, p. 173.

5. Thomas, p. 147.

6. Ray Simpson, *Exploring Celtic Spirituality: Historic Roots for Our Future*, Hodder & Stoughton, 1995, p. 146.

7. Thomas, p. 148.

8. Alwyn Marriage, 'The Celtic fringe' [editorial], *Christian*, Summer 1992, p. 1.

9. De Waal, *A World Made Whole*, p. 82ff.

10. Davies and Bowie, p. 171.

11. Davies and Bowie, pp. 182–3.

12. Marriage, p. 1.

13. Esther de Waal, *God Under My Roof: Celtic Songs and Blessings*, Marshall Pickering, 1984, p. 22.

14. Cited in Simpson, pp. 57–8.

15. De Waal, *God Under My Roof*, p. 23.

Mission, Inculturation and Black Communities

Joe D. Aldred

I find this topic problematic because it revives what are, for me, latent sensitivities concerning these matters, which in turn challenge my objectivity and capacity for detached analysis. My mother had a saying that 'who feels it knows it'. And Black people of every generation and of every location know, either by instinct or by experience, the repercussions of White missionary activities that for centuries have ridden roughshod over Black cultural heritage in their quest to establish their version of the truth of the gospel of Jesus Christ. So again, I say simply that it does not come easily to deal with this subject in Western academic circles where the vast majority of references at one's disposal are written by the very people who have participated, directly or indirectly, in the 'bad treatment' about which I am sensitive.

Whites tend not to be able to observe the many anomalous assumptions implicit in even the most apparently objective pieces of work in this area. It is sufficient to say that usually, after even the most voluminous missiological theses, White hegemony remains the basic immovable assumption with which the Black person is faced. In this context, therefore, I recall extracts from the classic work of W. E. B. Du Bois, in *The Souls of Black Folk*, where he describes the Black American problem with 'double-consciousness'. Du Bois describes his society as

> a world which yields him [the Black man] no true self-consciousness, but only lets him see himself through the revelation of the other world.
>
> It is a peculiar sensation this double-consciousness, this sense of always looking at one's self through the eyes of others, of measuring one's soul by the

> tape of a world that looks on in amused contempt
> and pity.[1]

Du Bois was not writing in a missiological context, but his description of the dilemma of Black American folks at the turn of the century continues to resonate with Black people of this generation who interact with White society. The context of engagement matters little, if at all; 'Black' appears distinguishable only in relation to 'White'. I find myself unable, therefore, to deal with mission and inculturation if my frame of reference has to be in relation to good or bad practices of Whites. What Du Bois calls 'the contradiction of double aims'[2] is a handicap that stifles Black academic creativity and denudes Blacks of self-worth and self-contained uniqueness, qualities that are not the subject of human generosity but derive from being made in the image of God.

It seems appropriate also to make reference to David J. Bosch's reminder that over the past five centuries the meaning of mission has shifted from a theocentric premise, that 'of the sending of the Son by the Father, and of the Holy Spirit by the Father and the Son'. He argues that during these years, mission has become Eurocentric with 'a fairly circumscribed set of meanings',[3] for example, the sending of missionaries, mission activities, the location of missionary activity, missionary agencies, the non-Christian world becoming known as a 'mission field'. This understanding was inextricably linked to the West's imperialist activity in 'heathen lands'.

According to Bosch, since the mid-twentieth century, 'the Christian Mission – at least as it has traditionally been interpreted and performed – is under attack not only from without but also from within its own ranks'.[4] Some of us say, 'and not before time'. To mourn the passing of such an epoch is to demonstrate a glaring insensitivity towards the victims of those years, and to remain unrepentant. The unsustainability of European mission practice over the past five hundred years was due to its generic unrighteousness. A new model was needed if the integrity of Christianity in the West were to be redeemed, one which demonstrated what we call in Jamaica 'manners', or in another idiom, 'respect'.

It appears to me that what is now necessary is a re-examination of, and attempt to reappropriate, the biblical mission paradigms, in which we use the Bible as our mission document. Certainly, the model of the last five hundred years of European mission offers us little by way of a suitable example. I contend, however, that although they have been suppressed and have never been written up, either by the practitioners or by their oppressors, biblical models of mission have been at work during those dark ages. So I, a diasporan African, wish to admonish – with righteous indignation – my White brothers and sisters not to spend their time and mine sanctifying by academic discourse a period of religious sins for which they ought to be repenting in sackcloth and ashes.

The peoples of cultures other than White European are much more than the 'victims' of White missionary activity: they have been missionary practitioners, too. To acknowledge this, all of us need to make a radical shift of perception away from the notion of 'mission' as being related to 'foreign fields'. I cannot bring myself to study a missiology that denies my people's existence as full participants in Jesus' missionary call to his church and its activity in the world. Nor am I satisfied with an academically enforced juxtaposition in which we are perpetually ascribed the status of 'subjects' of the activities of others, never fully participative 'objects'. My dilemma is compounded when my people absorb, and accept as normative, practices and propositions that are incongruous in a kingdom of God which has no place for superior/inferior relationships.

You may begin to understand my reasoning in now going on to attempt, in an almost sectarian way, to articulate an understanding of the mission work of Black communities in Britain, in particular the work carried out by people from the Caribbean since the 1950s. I offer here a different perspective, the Black point of view.

The victors, it has been said, write history. The victors, too, over recent centuries, have written theology and missiology – the 'voice' of their victims systematically suppressed. As I have noted, this should not lead us to accept the false proposition that nothing has been written because nothing has happened. Nor should we unquestioningly accept the victor's version of events. In fact, there is every reason for suspicion! On the spurious assumption that Caribbean people, for example, come from an 'oral' tradition, others have felt at liberty to articulate for us what we are evidently unable to write for ourselves. Lack of access to writing, printing and publishing facilities are rarely cited as the premier reasons for the lack of visibility of books by Black British authors. The assumption is that we just do not write, we are an oral people. And while all cultures have an oral history, it is with Blacks that Whites insist this tradition remains a permanent feature. So, once again, Black life, of necessity, is seen through White expressions. Some revision of our common sense of history is necessary – a revisionism which removes the notion that White European activity is normative.

The rebellious overtone in this chapter so far is echoed by the editorial in *A Time To Speak*:

> Black Christianity in Britain has had many exponents and apologists. Many have made their reputations and careers from 'interpreting' Black faith to indifferent intellectuals and earnest clerics. We, the victims of this spiritual 'colonisation', have been observed and pronounced upon. We have read what has been said about us and been impressed that something has been learnt, but disappointed that this is where it usually stops. Others have been angered by the fact that yet again we have been the objects of exploitation from theses material, for 'street credibility' or for conscience-salving. Over the years many of us have accepted this as the price we must pay for Christian unity. However, this 'colonisation' of our Black hearts is no longer acceptable to us: it's time to speak for ourselves.[5]

This is what I attempt to do in the remainder of this chapter.

Black mission activity in Britain

The contemporary period of mission activity in Britain by Black people began in the 1950s. I find myself in agreement with Bosch when he states: 'An inadequate foundation for mission and ambiguous missionary motives and aims are bound to lead to an unsatisfactory missionary practice.'[6] It is therefore worth reflecting on what the foundation, aim and nature of Black missionary activity in Britain have been.

John Mbiti points to an intrinsic African religiosity so deep that the African, whether at home or in the diaspora, does not know how to live without religion. Whether this is any more than a generalization, equally applicable or equally inappropriate to all people groups, is open to conjecture. However, it is true that Black people's sense of the divine appears to be virtually all-pervasive. There is in almost all Black people known to me a love and appreciation for God as creator, saviour and sustainer that defies the logic of Black experience at the hands of those who came in God's name.

This love for God is virtually impossible to describe other than to say that it is Christocentric to its core. It is this 'God-love', expressed in and through Jesus, that constitutes the kernel of Black missionary activity in Britain from its genesis to this time. Elaine Foster writes: 'Historically, it is a matter of record that Black settlers from the Caribbean were deeply spiritual people and had a dynamic faith before they left their homes to journey to Britain.'[7]

Second, Caribbean people were and to some extent still are fiercely denominational. In 1997, Robinson A. Millwood set out as his purpose for writing his account of his mission activity in London the encouraging of Black people 'to remain consistent and assiduous to their commitment to the Methodist Church, [and] to remind my indigenous brothers and sisters that the Methodist Church is symbiotically ours'.[8] The denominational allegiance apparent here in a White-led denomination is no less the case in other circles. In fact, among several of the Black-led denominations, some of which operate under a White-led American hierarchy, ecclesiastical exclusivism has been embraced with vigour. The Apostolic denominations, the Adventists and the Church of God of Prophecy were, and in some cases still are, renowned leaders in this field.

Let me deal here with two popular myths about Black Christianity in Britain. First, the notion that Black churches started in Britain primarily due to White rejection. This is an extravagant myth. Someone has commented that if this were true, that would make the Black church movement in Britain a church by default. Mythical, too, is the notion of a Black interdenominational mission, which was subverted and denominationalized by outside forces in the interest of a 'divide and rule' policy. Neither of these factors carries the weight ascribed to it by White observers and some Blacks who have echoed their thoughts.

Gerloff points to the 'small informal gatherings, street and house meetings in the Inner Ring of the cities, where face-to-face evangelism took place regardless of colour of skin, cultural background, nationality or denomination'.[9] What people sought was the re-creation of their worship and mission environment, a means of responding to the God they knew through the denomination they knew. An integral part of that worship of God and allegiance to denomination was a reaching out in evangelistic fervour to those around them. A willingness to worship (temporarily) with others was not an indication of abandonment of one's denomination, but rather an act of ecumenism and recognition of the oneness of God and the unity, universality and variety of the one catholic church.

From a mission perspective, what has driven Black Christians, I contend, has been their innate sense of love for God and loyalty to their denomination, which were and are distinguishable by a particular liturgy, theology, doctrine and cultural norm.[10]

The aims of Black missionary activity in Britain were never grandiose. The pioneers of this movement initially conceived no grand design. In recalling the early life of the New Testament Church of God in England, Oliver Lyseight demonstrates something of the motivation and progress of the premier Black-majority denomination in the country. It commenced in 1953 in rented accommodation with seven people, in Wolverhampton. When Lyseight retired in 1984, the church's records showed 89 congregations, 50 buildings owned, more than 6,000 members and a Sunday School enrolment of 11,000. He recalls:

> The YMCA Hall was obtained about the third week of September 1953, and there we started our campaign amongst the West Indians who had come to make this land their home. ... It was not easy, but we trusted the Lord and His presence was always with us. He inspired and anointed us with the Holy Spirit to do the 'will of Him that sent us while it is day for the night cometh when no man can work'.[11]

The expressed aim of Black mission was to meet the salvific needs of Black people. According to Io Smith, 'Before we left Jamaica we were forewarned about the Christians who came to Britain and fell by the wayside.'[12] In pursuit of the saving of Black souls – to which might be added worshipping God and promoting the denomination – emerging leaders did not shun proselytizing. Hence, when Black Christians were 'cold-shouldered' out of White-led churches they were most welcomed in the new Black-led congregations. As one eminent Black bishop commented at a recent leaders seminar, 'White churches helped to build Black churches by their negative comments about Black people.'[13]

In the case of all Black-led churches, a Black focus has never meant White exclusion. The gospel preached has always been for the 'whosoever will'. However, that focus on the Black community has shifted little, if at all – even in the case of the Black denomination that for decades has had a White American 'national overseer' imposed upon it. In spite of strenuous efforts towards attaining multiracial growth, the mass of the Black membership remained Black both in its constitution and in its focus. The Black mission has operated more as a symbol to White Christianity in Britain of zeal for the things of God, rather than as a tool of integration and sameness.

The nature of Black mission is identifiable both in its particularity and in its generality. At the micro level, there is intensive spiritual and social care for the well-being of individuals. This has at times led to strong discipline being meted out to members and non-members of a congregation. Much time is spent with individuals, first in 'bringing them to the Lord', and afterwards in prayer and other forms of support.

A second aspect of particularity, already mentioned, relates to the denomination and local congregation to which a person converts. A high level of loyalty is extended and expected in many areas of both the church's life and the individual's. Tim Ward notes five factors, natural to Black churches, that he believes explain their success:

1. Church doctrine and membership rules require deep personal commitment; thus once a member, one is likely to stay.
2. They have a well-developed pastoral care system that is 'individual-centred'.

3. The generations are fully integrated and the churches are, therefore, anti-ageist in nature.
4. They have vibrant musical worship.
5. They engender a sense of identity and belonging.[14]

At the macro level, the Black church is extremely varied. Some see this as a fragmentary tendency; Black people generally view this as dynamism. In 1992, Gerloff estimated, there were more than 1,000 Black congregations in about 300 organizations. Gerloff further identifies eleven independent Black church traditions in Britain: (1) African Methodist Episcopal and African Methodist Episcopal Zion, (2) Revivalists and Spiritual Baptists, (3) Sabbatarians: Seventh-Day Adventists, Church of God Seventh Day, Seventh-Day Baptists, (4) Holiness Movements, (5) Trinitarian Pentecostals, (6) Oneness (Apostolic) Pentecostals, (7) Revival (Healing) Pentecostals, (8) African Indigenous Churches, (9) Rastafari, (10) Anglo-Catholics, and (11) Asian Independent Fellowships.[15]

The variety of denominations and streams means that Black people are well catered for in terms of mission, whatever their 'tastes' or historical preferences may be. Added to this, of course, is the fact that in inner-city Britain, England in particular, almost all of the major White-led British churches now have some Black-majority congregations. As Millwood puts it: 'In plain unequivocal English, Indigenous Methodism is dead and gone. Methodism as we know it today in London is African and West Indian.'[16] Black mission in and to Britain may yet prove to be not just the salvation of Blacks but of the entire country, as Blacks rescue dying White-led denominations and congregations.

Black inculturation in Britain

As a Black person, I am of the view that when White Christians repent for the crimes committed against the subjects of past and present discrimination, their intentions may be good, but much of the assumption behind their repentance appears to be misplaced. I say this because, for example, it is folly to suppose that White missionaries could have taken the Christian faith abroad and left their culture behind. The sin is other than that they took their culture with them. It is partly in the understanding that 'mission' is synonymous with 'overseas' or 'foreign', and most particularly in that their 'mission, as a matter of course, presupposed the disintegration of the cultures into which it penetrated'.[17] The sin of disrespect for others and the negation of the inherent value of other forms of God-given culture was at work.

When Black people began to engage in mission in Britain, the gospel was equally wrapped in the covering of their cultures. It follows that those who attend a Black-led church enter into its culture. There are, of course, elements of Black culture that are similar to White culture, but there are also sharp divergences. For example, the Black church's music, singing, attitude to time, funerals and dreams are starkly different from White people's.[18]

Neither is Black culture monolithic, and one is likely to find wide variations in cultural norms throughout the Black church. A distinction can easily be made between church and secular Black culture, despite attempts to demonstrate that such classifications are not borne out of the best traditions of Africa. Inevitably, church attendees will fashion a culture in their own image, since 'culture includes the concept of an integrated system of learned pattern of behaviour, ideas, and products characteristic of a society'.[19] Any attempts by the missionary, Black or White, individual or church, to become non-cultural will end in frustration and disillusionment. Culturally, Black missionary activity has remained consistent with the words of the Jamaican saying that is applicable to both secular and religious realms: 'Be yourself, man.'

The present state of affairs

Describing the present state of affairs regarding mission, inculturation and Black communities is a complex task. First, within White-led denominations in Britain there are matters that are crying out for attention. These are missiological issues. For example, wherever Blacks are in a minority in the denomination of their choice, the gospel in almost all of its practical outworking is clothed in the garb of the majority culture. Therefore, in the church at least, such people are starved of their cultural nourishment. Some have been known to travel to and fro between their main church and a Black-led church, sometimes attending two services on a Sunday. Then, in almost all White-led denominations in which there are Black-majority congregations, the dearth of Black ministers invariably leads to a situation of White leadership and Black follower-ship. Black people in these situations often complain of feeling culturally suppressed and subscribing to a framework that serves the cultural needs of the minority White membership and its White minister rather than those of the majority Black constituency.

In both the above situations mission is hampered, as neither Black nor White participants appear willing to take the risks necessary to go forward. This becomes apparent even in the unwillingness to invite family and friends into an uneasy environment. The time surely must come, the point be reached, where all members create space for full gospel and cultural expressions. Some feel that this points to the American segregationist scenario, where Blacks and Whites will desire separate worshipping conditions – even while remaining in the same denomination.

Within the Black-led denominations there are emergent missiological and cultural issues, too. There has almost always been a small White presence in Black-majority churches; however, the ethos has been overwhelmingly Black in both cultural and missiological terms. Whites in these churches have learnt to lie low or have elected to leave. Some have even become Caribbeanized in order to remain in what are, after all, joyful and liberating environments.

But the real challenge to the British Black church movement is a generational one. It has to do with the different perceptions and expectations of older and younger Blacks, and covers a wide range of concerns: religious, political, sociological, psychological and so on. Will the pioneering generation, still with us, allow the emerging generation to theologically and missiologically remould the Black church in their image?

NOTES

1. W. E. B. Du Bois, *The Souls of Black Folk*, New York, 1994, p. 2.
2. Du Bois, p. 3.

3. David J. Bosch, *Transforming Mission,* Maryknoll, New York, 1996, p. 1.
4. Bosch, p. 2.
5. Paul Grant and Raj Patel (eds), *A Time to Speak: Perspectives of Black Christians in Britain,* Nottingham, 1990, p. 1.
6. Bosch, p. 5.
7. Elaine Foster in *A Time to Speak,* p. 57.
8. Robinson A. Millwood, *Liberation and Mission,* Kent, 1997, p. xiv.
9. Roswith I. H. Gerloff, *A Plea for British Black Theologies: The Black Church Movement in Britain in Its Transatlantic Cultural and Theological Interaction,* Frankfurt, 1992, p. 55.
10. Joel Edwards (ed.), *Let's Praise Him Again,* Eastbourne, 1997, p. 67.
11. Oliver A. Lyseight, *Forward March,* United Kingdom, 1995, p. 36.
12. Io Smith with Wendy Green, *An Ebony Cross,* London, 1989, p. 41.
13. Sydney Dunn, from minutes of 'That Birmingham May Believe', Selly Oak, 1997.
14. Tim Ward, *Where the Saints Have Trod,* Selly Oak, 1992, pp. 15–16.
15. Gerloff, p. xv.
16. Millwood, p. xiv.
17. Bosch, p. 448.
18. See Clifton Clarke, *The Reason Why We Sing: Introducing Black Pentecostal Spirituality,* Cambridge, 1997, pp. 20–24.
19. Len Anglin in *Let's Praise Him Again,* p. 97.

One Gospel, One Voice? A Response to Joe D. Aldred

Allan Anderson

In spite of significant numbers of people of African descent in some of the older denominations, the dominant expression of Black British Christianity is Pentecostalism, of which Joe Aldred is a prominent representative. Of this British phenomenon I know little, and my response will consist of suggesting parallels with that form of Pentecostalism in Africa with which I am most familiar. Not everyone is in agreement (particularly not Western Pentecostals) as to what may be defined as 'Pentecostal', but I argue for an inclusive understanding of the term to embrace those many indigenous movements in the Third World that have at most only remote connections, or none at all, to Western forms of Pentecostalism.[1]

It seems necessary, first, to place British Black Pentecostalism within its global context. According to David Barrett, there were an estimated 74 million 'Pentecostals/ Charismatics' – 6 per cent of the world's Christian population – in 1970. By 1996 this figure had reached 480 million, or 27 per cent, more than the total number of 'Protestants' and 'Anglicans' combined. Barrett calculates that if present trends continue, the figure is likely to rise to 1,140 million, or 44 per cent of the Christian world total, by 2025.[2]

This contemporary and complex movement is the fastest-growing section of Christianity and one of the most extraordinary religious phenomena in the world today. It is not always easy to define what is meant by Pentecostal, as the term refers to a wide variety of movements scattered throughout the world, ranging from fundamentalist and White middle-class 'megachurches' to indigenous movements all over the world which have adapted to their cultural and religious contexts to such an extent that many Western Pentecostals (including some Black Pentecostals) would probably doubt their qualifications as 'Christian' movements.

Aldred certainly represents the mainstream or 'classical' Pentecostal tradition in the Black community,[3] being a bishop in the second largest Black-led denomination in Britain – although the expression 'Black-led' may be a misnomer, especially as the two largest 'Black-led' denominations are overseen by White North Americans.[4] This is why the terms 'Black-majority' and 'Black-initiated' are also needed.

I think Aldred's background partly explains his eagerness to discuss the growth of Black Pentecostalism in terms of its own internal dynamics rather than as a result of external factors. He has pointed out a weakness that is also true of other African religious studies. For example, some researchers (mainly White outsiders) have suggested that racism is the main cause of Black Pentecostalism, and Aldred is right in suggesting that this might be a sop to their collective conscience.

Researchers of African Pentecostal churches have also pointed to colonialism and racist (or paternalistic) mission practices as causes for the emergence of this prominent type of African Christianity, perhaps for the same reasons. Such theories tend to detract from the creative energy that these movements contain *in themselves* to engage in mission in their societies. Seeing African Pentecostalism mainly as a reaction to Western missions and colonialism, although having some validity in the case of the earliest movements, obscures the fact that long after these initial secessions from Western mission-founded churches, Pentecostal churches went on proliferating and changing the face of African Christianity without any reference to European missions whatsoever.

The growth of all types of Pentecostalism should be seen as the result of the inculturation of a positive proclamation by its own indigenous missionaries rather than as a negative reaction to Western missions. However, I do not think we should dismiss the racism factor altogether, although it may indeed not be the *primary* factor, as Aldred observes. My short sojourn in Britain, and the more considerable experience I have in southern Africa, make me acutely aware of the ugly and insidious power of racism in the church. Robert Beckford, with his outline of the implicit theology of the Rastafarian reggae singer Bob Marley and his own 'Jesus is

Dread' Christology, has shown us another facet of Black Pentecostalism that affirms Blackness and Afrocentrism in the face of White racism in Britain. Although this view might represent a minority of British Black Pentecostals, it should not be marginalized.

In Third World Pentecostalism, experience and practice are far more important than dogma. Whereas Western 'classical Pentecostals' usually define themselves in terms of the *doctrine* of the 'initial evidence' of speaking in tongues, the Pentecostal movement is more correctly seen in a much broader context as a movement concerned primarily with the *experience* of the working of the Holy Spirit and the *practice* of spiritual gifts.[5]

Pentecostalism today is both fundamentally and dominantly a *Third World* phenomenon. In spite of its significant growth in North America, less than a quarter of its members in the world today are White, and this proportion continues to decrease.[6] Walter Hollenweger considers the growth of Pentecostalism in the Third World to have taken place not because of adherence to a particular doctrine but because of its roots in the spirituality of nineteenth-century African-American slave religion.

I do not think that Aldred has paid sufficient attention to this in his chapter, even though he refers to the pervasiveness of the divine in African religion. Some of the main features of this spirituality are an oral liturgy, a narrative theology and witness, the maximum participation of the whole community in worship and service, the inclusion of visions and dreams in public worship, and an understanding of the relationship between the body and the mind manifested by healing through prayer.[7]

Clifton Clarke, another Black Pentecostal from the largest Black-majority denomination in Britain, has recently published a booklet on Black Pentecostal spirituality, in which he points out the formative elements of African and Black slave religion in the Pentecostal movement. Included in these formative features are an awareness of the immanence and transcendence of God, an oral culture, a sensitivity to the spirit world, worship involving the whole being, and the minister as the agent of healing.[8] Aldred alludes to these features in his description of the differences between 'Black culture' and 'White culture'. Orality, as Clarke has observed, does not imply being 'illiterate' or 'inferior' but refers to a mode of living and dynamic communication.

There are many movements throughout the world, like most of the thousands of African-initiated churches, that are phenomenologically 'Pentecostal' movements, in which the features outlined by Hollenweger, Clarke and others have persisted, and which have developed a form of Christianity quite different from Western Pentecostalism. The African features of Pentecostalism have been absorbed into the whole Pentecostal movement, although some forms of Western Pentecostalism are more cerebral and capitalistic in their orientation. It is a fact that where Pentecostalism has departed from its original spirituality, particularly in the West, its mission has been corrupted.

In recent years, the greatest increases in the Pentecostal movement have been in sub-Saharan Africa, Indonesia, South Korea and, especially, Latin America, where the growth has been so phenomenal that scholars are asking whether the continent is turning 'Protestant'. The largest Christian congregation in the world – with 800,000 members in 1995 – is a Pentecostal one, the Yoido Full Gospel Church in Seoul, Korea. Opulent buildings holding thousands of worshippers reflect the emerging Pentecostal middle class in some parts of the world. These superchurches notwithstanding, Pentecostals in the Third World are usually and predominantly a grassroots movement appealing especially to the disadvantaged and underprivileged. Many, if not most, of the rapidly growing Christian churches in the Third World are Pentecostal, indigenous and operate independently of Western Pentecostalism. This phenomenon is so significant that the author of *The Secular City*, Harvey Cox, has written a book entitled *Fire from Heaven*, with the intriguing subtitle *The Rise of Pentecostal Spirituality and the Reshaping of Religion in the Twenty-first Century*. In this fascinating study, Cox virtually reverses his well-known position on secularization and speaks of Pentecostalism as a manifestation of the 'unanticipated reappearance of primal spirituality in our time.'[9]

Pentecostalism's roots in the African-based slave religion of the United States and the genesis of the movement in the Black-led Azusa Street revival in a Los Angeles ghetto (in itself a model of interracial harmony during one of North America's worst racist periods), together with an emphasis on 'freedom in the Spirit' that rendered it inherently flexible in different cultural and social contexts, made Pentecostalism remarkably successful at inculturation. This fact must be assessed in any consideration of inculturation and Black communities. Cox observes that 'the great strength of the Pentecostal impulse' lies in 'its power to combine, its aptitude for the language, the music, the cultural artefacts, the religious tropes ... of the setting in which it lives'.[10]

The manifestations of Pentecostalism's flexibility, however, did not always satisfy Western missionaries, who were drawn by their own cultural contexts towards promoting a more rational and less emotional expression of Pentecostal practice in keeping with their sense of decorum. This, too, was the 'sin of disrespect' of which Aldred speaks. It may not be too far-fetched to suggest that the ability or inability of churches in the West to adjust to their new context is directly related to their relevance and impact in mission. This is just as true of Black British churches as of any others. The success of missionary activity in Britain amongst African-Caribbean people from the 1950s onwards, to which Aldred makes reference, is at least partly due to their ability to adjust to a changing cultural context whilst appreciating the deep spirituality that had existed for generations. As he puts it, the gospel was wrapped in the covering of Black people's cultures. Beckford's work illustrates that this form of Black Pentecostalism may not be sufficiently addressing the Black community's context today.

Pentecostal churches in Africa itself were also founded on innovative initiatives unprecedented in the history of mission, motivated by a compelling need to preach and, even more significantly, to *experience* a new message of the power of the Holy Spirit. The effectiveness of these mission initiatives was based on this unique message, which was both the motivation for the thousands of grassroots emissaries and their source of attraction. All the widely differing African Pentecostal movements have important common features: they all regard themselves as 'churches of the Spirit', they proclaim and celebrate a salvation (or 'healing') that encompasses all of life's experiences and afflictions, and they offer an empowerment that provides a sense of dignity and a coping mechanism for life and drives their messengers forward into a unique mission.

Their mission was to share this all-embracing message with as many people as possible, and to accomplish this, African Pentecostal missionaries traversed the continent. The astonishing journeys in 1914 of the famous Liberian prophet William Wade Harris throughout the Ivory Coast to western Ghana, which have been described as 'the most remarkable evangelical campaign Africa has ever witnessed',[11] resulted in tens of thousands of conversions to Christianity. A year later, Garrick Braide in the Niger Delta area of Nigeria conducted a similar crusade, with thousands becoming Christians. Braide was barred from the Anglican church because of his practice of healing the sick and tolerance of polygamy, and because he called himself a prophet.[12]

These and other African missionaries demonstrated their proclamation in emphasizing the manifestation of divine power through healing, prophecy, speaking in tongues and other Pentecostal phenomena. The message proclaimed by these charismatic preachers of receiving the power of the Holy Spirit to meet human needs was welcomed in societies in which a lack of power was keenly felt on a daily basis. These preachers, like their contemporary Western Pentecostal missionaries, often rejected all forms of medicine, whether Western or African, and some, like the Christ Apostolic Church in Nigeria, later seceded from Western Pentecostal mission churches who had become more tolerant of medicine use.[13]

Healing and protection from evil are the most prominent features of the proclamation of these Pentecostals and are probably the most important part of the liturgy in their evangelism and church recruitment. The central place given to healing is no longer a main feature of Western Pentecostalism, but in Africa the problems of disease and evil affect the whole community and are not simply a private domain relegated to individual pastoral care. As Cox observes, African Pentecostals 'provide a setting in which the African conviction that spirituality and healing belong together is dramatically enacted'.[14] Traditional African communities were to a large extent health-orientated communities and in

African traditional religions, rituals for healing and protection were the most prominent ones.

African Pentecostal missionaries responded to what they experienced as a void left by a rationalistic Western form of Christianity, which had unwittingly initiated what was tantamount to the destruction of African spiritual values. Africans were able to declare a message that reclaimed ancient biblical traditions of healing and protection from evil, to demonstrate the practical effects of these traditions, and by so doing to be the heralds of a Christianity with an implicit theology that was really meaningful to Africans. African experience is the crucible in which a genuinely African theology is made. African Pentecostal movements have gone a long way towards meeting the physical, emotional and spiritual needs of Africans, offering solutions to life's problems and ways to cope in a threatening and hostile world. African missionaries proclaimed that the same God who saves the 'soul' also heals the body, delivers from evil forces and provides answers to human needs.[15]

NOTES

1. Allan Anderson, *Bazalwane: African Pentecostals in South Africa*, Unisa Press, 1992, pp. 2–5.
2. See further David B. Barrett, 'Annual statistical table on global mission: 2000', *International Bulletin of Missionary Research*, January 2000.
3. This term denotes the Pentecostal denominations originating in the early North American movement, the largest being the Assemblies of God and various Church of God denominations.
4. Clifton Clarke, *The Reason Why We Sing: Introducing Black Pentecostal Spirituality*, Grove Books, 1997, pp. 3–4.

5. Robert M. Anderson, *Vision of the Disinherited: The Making of American Pentecostalism*, Hendrickson, 1979, p. 4.
6. Steven J. Land, *Pentecostal Spirituality: A Passion for the Kingdom*, Sheffield Academic Press, 1993, p. 21.
7. Walter J. Hollenweger, 'After twenty years' research on Pentecostalism', *International Review of Mission*, 1986, pp. 5–6.
8. Clarke, pp. 7–8.
9. Harvey Cox, *Fire from Heaven: The Rise of Pentecostal Spirituality and the Reshaping of Religion in the Twenty-first Century*, Cassell, 1996, p. 221.
10. Cox, p. 259.
11. Adrian Hastings, *A History of African Christianity 1950–1975*, Cambridge University Press, 1979, p. 67.
12. Adrian Hastings, *The Church in Africa 1450–1950*, Clarendon, 1994, pp. 443–6.
13. Hastings, *The Church in Africa 1450–1950*, p. 514.
14. Cox, p. 247.
15. Allan Anderson and Samuel Otwang, *Tumelo: The Faith of African Pentecostals in South Africa*, Unisa Press, 1993, p. 32. See also Allan Anderson, *Pentecostals After a Century*, Sheffield Academic Press, 1999. I am currently working on African initiatives in Christianity.

The Liberation of Genders: Feminist Theology as a Challenge to Inculturation

Ann Loades

I write from within the Christian tradition, as I have no first-hand knowledge of any other. There are complications enough in speaking or writing for women within the Christian tradition, including the possibility of accidental anti-Semitism, without risking accidental misrepresentation of other religious traditions as well.

Let us, then, begin with an invitation that came to me to assist the House of Bishops of the Church of England with some preliminary advice and reflections in relation to a July 1991 General Synod resolution couched in the following terms: 'That this Synod notes the concern about feminist theology expressed in various quarters of the church and asks the House of Bishops to examine and report on the issues raised, ensuring that the views of women as well as men are taken into account in that process.'

Feminist theology here is very probably associated with post-Christian feminism, and whilst the most formidable post-Christian feminist known internationally is Mary Daly,[1] in Britain it is Daphne Hampson who occupies that position. So I will begin with some observations about her major book, *After Christianity* (1996), so that we may appreciate something of the force of the post-Christian option for women, at least – and presumably for feminist men.

Hampson is correct in her observation that no major feminist thinker is Christian (p. 252), and her book explains why that is. The bones of her position are that Christianity is both untrue and profoundly unethical in its devaluation of women. Much of her book would be worth attention quite irrespective of her understanding of feminism and its consequences, though her position is inevitably fraught with certain difficulties. For Hampson, like the rest of us, inhabits the Enlightenment and post-

Enlightenment world, including its liberalism and epistemological scepticism. And yet Enlightenment rationalism and the modes of thinking Hampson herself employs have, like ours, been constituted by the exclusion of, or in opposition to, the 'feminine'.

Only in the latter part of the twentieth century have the insights of certain forms of psychoanalysis, as appropriated by so-called 'French feminism', begun to impinge on what has for so long seemed to us to be 'rational' and to make us begin to think differently about the supposedly gender-free character of reason itself. Thus Hampson appeals to 'autonomy' (still hardly understood by many women in their inability to take responsibility for themselves and what they think and do) and devalues hierarchy and heteronomy. Autonomy, however, is qualified as that of a centred self in relation, responding not merely to other human persons but to the beauty of the world. Attention to others as to self, honesty and a determination to order one's life are marks of a spirituality of the kind we should foster in our time.

Much of Hampson's argument about the 'untruth' of Christianity is familiar enough to anyone who knows the sort of British philosophy of religion current (pre-Wittgenstein) for the last century or so. What will be unfamiliar is the way she presses her case about that 'untruth' with the devaluation of women so characteristic of Christian thinking in a whole variety of contexts. Whilst she acknowledges that variety (p. 119) and the richness of Christian history, she does not think that it offers anything worthwhile to women.

In her dismissal of the past, she again is marked by 'enlightenment', but the force of her contention stands. And its core is that the hierarchy and heteronomy utterly characteristic of Christianity are integral to the subordination of women by men and to the way men have construed the meaning of women's lives as lesser persons, as 'outsiders'. Since women need justice and not consolation (p. 272), the role models of those who have negotiated their way within patriarchy are not what feminists need. Rather, they need to be clear of the whole interrelated symbol system and institutions which have done them so much damage.

However contentious some of her comments (for instance, her treatment of the Lord's Prayer, pp. 129–30), her argument remains a powerful one and is at its best in Chapter 6 on 'Christian idolatry', which should become recommended reading for those who stay with the Christian tradition as well as those who are in the process of leaving and want to articulate why! Her most devastating criticism is that women are those who are renounced in loving such a God as is portrayed in Christianity (p. 159), for we turn to the divine for the satisfaction of those needs and wants which are improperly denied, and which could and should be acknowledged and met in human reality. Their denial is crucially connected with the devaluation of women, and the separation of the sexes sustains denigration of women's sexuality at the same time as the doctrine of the Trinity externalizes male experience of male sexuality. The doctrine, moreover, provides a form of therapy to alleviate fear of the father whilst experiencing the loss of the maternal and the desire to regain it.

There are no easy shortcuts, however. Notably, calling God 'mother' has, or could have, revolutionary potential if and only if 'God' named female/feminine agency and power, and not simply the mediation of male–male relationships. Thus, for women to come into their own is simply the most revolutionary thing they could do (p. 207), not least if 'God' means no less than what is intrinsic to women themselves. For the appearance of independent and self-actualizing women on the public scene would not only disrupt the whole Christian symbol system but much of our secular symbol system and institutions as well.

Such a summary version of Hampson's points can by no means do justice to the power of her case but will perhaps suffice to make my initial point: that feminist theology is too readily associated with post-Christian feminism, and such an association inhibits even the most minimal attempt to understand it as a movement. For a movement it is, and a complex one at that. Just as there is no one thing meant by 'theology' or 'Christian', so there is no one thing meant by 'feminism'. In principle, if Christianity is to fulfil the promise of full human dignity it professes on at least some occasions and in some circumstances, a Christian feminism might be possible. It might be as easy to say of a bishop, 'As a feminist, he ... ' as it would be to say, 'As a Christian feminist, she ... .'

We could spend a lot of time elaborating the different varieties of feminism, but what they all have in common, so far as I can see, is a determination to secure change for the better in terms of justice for women. In principle, therefore, a feminist need not be female by sex, but it is crucial to feminism that women's perspectives and responsibilities are taken into account – an acknowledgement that needs to be made more tactfully than in the General Synod resolution with which I began.

We need to note that 'feminism' can itself be an offensive term, if 'White' feminism (White indicating those with 'imperialist pink skin') presumes to speak for 'womanists',[2] for 'mujerista'[3] or for women of Far East Asian Christianity[4] as they develop their theologies in context. Complications of race, class and colonial expropriation abound. That said, so many 'feminist theologians' (I shall continue to use the phrase without presuming to speak except so far as I can for and from my own location) have received much the same sort of theological education that, despite appeals to context and culture, they can easily end up sounding much the same! No doubt this situation will change over time. In whatever context or circumstances, however, the point remains that since being female is as much the predominant human experience as being male, the insights and experiences of women should be readily treated as being as valuable as those of men. The challenge to the Christian tradition is to come to terms with this reality in a way it simply has not done before.

It is equally important to notice that not every female theologian is a feminist theologian, in the sense that she does not necessarily have feminist issues at the top of her theological agenda all the time – any more than if one were discussing an equilateral triangle, for instance. Feminism will not necessarily enlighten every issue, though we may not always be able to specify in advance what those issues will be.

Within the churches, feminist theology is inevitably primarily a lay movement, not least in those churches in which women are irretrievably lay simply by virtue of their sex. (I will return later to the distinction between sex and gender commonly employed.) As laity, women do not necessarily find themselves affirmed, since both liturgy and teaching tend to exclude them, to diminish them. To give a simple example, we hear of the God of Abraham, Isaac and Jacob, but not of the God of Sarah and Hagar, of Rebecca, Leah and Rachel.

The tradition is powerfully ambivalent for women, both (in some ways) affirming them and (in other ways) diminishing their worth and value by treating the male as normative. Baptism into Christ's body is not, it seems, enough as an expression of women's dignity. In so far as they have been positively affirmed, however, women have developed very strong convictions about what they may have to offer to one another and to their ecclesiastical institutions (assuming they continue to struggle with these). They and their lives are gifts to the church, by which they are graced in turn.

Women are also likely to value a learning style associated with adult education, which places priority on the members of a group setting their own agenda, on hearing everyone's voice, and on the creative and practical testing and development of what is said, free of clerical control. The 'clerks' here may include 'professional' academic women theologians such as myself as much as male theologians, since some would certainly suppose that we are tokenized women in the theological scene, having capitulated too much to the world we might like to transform.

Being free of the 'clerks', however, has its disadvantages – such as having perpetually to reinvent the wheel. Not to inhabit one's tradition may leave one without resources, without the stimulus of evaluating women's lives and teaching in the past, without the capacity to generate critical dissonance with the present, to open up new vistas and walkways, generate new insights, negotiate dead ends, endure experiences of profound alienation and live with changing criteria.

Feminist theology is now sufficiently inculturated in the academic theological scene to be a regular feature of teaching programmes. And it should be noted that long before a specifically feminist theology developed, it was secular universities and colleges, and not seminaries (seedbeds!), which first gave women the opportunity to teach theology – though they were more readily accepted in some areas of the discipline than others ('pastoral' theology, of course, was acceptable). Given the abysmal depths of suspicion of what women might say if allowed to open their mouths (using 1 Timothy 2.12), we still do not know how to evaluate the fact that it is both recent and still rare for women to be permitted to teach theology, let alone preach. Some of us, at least, have non-ecclesiastical institutions to thank for the privilege.

Since feminist theology may now be taught not merely as a separate aspect of theology but as integral to the mainstream, it will be inculturated through some forms of theological education, as it should be, given the unambiguous evidence of the academic standard of writing and publication in this area. And there are now at least two organizations that link women in churches with women in educational institutions: the European Society of Women for Theological Research, and the Britain and Ireland School of Feminist Theology (both draw on resources worldwide).

On the one hand, therefore, there is a problem about the 'inculturalization' of Christianity for women, a problem represented by those who leave the tradition, such as Daphne Hampson. On the other, there is another sort of problem, about the inculturalization of feminist insight into the world of those who remain. Either way, feminist theology now exists and is not going to go away.

There is, of course, the question of whether – somewhat analogous to 'just war', perhaps – 'feminist theology' is a contradiction in terms, and to this I shall return very shortly. To concede the point that theology – from *theos*/god-male – is irretrievably a male project would necessitate leaving the tradition: it would be necessary for one's well-being that one should. It would be betraying other women and their needs to stay and, importantly, be doing nothing to transform relationships between women and men.

Those who stay with the tradition in the face of the feminist critique may well find it painful to do so, for their critics may be right. Women may be incapacitating themselves by hoping that the Christian tradition is capable of reform and by making such efforts as they can to contribute to that reformation. To leave is not as easy as giving up belief in Santa Claus, and even Santa Claus has his point, in reminding us to give to poverty-stricken and vulnerable children. My position presupposes the hope that it is possible to inculturate feminist theology within the Christian tradition that has given it birth and within the lives of women outside the tradition at present, though this will be a long haul in both cases.

To turn now to the history of feminist theology, we should note that it has its origins in such nineteenth-century social movements as the campaigns against slavery and for the vote, and the campaign spearheaded by Josephine Butler for the repeal of the Contagious Diseases Acts. If we now find the fight for the vote almost incomprehensible, we need to recall that it had a symbolic importance – that women had minds and wills of their own, and could and would exercise them independently. Elizabeth Cady Stanton is the name to conjure here, and the whole movement of feminist critique of biblical texts that has developed since she and her collaborators published *The Woman's Bible* in 1895.[5]

Post-World War II, the catalysts were Roman Catholic women responding to the work of the second Vatican Council, coincidentally with campaigns for equal rights by those devalued on account of their sex or race. Access to education, and to theological education in particular, has over the course of a century brought the central theological issues into focus. Whereas women quickly learned about their church's devaluation of women, they had not earlier made the connection between that devaluation and its 'theological' justification. Here the key initiators of the movement were Rosemary Radford Reuther, Elisabeth Schüssler Fiorenza and, in Old Testament studies, Phyllis Trible – now joined by many more.

What is important is to realize that feminist interpretation and evaluation of both Bible and tradition is essentially a theological task, with issues about justice to women and the symbolism used for God and God's relationship to God's creatures entangled with one another and needing scrupulous attention at all times. Take one recent example, Renita J. Weems's *Battered Love: Marriage, Sex and Violence in the Hebrew Prophets* (1995). As she says, to the extent that God's covenant with Israel is like a marriage, and to the extent that divine retribution is theologically acceptable, the image of a husband physically retaliating against his wife becomes unavoidable (p. 112). The marriage metaphor requires particular vigilance whatever its original point – such as, by a male author for the male imagination, that 'God is as outraged at what you're doing as any one of you would be if your wives were acting the way you are acting' (p. 42). Feminist exegesis has great potential not only for opening up new ways of reading texts but also for persuading us to look differently at our relationships and, importantly, at how we symbolize God.

A core issue, indeed, is the unease in the Christian tradition about the association of the female and the feminine with the godlike and the divine, tackled in scriptural exegesis by, for example, Phyllis Trible in *God and the Rhetoric of Sexuality* (1978). In the second chapter, she tracks the journey of a single metaphor (womb/compassion) that highlights female/feminine-related imagery for God, metaphor that is reality-depicting as much as any language for God may be.

Another example of scriptural and theological re-evaluation of this, this time in the New Testament, is the section 'The Sophia-God of Jesus and the discipleship of women' in Elisabeth Schüssler Fiorenza's *In Memory of Her* (1983). The notion of Sophia-God is important to express the gracious goodness in the divine by selective use of Jewish 'wisdom' theology, which arguably used elements of 'goddess' language to speak of God and made possible Jesus' invitation to women to become his disciples.

That such exegesis should only now become possible itself illustrates the point that whereas it is arguable that feminist theology is a contradiction in terms, feminist *thealogy* would not be. The word theology needs to be qualified as 'masculinist', perhaps, to make clear that it is not deemed to be humanly inclusive in its metaphorical or analogical range. I shall continue to use the phrase feminist theology to indicate the hope that God is given to us and can be imaged/symbolized in gender-inclusive ways. I will come shortly to explain the perhaps too conventional way of making the distinction between sex and gender that lies at the heart of much of the discussion.

So far as I know, it is perfectly orthodox to affirm that God transcends both sex and gender. Some, indeed, will retain the convention of writing 'he' and 'him' for God precisely as a reminder that God is not anthropomorphically masculine. The problem is that we seem to be incapable of acting on that acknowledgement, even though (theology apart) we know perfectly well that grammatical gender tells us little about some subjects of our attention. 'Majesty', for instance, is 'feminine' in French, even when used of Louis XIV.

Assuming that we want to continue to use anthropomorphic (let alone parental) language for God at all, we might argue that the mystery of God positively requires a variety of names, each of which acts as a corrective against the tendency of any particular one to become reified and literal. An alternative is to opt for a kind of intellectual and spiritual asceticism here, at least for the time being – that is, for a kind of 'negative way' which recalls us not merely to the mystery of God but to God's incomprehensibility.

But the fundamental principle that has emerged is worth emphasizing: that the female/feminine can, of and by itself, image God in as full and as limited a way as God is imaged by the male/masculine. The most sustained exposition of this case has been made by Elizabeth A. Johnson's outstanding book *She Who Is: The Mystery of God in Feminist Theological Discourse* (1993). This is not a matter of simply adding a feminine dimension to a God basically imaged as male despite all disclaimers to the contrary, as in 'brothers and sisters' in a liturgy that otherwise remains the same (the 'add women and stir' principle). It is a matter of enriching the Christian theological tradition, as it has flowered in gender-fluid devotion and prayer throughout the centuries, without inevitable error and irretrievable spiritual corruption. In using (if we do) the metaphor of 'Father' for God, we note that there is, of course, no absolutely necessary association of the word with being dominant, implacable, distant, unrelated and controlling, given its notes of intimacy and accessibility as well as of righteousness (as, for example, in John 17.25,26). That said, the language of divine 'mothering' derived from Scripture and tradition needs to be honoured also, no less than the lives of human mothers. There are other consequences for theology, too, also affected by attention to gender matters.

The distinction between sex and gender commonly employed is between basic biological differences (such as that men ejaculate and women menstruate, gestate and lactate) and what particular societies make of these differences in various social, cultural and economic ways, given the power issues at stake. The nursery rhyme 'What are little girls/boys made of?' expresses one such gender construction. Little girls stay clean, stay home and smell nice. Little boys muck in with one another and their world and learn to find their way about in it. Just how much they depend on female support and 'mothering' to do so safely is obscured in the rhyme.

Another classic example is a preacher's commendation of Teresa of Avila in a 1627 sermon in honour of her nomination as co-patron of Spain. On the one hand, 'sanctity in women usually consists in being quiet, obeying, staying in a corner and forgetting about oneself', whereas Teresa had become saintly (in an implicitly masculine way) 'not by keeping quiet, but by speaking, teaching and writing; not only by obeying, but by ordering, commanding, governing; not by observing enclosure, but by travelling, disputing'. That Christian gender constructions still affect us is evident in Janet Daley's remarks, quoted in *The Times* of 10 March 1992: 'Self-effacing invisibility in public combined with sympathetic support in private is the ideal helpmeet face of the working woman.' Unsurprising, then, that it seems easy enough to redesignate the Spirit as 'she' in some theologies, since 'she' clearly plays nothing more than a go-between role between Father and Son.

The worst-case scenario so far as the Christian gender construction for women is concerned is that women are derivative from and hence secondary to men, that they are characterized by passivity, that their bodily difference from men symbolizes lesser intellectual functioning, and that they cannot be associated with transcendent 'mind'. It follows from this that Christian theology has 'genderized' appropriate ways of thinking about and actually experiencing divine presence and immanence as well as transcendence, sacramental or otherwise – another area to which feminist theologians are turning their attention. Put another way, it can be argued that the dominant gender construction for Christian men is that they are active, independent, intelligent, brave, strong, good and godlike, with God in turn being male-like, as well as being all-powerful and all-knowing. Males are always more godlike than females could ever be, since women's religiously sanctioned gender construction has been that they are passive, dependent, bodily, emotional, weak, peculiarly responsible for evil (though not, of course, for pride – that sin of the intellect – since they fail to use whatever brains they have) and childlike, in the worst senses of that word.

That this sort of nonsense is still current was fairly recently exhibited in the work of a former Church of England bishop, who wrote both irresponsibly and unacceptably that 'in the whole of human instinct and understanding it is the masculine which is associated with giving and the feminine with receiving'. To be fair, this prompted another bishop to point up the underlying sexual ideology of the claim by saying that Bishop X might wish to describe what happened in his own bedroom, but he was not going to prescribe what happened in anyone else's!

The association of the masculine with giving and the feminine with receiving is manifestly false as description: that is to say, it is self-deception to suppose that women and men relate to one another in this simplistic way. It is also thoroughly bad as prescription: if human beings try to relate to one another in this simplistic way, disaster may well follow, with exhaustion for the giver and helplessness intrinsic to the recipient. Consider, for instance, Cinderella, Snow White and Sleeping Beauty, sitting in the ashes, sleeping under a glass coffin lid and behind a thorn hedge, waiting for Prince Charming to ride by and pick them up and out. There could be no conceivable justification for placing such an intolerable burden on men, and for erecting such barriers as these fantasies portray to the self-actualization and responsibility of women for themselves and their own lives.

Tangled up in the gender construction of the mainstream tradition is an assumption wholly at odds with what is now known to be the case about the role of women as co-procreators with men of new human life. The pre-Christian assumption, incorporated into Christianity and based on the best available biology of the day, was that it was males who were primarily creative (as in 'Lord and Giver of Life') and that children originated essentially from only one source. This assumption, that it is the male who has the primary and essential role in reproduction and that a women is merely a nurturing receptacle for 'his' child, is well worked into our symbol system and profoundly affects discussion of ordained and other forms of ministry, of marriage and family life in all their variability, and of appropriate language for God, as we have already seen.

Yet again, we can see that feminist theology is bound to make a difference to some of our most fundamental institutions. The agenda, however, is not to pretend that sex/gender differences can be or ought to be obliterated, whatever the balance of 'nature' or 'construction' involved, but to find ways of celebrating difference. This would enable us to speak theologically with a proliferation of the names of God, which we noticed earlier. Crucial, then, would be to avoid locating all the values associated with males/masculinity at the top of some hierarchy of value, with those associated with females/femininity at the bottom. It must be obvious that we are all at some time or other emotional, intelligent, passive or active, dependent and interdependent as well as independent in relation to one another, and so on and so forth. All these are simply aspects of being human, for members of both sexes.

Manifestly, feminist theology integrates ethics with theology and wants the reintegration of liturgy, pastoral practice and spirituality with theology, too frequently construed as doctrine in isolation from other areas of reflection. To give one example of the sort of topic that needs to be tackled: why, in the light of the divine 'fatherhood', are the churches so insistent on the genetic connection between fathers and children (the figure of Joseph notwithstanding) and so remiss about the nurture, education and socialization of children by their fathers, not least what now seems to have been established about the importance to daughters of their fathers' actual presence? There is an area here of acute disjunction between the language of 'fathering' for God and lived experience for women.

If, unfortunately, feminist theology continues to mimic the agenda of non-feminist theology, the interests of children will be as disregarded theologically as they have been so largely up to now. Theology has been concerned with the 'unborn' and with adolescent sexuality and its control, but remarkably little with the lives of actual children as responsibilities of both their parents – rather than, for example, as merely appendages of their mothers. Matters such as the sexual abuse of children, for instance, are almost impossible to think about until we understand and imagine the lives of children themselves.

It is also noteworthy that feminist theological ethics typically attends to the values of which women are culturally the bearers, such as care, connectedness, relationality, interdependence and so forth. These aspects of relationships are of crucial importance, but are themselves already manifestations of gender if they are seen to be primarily the responsibility of women, and of women confined to the private sphere – despite their major contribution to the well-being of their households by the work most of them for many generations have undertaken outside their homes as well as within them. An emphasis on justice in the private realm, and affirmation of women's vocal presence in the struggle for public justice, is essential if change for the better is ever to be a realizable goal.

At least one objective of feminist theology must be to find some social and political 'edge' to make an impact on long-term change in society as well as in ecclesiastical institutions. Without such an edge, no feminist worth her salt will give the Christian tradition a thought. There has so far been little attention to economic and social injustice and its connection with pregnancy termination; to what is euphemistically referred to as 'foetal tissue use'; to the burdens associated with developments in artificially assisted human reproduction; and to the new ethical issues arising from developments in human genetics, especially in respect of socially constructed attitudes to the 'disabled'. In other words, if feminist theology to some degree equips people to contribute to life beyond their own selves in imaginative and constructive ways, we might hope to find invigorated debate, and action flowing from such debate and in turn enlivening it. In such ways, feminist theology might be seen to be at the core of theology in the churches' endeavours to 'inculturate' Christianity in this new millennium. If feminists continue to distance themselves from the Christian tradition, the outlook may be grim indeed.

NOTES

1. See, for instance, 'Beyond God the father: an introduction to Mary Daly's view of Christian tradition', in A. Linzey and P. Wexler (eds), *Fundamentalism and Tolerance*, London, 1991, pp. 113–22.

2. Alice Walker's *The Color Purple* is the classic text here. See also L. M. Russell and J. Shannon Clarkson (eds), *Dictionary of Feminist Theologies*, Louisville, 1996; S. Jones, 'Women's experience: between a rock and a hard place – feminist, womanist and mujerista theologies in North America', *Religious Studies Review* 21(3), 1995, pp. 171–8.
3. A. M. Isasi-Diaz, *En La Lucha. In the Struggle: A Hispanic Women's Liberation Theology*, Minneapolis, 1993; see also A. Loades, 'Feminist theology' in D. Ford (ed.), *The Modern Theologians*, Oxford, 1997, pp. 575–84 for further bibliography.
4. As above in Loades; see also U. King (ed.), *Feminist Theology from the Third World*, London, 1994.
5. See the material in A. Loades (ed.), *Feminist Theology: A Reader*, London, 1990, pp. 13–80; C. A. Newson and S. H. Ringe (eds), *The Women's Bible Commentary*, London, 1992; and further bibliography on Old Testament texts in J. Cheryl Exum, *Fragmented Women: Feminist (Sub)versions of Biblical Narratives*, Sheffield,1993, and the two volumes of E. Schüssler Fiorenza (ed.), *Searching the Scriptures*, London, 1993–4.

ADDITIONAL BIBLIOGRAPHY

R. Nakashima Brock, C. Camp and S. Jones (eds), *Setting the Table: Women in Theological Conversation*, St Louis, 1995.

A. O'Hara Graff (ed.), *In the Embrace of God: Feminist Approaches to Theological Anthropology*, Maryknoll, New York, 1995.

L. Isherwood and D. McEwan (eds), *An A to Z of Feminist Theology*, Sheffield, 1996.

C. Mowry LaCugna (ed.), *Freeing Theology: The Essentials of Theology in Feminist Perspective*, San Francisco, 1993.

M. Stewart Van Leeuwen (ed.), *After Eden: Facing the Challenge of Gender Reconciliation*, Grand Rapids, Michigan, 1993.

Mission Beyond Modernity: A Global Perspective

Bert Hoedemaker

The term 'world Christianity' refers to the worldwide and pluriform manifestation of the Christian religion, but not in a general and neutral way. It evokes a specific history that is marked by two influential Western projects: Christianization and modernization. Both projects have shaped Western culture in a definitive way and have determined the development of contemporary world society. As such they remain inescapably present in contemporary Christianity as well. It is important to keep both projects in view and not limit our focus to modernization: modernization has incorporated the earlier heritage of Christianization to a large extent, but not completely, as the history of modern Western Christianity testifies.

The problem that needs to be addressed is that, for the interpretation of the present dynamics of world Christianity, the two projects are beginning to run out of defining power. The new reality of globalization, which results worldwide in a large number of uneasy marriages between the global and the local, surpasses the usefulness of older distinctions such as Western versus non-Western, colonizer versus colonized, perhaps even secular versus religious. There is much religious reality – in both the Western and non-Western world, inside and outside Christianity – that challenges the traditional frameworks of definition.

All this has important consequences for the conceptualizing of world Christianity. It forces us to question customary assumptions and to look for paradigms that take new experiences seriously and transcend the limits of the (relatively recent) projects of Christianization and modernization. This is necessary both for the ecumenical debate on the unifying identity of Christianity and for the missionary question of the orientation towards the unity of humankind.

The modern construction of religion

The agenda of modernity

At the heart of modernity is the desire to master a complex world with the aid of universal rational concepts and a technology developed on the basis of those concepts. Its hidden agenda[1] is to conquer ambiguity and messiness by decontextualizing human thought and to create a stable world order on the basis of rationality and experiment. The birth of the modern concepts of *culture* and *religion* must be understood in this framework: these concepts were essentially modernizing tools. As such, they were the instruments of the *elite* in organizing and controlling social life. Socially speaking, modernization is a project of civilization, aimed at the uneducated masses within the orbit of the Western world and then at the unconverted heathen outside this orbit.

Closely linked to this modern emphasis on universality and rationality is the elevation of the individual. Rationality involves a personal duty to come of age (Kant); analogously, religion involves personal conversion. There is an important relation between modern notions of personhood and the missionary project of conversion.[2] Mission and modernization share the desire to define and to order. The identification of 'other' cultures and 'other' religions has an important function here: it is an aspect of a totalizing project of reconstruction[3] and of the incorporation of the peoples of the world into basically Western definitions. Other cultures and religions become visible and definable either as allies or as adversaries in the project of modernity.

The project of modernity is history-creating in the sense that it draws the world into the Western historical narrative. The cultural and religious reality of the non-Western world is brought to consciousness in the context of this narrative. Everything that cannot be brought to consciousness in this way remains undetermined, and in a way non-existent.

Modern rearrangement of rationality, religion and faith

Rationality and religion are basic features of human society. Rationality is the ability to organize, to structure reality according to principles and goals. Religion is the permanent struggle with contingency and the attempt to make sense of life by reference to a reality that transcends it. Rationality and religion always function in mixtures, both in individual efforts to give meaning to one's context and in the organization of social life, and there is an original, healthy tension between them. A culture lives and survives with the aid of this tension and of the balance that it presupposes. It is the function of *faith(s)* to build bridges between rationality and religion: to structure religion with the aid of a narrative, a community, a conceptual system, and to keep it on speaking terms with rationality.

Since the advent of modernity, however, this triangular balance is somehow characterized by disarray. (In a sense, the possibility of discussing rationality, religion and faith as distinct elements is dependent on this disarray.) In modern Western culture, rationality turns against religion in two ways: first in the sense of emancipation, of liberation from dogma and superstition considered to be a hindrance to the development of autonomous reason; then in the sense of a systemic functionalism that prides itself on its ability to organize life without reference to the transcendent. The systems of this functional rationality have colonized and are still colonizing the 'life worlds', the primary contexts of daily living (Habermas). The expanding and globalizing drive of the project of modernity has brought this Western unbalance to the ends of the earth: it has become worldwide.[4]

To call it an unbalance, however, is already a postmodern judgement. In the self-definition of modernity, the rearrangement of rationality, religion and faith presented an advance over previous balances. It created a 'higher', a more mature synthesis than the one created by Christendom, as it was based on the autonomous development of rationality and a redefinition of religion as a project of essentially subjective design. Generally speaking, the dominant Christian traditions accepted the new synthesis, and even where it was perceived and distrusted as a colonizing instrument (for instance, in some parts of North American evangelical Protestantism), it still remained the framework for the articulation of Christian identity.

Christianization and modernization

The advent of the modern synthesis can also be viewed from a different angle. At the time of the Reformation, the spread of Christianity in Europe was still quite limited, both quantitatively and qualitatively. Both the Reformation and the Catholic renewal that began in the sixteenth century were major efforts to push the project of Christianization forward, and the same can be said of later movements such as Puritanism, Pietism and Revivalism.

From the seventeenth century onward, however, the project concurred with the project of modernization, and the two became, to a certain degree, intertwined. It is important to see why and at what points they concur, even though they obviously presuppose different syntheses and different arrangements of rationality, religion and faith. *It is the containment, the taming of local, plural religion in an overarching cultural system, that is their common motivation.* This is precisely the reason that both syntheses are also precarious: they make themselves dependent on the possibility of containing religion, that is, of defining it from the point of view of some 'centre'.

The difference between Christendom's synthesis and modernity's – and, analogously, between the projects of Christianization and modernization – can be formulated as a difference in ways of containing religion. In Christendom, it is basically the authority of the church that unifies religious practices and 'redefines religious spaces'.[5] In modern times, the universalization and personalization of the concept of religion performs the same function. From the 'Christian' point of view, religion is truly religion when it fits into the authoritatively defined framework of Christianity; from the 'modern' point of view, religion is truly religion when it can be articulated and accounted for in beliefs and personal conversion. In short, in the Christendom synthesis *faith* is the dominant element; in the modern synthesis, it is *rationality*.

Both the concurrence and the fundamental difference, the kinship and the rivalry, between the two projects are visible in the history of modern Christianity. Both function as 'grand narratives' (Lyotard), and occasionally they merge into one. The *conquista* of Latin America is a good example of Christianization in its pure form, based on the premodern synthesis and on the discourse of authority. The modern missionary movement, with its emphasis on conversion as distinct from political or commercial gain, has much more affinity to the project of modernization. In nineteenth-century movements of 'civilization', in which Christian revivalism joins hands with cultural education of the people, we often find the two projects working together in harmony, although religious distrust of the modern synthesis is never absent. Christianization is not completely absorbed into modernization, although it is marked and transformed by it in a definitive way.

The colonizing project

What is often massively called 'the West' or 'modern Western culture' is, in fact, an uneasy coexistence of several layers and projects, an open-ended process of forming, reforming, rejecting and reinterpreting ethnic and cultural identities, that never came to completion or even coherent self-definition. The colonizing project was an extension of this disorderly establishment into the world outside Europe and at the same time an instrument in creating some order and identity for 'the West'. It produced a certain unity rather than being the product of a pre-existing unity. In this process, the premises of modernity were dominant, including the premise that the premodern world, in both its Western and non-Western forms, needed to be conquered and transformed. This 'conversion to modernity' further confirmed and strengthened, and even helped to create, modernity.

For the non-Western world, colonization meant pressure to give an account of itself in terms introduced by an outsider. At the same time, the possibility of giving this account implied space for creative self-assertion. Colonization, conceived in this way, is certainly not one-sided oppression. It is the introduction of a framework for self-definition and, on this basis, for effective participation in a wider global, modern community of humankind.

Anti-colonial movements of nationalism and nation building are primary examples of this creativity of self-definition within the framework of (introduced) modernity. To a large extent, non-Western nation building mirrored the modern Western nation state. The modern synthesis remained the objective even when there were appearances of difference, for instance, with regard to the religious identity of the emergent states. The new nationalist movements (in India, Pakistan and Indonesia, for example) were avowedly religious, and even the secularity of formally secular states rested on compromises with powerful religious groups.

Yet it is precisely this political mobilization of religion, this assignment of a constructive role to religion in the process of nation building, that is typically modern. It is a new element in the history of the non-Western world, and it represents a major step in the direction of the modern synthesis, even though it also provides a certain continuity with the premodern past. The heart of colonialism is a transformation of the religious domain.[6]

This is also true for Islam. In the case of Pakistan, Islam became a nationalism. In the Arab world, it transformed itself into an ideology of guided reformation, aimed at unity and identity. All these developments confirm the premises of the modern construction of religion.

The missionary movement shared with the overarching projects of modernity and colonialism at least the desire to define, order and in a sense contain religion. They were all, in a way, conversion movements; they shared the need to speak of *religions* as large units, as definable configurations of religion, rationality and faith, and to impose on those units the need to give account of themselves through the articulation of beliefs and personal commitment. They wanted those units (Hindu*ism*, Buddh*ism*, Mohammedan*ism*) to be compatible with what they conceived Christianity to be.

For the non-Western religious world, all this provided an opportunity for a new self-consciousness, new self-definitions and renaissance movements. Inevitably, however, much religious reality had to remain undefined and, as such, invisible in this effort. For, unlike the modern West, the non-Western religious world does not have a history of authoritative redefinition of religion that could have prepared it for the redefinitions of colonial modernity. Outside the orbit of Western culture, plurality and locality were basically untamed (with the possible exception of China), and the taming efforts of modernity could only reach part of this.

This is not to say that religion beyond modernity is merely an untamed remnant of religion, that which has remained untouched by the modern world. The point is that the conditions for the self-definition of religion are changing – better, that the modern conditions for the definition of religion are losing credibility. Religion today is challenged to conceive of itself in interaction with global systems of survival. In this process, some religious reality will break away from larger modern frameworks or even become visible (definable) for the first time. In the long run, the whole world map of religion is likely to change.

Deconstruction of modern religion

Deceptive appearance of synthesis

The preceding sketch of the modern construction of religion suggests that the construction was successful only to a certain extent. Behind and beyond the grip of modernity, local and plural forms of religious reality survived, eschewing modern redefinition, waiting for new chances to make themselves visible and audible. Perhaps this is a sign of a basic paradox in the project of modernity itself: in its actual effects, it tends towards containment of religion; in its utopian aspects, it keeps provoking it. As Hervieu-Léger has noted, 'Modern societies may well corrode their traditional religious base, but at the same time they open up spaces or sectors that only religion can fill.'[7] In the colonial world, this paradox manifests itself particularly in the remaining tension between the need to organize public life along modern lines and the need to define identities along the lines of a particular religious tradition.

The history of modern (specifically Protestant) Christianity in North America provides interesting illustrations of these points. On the one hand, North American Christianity is a good example of the modern synthesis because of its un-European alliance between Christianity and Enlightenment, and the development of a widespread 'civil religion' on that basis. On the other hand, its explosions of plurality have produced and maintained important pockets of suspicion with regard to this alliance, particularly in the 'religions of the disinherited', to use H. R. Niebuhr's term, and the movements of evangelicalism.

In a real sense, evangelical suspicion belongs to the sphere of modernity and confirms it: its eschatological and dispensational theories still presuppose a certain coherent framework in which the converted believers and the 'evil world' belong together, and which even makes political action possible. At the same time, evangelical suspicion maintains and creates reservoirs of 'displaced religion' that cannot be accounted for in modern terms and that refuse to be trivialized by civil religion or by a national identity that needs religious legitimation. These reservoirs can perhaps be explained as remnants of the project of Christianization that could not be covered by modernization, or they may just represent basic forms of religious life for people seeking an identity in a new situation. In any case, they tend to leak away to fundamentalism, but they also provide important links to 'religion beyond modernity'.

The modern synthesis is widely desired and accepted, and it is no doubt attractive – even for religious institutions. Modernity provides for them a certain freedom of development and self-assertion, and in some cases the semblance of public significance. The synthesis, however, is constituted on the basis of a rationality that suspects religion and seeks to contain it. In other words: *in so far as religion supports and confirms the modern synthesis, it is suicidal.*

Noticing the 'cracks' in the modern construction of religion and being alert to forms of religious life that are local, plural and vital – behind, beyond and in spite of this construction – we are driven to the conclusion that its appearance of synthesis is deceptive, even though its power to maintain and reproduce itself is considerable. In the latter days of the project of Christianization, the grip of *faith* on religion loosens; a similar thing happens with the grip of *rationality*, when modernity is no longer a self-evident framework.

Deceptive appearance of difference

Once the shakiness and deceptiveness of the modern synthesis comes into view, it becomes tempting to locate the 'limits of modernity' at the borderline between Western and non-Western establishments, because of their different histories with regard to configurations of rationality, religion and faith. This, however, would be a mistake: the differences are overarched by a common problem. There is 'modern' containment of religion on both sides of the line, and there is 'untamed' religion – uncolonized life-worlds, loose ends that escape modern definition – on both sides as well. In this perspective, the difference between the supposedly *religious* character of non-Western establishments and the supposedly *secular* character of Western ones needs to be relativized. In 'religious' cultures, too, the alliance between religion and a society or a state that aspires to development in a modern sense involves containment of religion and assumes the possibility of 'modern synthesis' – even when in practice the syntheses remain precarious.

Indonesia presents a good illustration of this point. Here, the construction of the modern nation has co-opted religion, in the sense that typically modern values such as humanism and democracy are seen as embedded in an encompassing belief in 'the one God'. This embedding becomes explicit in the official recognition of three 'major' religions. Indonesian citizens are expected to belong (by personal commitment and belief, that is, in a *modern* sense!) to one of these, and the religious institutions are expected to support the nation. The most influential variety of Islam in this context is a tolerant, modernizing variety that is intent upon taming the folk-religious layers. There are obviously great social and political tensions behind this façade, and tensions such as these may be stronger in the non-Western world than in the West. Nevertheless, they are inherent in the project of modernity as such and not exclusively typical of the so-called Third World.

Considerations such as these should lead us to a certain scepticism about contemporary tendencies in world Christianity to contrast the cultures of Asia and Africa with those of the West as 'profoundly religious' cultures over against 'profoundly secular' ones, and to suggest on this basis that Asian and African Christianity can 'save' Western Christianity from its captivity to the Enlightenment by restoring the balance between religion and rationality. Apart from other considerations, there is a danger of caricature here, similar to the way in which the colonizing project was inclined to caricature the non-Western world. It seems as if the ingrained tendency of the project of modernity to stigmatize the 'other' as explicitly *non*-Western now turns against modern Western culture itself in this reversed caricaturing ('occidentalism' after 'orientalism'?). It remains, nevertheless, a tendency of *modernity* (stigma and caricature are forms of taming), and it ignores the more complex problem of religion in which all of global society is involved.

It would be interesting to review the discussions about the specific identity of 'Third World theology' in this perspective. For one thing, it would probably not be very difficult to show that Latin American liberation theology, for all its crucial opposition to Western academic theology, shares fundamental *modern* presuppositions with it. As a rapid radicalization of the traditional Roman Catholic (premodern) position, it remains within the confines of the modern construction of religion, even as it turns against its exclusive and oppressive features, and it still presupposes – to some extent with the aid of Marxist categories – the possibility of speaking of '*one* (liberation) history' of humankind. Especially in its early manifestations, liberation theology is/was inclined to ignore or undervalue popular (folk) religion, if not to contain and tame it. The 'success' of Pentecostalism in Latin America, which seems to depend largely on a mobilization of the religious 'reservoir' left aside by modern construction, makes this problem visible.[8]

Discussions in the Ecumenical Association of Third World Theologians (EATWOT) have, over the years, highlighted the difficulty of establishing the identity of a truly non-Western theology. These discussions have revealed important differences between Asian and African approaches to problems of culture, religion and justice on the one hand and Latin American approaches on the other hand. But they have, generally speaking, not moved outside the framework of modern discourse. To some extent, the EATWOT adventure is caught in contradictions. On the one hand, it is an important and impressive attempt to claim attention for the problem of contextuality and for the local and plural nature of religion resisting larger frameworks. On the other hand, it constructs contextuality as *anti-Western* rather than *anti-modern*. The presupposition that a general non-Western alternative can be found to Western theological methodology keeps it firmly within modern discourse. It does raise the problem of colonizing, containing and taming by highlighting the specific histories of non-Western Christianity, and as such it points the way to new conceptualizations of world Christianity; but it precludes significant movement in that direction by still seeking to unite those histories in one definition.

When, for example, Aloysius Pieris defends the position that poverty and religion as the dominant characteristics of the Asian people should become the starting points of Asian Christian theology, he is still responding to a *modern* perception of religions and cultures as definable (and manageable) wholes.[9] The triad poverty–religion–liberation remains the overarching concern. And when African theologians such as Lamin Sanneh and Kwame Bediako claim that the African way of permeating public life with religious spirituality provides an alternative for the 'Western sickness' of separation between public secularity and private religiosity, they do not go beyond the *modern* effort to assign a specific role to religion in the project of organizing society.[10] In all these and similar cases, the anti-modern appearance is deceptive.

All this is not to deny that the emergence of Third World theologies is much more than a nuance within the discourse of modern theology. It is evident that the anti-Western agenda of these theologies is strongly motivated by an experience of the *limits* of the discourse of modernity, particularly in its ambition to chart all cultural and religious reality. Perhaps these limits are felt more strongly in the context to which Third World theology has to respond: a context characterized by the relative absence of a history of 'taming' and the close relatedness of Christianity to local and plural forms of religion. In that respect, even though it remains bound to modern discourse, Third World theology confirms 'between the lines' that there is religion that survives behind and beyond the defining and containing efforts of modernity.

Religion beyond modernity

The various manifestations of religion beyond modernity are often discussed against the background of the untenability of the so-called secularization thesis, according to which all religion is eventually doomed to disappear under the pressure of modern rationality and the disenchantment of society that it produces.[11] Religion beyond modernity is then called *desecularization* (Berger), and it is suggested that – in distinction from the secularization thesis – secularized contexts such as certain parts of Europe are the exception rather than the rule.

It must be stressed, however, that the point of desecularization is not that religion has a strong survival capacity over against the destructive forces of modernization, but rather that it could not be adequately perceived, defined and analysed on the premises of modernity. Desecularization is not simply the re-emergence of religion from a temporary shelter; it is the surfacing of types of religion that disregard the limits placed on them by modernity. Although this postmodern religious reality is linked to the remainders, the loose ends and the reservoirs mentioned in the preceding paragraphs, it is more than 'old-time religion'. It is religion challenged to reconstruction because of increasing tensions between global and local forms of life, between globalization and the need to maintain manageable individual and collective identities.

Among the 'globalized elite' we sometimes witness what might be called a 're-enchantment of the market'. Luck and success – and, conversely, uncertainty and failure and what Lawrence called the 'terrifying freedom of being left alone' – become religious categories, and established religious traditions are used in an eclectic way to provide a coherent world-view around these categories. Even within established Christian traditions, plurality and syncretism emerge, as well as a reluctance to define one's religious position with the aid of the modern tools of propositions and conversion.

In Islamic countries such as Iran and Pakistan, successful career people sometimes 'discover' Islam as a formula of personal meaning and a valuable instrument for coherence and direction in life. These personal 'conversions' sometimes ally themselves for pragmatic reasons with fundamentalist politics, but it is obvious that there is a vast difference in context.[12] Along the same lines mention could be made of a revival of interest in the Jewish tradition that is no longer (or less) preoccupied with the dramatic history of the Jewish people in the modern period (emancipation, exclusion, the Holocaust, nation building) but concentrates on the substance of the tradition itself.

Religion beyond modernity is, however, not confined to the globalized elite. The success of Pentecostalism in Latin America, for example, can be interpreted against the background of a leap from a premodern to a post-modern (globalized) economy, and the emergence of social and religious gaps because of that.[13] Individual universes of meaning are constructed out of a religious reservoir untouched by modernity and with the aid of a specific Christian tradition (Pentecostalism), itself born on the fringes of modernity. Mention could also be made of the tendency in countries such as Brazil to combine formal membership of the Roman Catholic Church with participation in an Afro-Brazilian cult. In the discourse of modernity, this is called syncretism or 'dual system', with the implication that it is less than adequate and that religious affiliation should be clearly defined and consistent. It is very possible, however, that the people concerned do not experience any problem of unclarity or inconsistency.

Religion beyond modernity, then, does not simply consist of leftovers or relics from premodern times. It is a *new* functionalization of reservoirs of religion, one might even say a new, though fragmentary, attempt to rearrange rationality, religion and faith. It is, of course, possible to attribute this to the ineradicability of human religion, as the permanent struggle with contingency and the attempt to make sense of life by reference to a reality that transcends it. But perhaps we should not overlook the role of *faith* as the bridge between religion and rationality, as the indispensable structuring of religion with the aid of narrative and belief and community. In the project of modernity, faith is extremely vulnerable. It is distrusted by rationality as a step backwards into the irrationality of religion, and by religion as another instrument of 'colonization'. Yet, through all this, faith also provides continuity and framework; and the persistence of faith narratives may well contribute significantly to the survival and new presence of religion beyond modernity.

Religion beyond modernity manifests an ineradicably *plural* character: it consists of hybridities, eclecticisms and syncretisms, and seems to lose all interest in defining itself according to the grand narratives of the religions. For the same reason, it is also primarily *local*: it lives in the life-worlds of people rather than in modern units such as societies or cultures. 'Local' does not necessarily mean geographically confined: a particular life-world may well extend beyond the place in which one lives. The defining category is *community* rather than *space*. In all this, religion beyond modernity undermines the typically modern desire to order and to define, and it rejects the necessity of a link with social or political construction.

A note on fundamentalism

Fundamentalism is certainly not 'beyond modernity', although it builds on dissatisfaction and disappointment with regard to modernity. It is not a step backwards into premodernity either, although it seeks to mobilize premodern reservoirs of religion in its vision of the true society. It is the effort to restore the balance between religion and rationality with modern tools, that is, not by claiming more space for religion but by proposing an alternative rationality. It is an effort to attack modernity with its own weapons and to conquer it in the name of an idealized religious tradition.[14] It is a counter-attack of the life-world on the systems of the modern world. The rationality it uses for that purpose is a common-sense rationality, in which the gap between faith and science disappears and all doubt about 'truth' is made unnecessary.

In this way, the various forms of fundamentalism present themselves as plausible alternatives to the project of modernity and as attractive solutions to the problems caused by the intrusion of modernity into premodern worlds and the containment of religion that this intrusion implies. It can only survive, however, as a variety of modernity, since it adopts the latter's presuppositions.

Its championing of a particular religious tradition can only result in other forms of containment of religion. Fundamentalism is suspicious of the local and plural character of religion and intends to tame it: spontaneous expressions of mourning on account of a martyrdom in Iran are manipulated into controlled revolutionary activity;[15] religious emotion is turned into a political instrument.

The containment of religion that takes place in fundamentalism is both premodern and modern. It is premodern in so far as plurality is brought into submission to the one valid tradition by decree of authority; it is modern in so far as it is brought to order with the aid of efficient, rational organization.

Fundamentalism cannot, therefore, be characterized as 'religion beyond modernity'. In North America, it stands in continuity with the modern/anti-modern currents of evangelical Protestantism; in other religions and in the non-Western world, it stands in continuity with the unconquerable fringes of the operational field of the colonizing project. In all these cases, fundamentalism seeks to emulate rather than to repudiate the project of modernity.

Constructions of world Christianity

The modern captivity of the ecumenical movement

The ecumenical movement began as a renaissance of Western Christianity under the impact of modern visions of unity. The classical meaning of *oikoumene* – the whole inhabited earth – came into view in the context of typically modern understandings of cultural development, economic progress, interreligious understanding and the elevation of the poor. The movement was motivated by a strong eschatological passion: a vision that held the kingdom of God and the unity of humankind together. After the learning processes of the 'ecumenical century' it is obvious, however, that the limits of the project of modernity challenge the identity of the movement in a fundamental way. The present crisis is more than institutional: it is about the possibility of constructing a world Christianity when the premises of modernity are no longer convincing.

The ecumenical significance of the limits of the project of modernity can be specified according to the three major streams in which the movement has taken shape. The *ecumenical missionary movement* was conceived as a worldwide network of witnessing churches and as a common global responsibility to proclaim the *one* message; its vision was expressed in formulas such as 'partnership in obedience' and 'mutual assistance'. Meanwhile, the 'Christocentric universalism' (Raiser) of this vision is gradually undermined by a growing awareness of contextuality and cultural plurality. The *social ethical movement* – strong in its presentation of formulas such as 'responsible society'; in its contribution to the consciousness of the evils of racism, classism and sexism; and in its programs for peace, justice and the integrity of creation – is confronted by the disparity of systems for setting ethical priorities and by searching questions about the anchoring of moral formation in church communities. The *unity movement*, strongly committed to the visible unity of churches through a gradual process of overcoming traditional controversies, is forced to realize that growing consensus at one level kept pace with growing pluralization at another, and that an understanding of the church (and the ecumenical movement itself) as a community of interpretation in a global context of pluralism might be a more adequate objective than the original vision of organic oneness. In all this, the traditional ways of defining the identity and unity of world Christianity are undermined.

Through the cracks of modernity we are beginning to see much original locality and plurality of religion, not only within the major religious traditions but also within the various Christian traditions. These traditions have been constructed as wholes, and although that has been enormously beneficial for the development of worldwide networks of understanding, communication and dialogue, the question of the presuppositions of this constructing activity inescapably presents itself. World Christianity has been constructed in the context of the two projects of Christianization and modernization. It bears the traces of both the premodern and the modern synthesis, and of the 'containing' that has taken place in these frameworks. The ecumenical movement was meant to bring this construction to completion. That is why it is so deeply affected now that the presuppositions are under fire.

It would be a mistake, however, to try to reconstruct world Christianity – and also ecumenism and mission – as a third project that might be a worthy successor to the two preceding ones. One cannot simply dispose of Christianization and modernization as worn-out tools. Not only is the way in which we perceive the various developments in world Christianity deeply and decisively conditioned by them, we will continue to need them as there are no other ways to speak of Christianity as 'one thing'. What can and must be done, however, is to encourage and develop a critical awareness of the *limits* of the projects, particularly of their limited capacity to define and to order religion.

The challenge of 'glocalization'

The term 'glocalization'[16] refers to the interaction between the processes of globalization and local situations. It is important to underline that globalization differs basically from modernization in the way it takes possession of the world. Unlike modernization, globalization is not the expansion, conquest or intrusion of an outside culture into relatively premodern worlds. Unlike colonization, globalization does not challenge local worlds to conversion or to new constructions of their identity. *Globalization is the ubiquitous self-expanding space of imagined communities.* It is an infinite number of localities, thrown together by the pressure to deal with the whole; it is the unavoidability of increased contact with global networks. It is not a local culture writ large, but a field in which cultural syncretisms and hybridizations are both formed and undone. Glocalization means that local constructions of common life – political, social, cultural and religious institutions – can only maintain their identity and impact if they enter the arena of competition with the forces of globalization and accept the accompanying risk of redefinition and reconstruction.

A major implication of the challenge of glocalization is the redefinition of culture. There is a growing consensus that cultures can no longer be dealt with as systemic, totalistic units that define themselves through 'boundaries', that is, sharp distinctions between inside and outside. On the contrary, distinct cultural identities can only emerge as (temporary) outcomes of preceding and ongoing processes of interaction. The adequate metaphor to grasp the reality of cultural identities is *eddy* rather than *island*.[17] For our discussion all this implies that what we have described as synthesis dynamics – the arrangement and rearrangement of religion, rationality and faith – takes place less and less in distinguishable units called cultures. In the situation of glocalization, to put it very succinctly, *rationality is global, religion is local.*

If this is true, the modern construction of religion is placed in an impossible position. One could also say that its problematic nature, which we have been surveying in the course of this argument, is confirmed once more by the processes of globalization. It is manifest in the increasing tendency of religion to withdraw from modern containment, to define itself without any need for synthesis. What remains of modern synthesis is pulled apart in local, plural religion on the one hand and global, secular rationality on the other. *Globalization itself diminishes the necessity of containment of religion.*

As I noted earlier in discussing religion beyond modernity, there are various ways to deal with this predicament. Obviously, large numbers of people are content with maintaining a kind of dual system: rationality for one's working life, religion for personal comfort. Others try to reinterpret religious traditions into an uncritical symbolic duplication of globalization ('constitutional religion', as Gellner calls it). Some yield to the temptation to construct a dualism, implying that globalization is a devilish scheme and that light and salvation are to be found only with the people who live close to nature and tradition. This is the field of choices in which new theological creativity is urgently needed, especially now that the modern schemes of ecumenism and mission can no longer be counted upon.

Ecumenism: networks of critical memory

World Christianity needs new conceptualization beyond the limits of the projects of Christianization and modernization, in a world in which the heritage of both these projects is still strong. Leaving it un-conceptualized, that is, without a master image of how all local manifestations of Christian faith belong together, would mean giving up the question of the identity of the 'one' tradition and – worse – failing to deal with the unity of humankind in a theological way. At present, two postmodern master images are available: they have been developed on either side of the mainline ecumenical movement, centred around the World Council of Churches. The first is Roman Catholicism, as remodeled during the pontificate of John Paul II; the second is evangelicalism, in its innumerable varieties.

Using the terms that have been prevalent in this argument, one might say that contemporary Roman Catholicism with its authority-centred definition of faith and its strong ecclesial institutionalization maintains a continuity with the premodern synthesis, yet in combination with a typically modern emphasis on universal human rights and norms. The strength of this combination could very well survive the dismantlement of the project of modernity. Evangelicalism, on the other hand, is a product of the modern/anti-modern currents in Protestantism; it mobilizes all kinds of suspicion and distrust with regard to modernity, and it takes the typically modern emphasis on conversion out of the modern synthesis, transforming it into an emotional movement that can be experienced both individually and collectively. Taken together, these contemporary forms of Roman Catholicism and evangelicalism present enlarged forms of aspects that are still held together in mainline Protestantism, namely institutional safeguard and spiritual experience. At the same time, they present enlarged forms of aspects of the modern construction of religion: propositional belief and conversion.

Searching for some kind of middle road between these two master images will imply at least two things. First, it will imply the relativization of 'unity' in the sense of a prior givenness that only needs to be applied to local situations and a shift of emphasis from tradition to communication: communication in the sense of an ongoing effort of locally rooted Christians or Christian communities to engage each other in the construction of a common identity. Second, it will imply a wariness of the evaporation of the common substance of faith into a common spiritual experience and an effort to bring many experiences together in a discussion about their effects on private and public life. Ecumenism will then mean the creation of networks in which a critical testing takes place of whatever presents itself as 'Christian faith' across the world, and in which a common memory is both constructed and maintained.

Mission: the localization of eschatological discourse

The effort to define mission beyond the projects of Christianization and modernization leads almost to a contradiction in terms. Bringing Jesus Christ to the world is a major motivation of most missionary activity, and therefore missionary activity will always maintain some continuity and resemblance with Christianization. In addition, the project of modernization has provided a supportive context for the modern missionary movement. Trying to define mission apart from this motivation and context, under the impression of the predicament of religion in globalized society, seems equivalent to giving up the whole idea.

However, if we understand mission in a very fundamental sense as the effort to hold on to a real connection between 'eschaton' and 'world' – bypassing the intermediary structures of Christianization and modernization – there might still be some room for redefinition. Of course, this fundamental theological understanding of mission was already developed to some extent in the ecumenical missionary movement: the *missio dei* formula was invented to express just that understanding. Yet *missio dei* thinking retains a measure of modern containment. It tends to ignore the locality, plurality and ambiguity of human struggles with the humankind perspective. It remains loyal to the project of modernity in its focus on a worldwide church, and especially in its persistent use of modern concepts of culture and religion. Even terms such as intercultural communication and interreligious dialogue presuppose these modern concepts: cultures and religions are conceived as definable units that can be brought into relation with each other.

How to break out of this captivity? Perhaps by reminding ourselves that the most fundamental polarity with which mission deals is not the polarity between human beings and church or Christianity, but between contextual human struggles for meaning and direction on the one hand and the vision of divine judgement and reconciliation on the other. Mission is the effort to localize and actualize the promise that God is constructing *one* heaven and earth for a *diverse* and *pluriform* humanity; it is the reflection of the dual movement of gathering and multiplying. It is, to put it differently, upholding the metanarrative of human suffering and final redemption that takes its clue in Jesus Christ.

In all human religion, inescapably local and plural as it may be, there is the drive to raise further questions about human existence and to keep alive a vision of a true unity of humankind. It is this eschatological drive of religion that needs to be activated in situations in which globalization misleadingly presents itself as the realized eschaton of human salvation, and that needs to be cultivated over against the temptation to accommodate religion to globalization or to construct a fruitless opposition between them. Mission is the effort to establish an explicit interaction between this eschatological activation of religion on the one hand and the eschatological content of the Christian faith on the other. In this way, mission is the subjection of the Christian faith to a worldwide test of relevance and to a learning process that draws humankind in the direction of a true unity. It will imply the creation of communities of interpretation and the formation of strong believers. This has always been the objective of the missionary movement, even when it was also moved by the visions of Christianization and modernization.

This is an edited version of a paper presented at a meeting of the Network of Theological Enquiry held at New Hall, Cambridge in March 2000. The network is sponsored by the Council for World Mission, and the original paper was published as 'Religion beyond modernity: a missiological perspective', in Philip L Wickeri, Janice K Wickeri and Damayanthi M A Niles (eds), Plurality, Power and Mission: Intercontextual Theological Explorations on the Role of Religion in the New Millennium, CWM, 2000.

NOTES

1. Stephen Toulmin, *Cosmopolis: The Hidden Agenda of Modernity*, Chicago, 1990.
2. 'Christian conversion is a "technology of the self"... which, under modern conditions, produces a new subjecthood that is deeply enmeshed in economic globalization and the emergence of a system of nation-states.' Peter van der Veer (ed.), *Conversion to Modernities: The Globalization of Christianity*, New York and London, 1996, p. 19.
3. Talal Asad, *Genealogies of Religion: Discipline and Reasons of Power in Christianity and Islam*, Baltimore and London, 1993, p. 252: 'My concern is to identify culture as part of a language of total colonial reconstruction.'
4. For an elaboration of this argument, see Bert Hoedemaker, *Secularization and Mission: A Theological Essay*, Harrisburg, Pennsylvania, and Leominster, England, 1998.
5. Asad, p. 37.
6. Van der Veer, p. 7.
7. Hervieu-Léger, quoted by Grace Davie, 'Europe: the exception that proves the rule?', in Peter L. Berger (ed.), *The Desecularization of the World: Resurgent Religion and World Politics*, Washington, D.C., and Grand Rapids, Michigan, 1999, pp. 65–83; 80)
8. D. Martin, *Tongues of Fire: the Explosion of Protestantism in Latin America*, Oxford and Cambridge, 1990; V. Garrard-Burnett and D. Stoll (eds), *Rethinking Protestantism in Latin America*, Philadelphia, 1993.
9. Aloysius Pieris, *An Asian Theology of Liberation*, Maryknoll, New York, 1988.

10. Lamin Sanneh, *Encountering the West: Christianity and the Global Cultural Process – the African Dimension*, Maryknoll, New York, 1993; Kwame Bediako, *Christianity in Africa: the Renewal of a Non-Western Religion*, Maryknoll, New York, 1995.
11. Jeffrey K. Hadden and Anson Shupe (eds), *Secularization and Fundamentalism Reconsidered: Religion and the Political Order*, New York, 1990; Phillip E. Hammond (ed.), *The Sacred in a Secular Age: Toward Revision in the Scientific Study of Religion*, Berkeley, 1985.
12. Examples of this can be found in V. S. Naipaul's *Beyond Belief* (1997), the report of his 'Islamic journeys'.
13. Bernice Martin, 'From pre- to postmodernity in Latin America: the case of pentecostalism', in P. Heelas (ed.), *Religion, Modernity and Postmodernity*, Oxford and Cambridge, 1996, pp. 102–46.
14. B. B. Lawrence, *Defenders of God: The Fundamentalist Revolt Against the Modern Age*, London and New York, 1990; M. E. Marty and R. S. Appleby (eds), *Fundamentalisms Observed*, Chicago and London, 1991.
15. The example is from M. Riesebrodt, *Fundamentalismus als Patriarchalische Protestbewegung: Amerikanische Protestanten (1910-1918) und Iranische Schi'iten (1961-1979) im Vergleich*, Tübingen, 1990, pp. 168f.
16. Roland Robertson, 'Glocalization: time–space and homogeneity–heterogeneity', in Scott Lash and Roland Robertson (eds), *Global Modernities*, London, 1995.
17. Zygmunt Bauman, *Culture as Praxis* (new edition), London, 1999, p. xlv.

Afterword: Re-engaging Mission with Theology in the West Today

Simon Barrow

The essays in this book do not pretend to constitute a comprehensive overview of contemporary issues concerning mission in the North Atlantic (and especially western European) region. That would be hopelessly ambitious. They are better viewed as signposts in a wide-ranging conversation that both precedes from and informs actual engagement: despatches from the front, if you will, from people who are either practiced reflectors or reflective practitioners. In this context, the purpose of an afterword is to link some of the particular arguments and inspirations of *Christian Mission in Western Society* to the wider challenges confronting mission theology at the moment, rather than to impose an editorial ideology on the collection. I will also suggest contours for further exploration and make reference to other important current research projects in the area of Western missiology.[1]

The theological task of missiology

Each essay in this volume illustrates the requirement for all mature Christian thinking to root itself in the contemporary theological questions arising from complex, plural, ambiguous and critical environments. Simply accusing 'our culture' of being 'gospel-unfriendly' will not do: it assumes too much about the unity of cultures and too little about the diversity of faith. Christian discernment takes place within a set of traditions that are engaged both internally and externally in reciprocal disputation as well as affirmation. This has always been the case. What is new in modernity/postmodernity is that everything is up for negotiation. None of the language that we use to describe the Christian hope or the Christian task is innocent, uncontested or easily translatable. It all has to be accounted for in the midst of whatever else is being said, and it must be related (however critically or challengingly) to the dominant languages and assumptions of our time. That requires an intellectual and spiritual exploration into some of the secular and religious confusions that characterize Western societies.[2]

It has to be admitted that missiology is not always as good at negotiating the frontiers as its rhetoric suggests. Its temptation is to shelter from the wider climate by inhabiting a safe, reassuring, confessional vocabulary. This often manifests itself in an exclusive understanding of the calling of the church, a pre-critical approach to the use of biblical texts, and a selective or impressionistic treatment of the other disciplines with which missiology needs to interact – philosophy, history, anthropology, literature and so on.[3]

In part this theological timidity stems from the predominance of a certain set of conservative instincts in missiological circles – witness the culture-hostile stances that Antonie Wessels, Werner Ustorf, Bert Hoedemaker and others challenge. Such defensive postures arise from the inherently intra-Christian nature of mission theology. When people serving the church discuss with each other what the church should be doing and thinking, those outside the faith are present in the conversation, if at all, only in the way they are imaged by one section or other of the Christian community. Contrast this with interreligious conversation (a source of alarm to some mission theologians,[4] though not to Jay Kothare here), where the communication system has to include the voices of those who are being encountered if it is to be regarded as having any legitimacy. This is an issue that Ann Loades also raises from the experience of feminist methodology.

Other factors producing a lack of more positive missiological engagement with developments in the modern/postmodern environment include the dominance of pragmatic and strategic considerations over theological concerns in some influential sections of the evangelical movement (mission as marketing), and the Western agency-led romanticization of Christianity in the South. Both these trends have had the effect of reducing the missionary question to one of simple absorption or hegemony, rather than allowing it to embrace the complexity of relationship and communication. They therefore consign difficult issues – of secularity, religious plurality and moral diversity, say – to a waste bin marked 'Western disease only'. This is unhelpful and misleading.

So insularity and evasion remain serious possibilities for missiology. Yet all who have written in this book are, in one form or another, protesting against such narrow-mindedness. The contributors are by no means uniform in their approach or theological tenor, but they all believe in taking risks for the sake of the gospel. Many would perhaps also share the conviction that God is the biggest risk-taker of all, and that fear is the largest single threat to critical faith in a climate in which fidelity to the constancy of the Christian story requires the continual negotiation of change.

Mission and the matrix of modernity

How, then, are we going to handle some of the most basic questions that those of other faith or no faith pose to Christians in Western society today: questions about the nature of belief in God in the face of techno-science, about the authority claims of traditions and scriptures in a 'virtual' world, about the identity of Christ in a plural society, and about the possibility of Christian community (or any kind of community) in the face of an atomizing global market? Here, as this book illustrates, both by commission and omission, even the most thoughtful Christians are still trying to get to grips with the issues. This ought not to be regarded as a surprise, an intellectual failing or a deficit of faith, since our time is marked by a strong sense that the old has passed away but that the shape of the new is not yet clear. Indeed, it may never become clear in the way that some would like, because the scale and diversity of what is coming into being in the late-modern, hyper-modern or postmodern urbanized world (take your pick from many analyses and descriptions) is beyond the capacity of modern instrumentalism and rationalism to capture – which is the one major point of agreement within the plethora of 'after modernity' theses.

If the whole idea of mission as it is discussed today emerged in the matrix of modernity, and if Christianity, by virtue of being an eschatological faith, is marked by a constant deferral of absolute judgement – as Hoedemaker suggests – such bold humility may turn out to be both a practical and a theological necessity. For whereas Western thought in the modern age has been characterized by an imperial tendency to universalize itself as the truth for all times and all places, it may now be that we are entering an era in which we are able to discover that many of our leading ideas (not least our ideas about God) are only just coming out of the kindergarten.[5] The real danger (and it is one endemic in our rationalistic, money-driven, technological and yet deeply emotive cultures) is that we fail to recognize this, opting instead for nostalgia, hubris or despair. In a Western Christian context, then, theologians have a particular duty to cry out when missiologists show evidence of – for example – seeking refuge in an imagined golden age (see especially Micheal MacCraith), resorting to mere assertion or abandoning ship altogether.

What, then, is the task of missiology today? An appropriate answer, I suggest, is 'to generate creative, practically tempered experiments in thinking out what the churches are called to be, do and say, contextually, in fast-moving societies'. It is this challenge that makes theology a missionary matter and mission a theological matter. But you cannot travel far without a set of maps. So missiology is that branch of the total theological enterprise that is specifically concerned with the 'somewhere' of the Christian community in relation to the 'somewhere' of its inheritance, all mediated through the multiple 'somewheres' of its (narrative) historical, political, social, economic, scientific, ecological, cultural and psychological contexts.

The missionary question is, therefore, both about the dynamic of churches in relation to the world (where they should be going, what they should be doing) and about the intellectual and spiritual contours of their stance (why they should be doing or standing for these things rather than others). As can be seen from the essays in this book, that means a conversational approach within and without. It is observable that fruitful discussion proceeds from the kind of relationship to truth that Wittgenstein spelled out in his river analogy – continuous and discontinuous flow within identifiable but changing processes[6] – as distinct from the fashionable neo-orthodox picture, which too easily assumes a hermetic, tradition-bounded 'gospel truth' encountering 'the world' with which it shares nothing of salvific value.[7]

By contrast, incarnational religion, though it is about God's love breaking through transformatively in the particular, cannot abolish the ambiguity and mess of the world without losing its focus on the very God who is committed to that world process in ways that we label 'creation', 'redemption' and 'consummation'. Moreover, as Hoedemaker suggests, there is an internal, eschatological self-criticism within the New Testament, which is made visible in Jesus' self-relativizing devotion to the kingdom of God. As the Gospels make clear, it is (paradoxically) this willingness to abandon ideas of separation or superiority that constitutes a massive critique of earthly strategies of lordship, revealing what Walter Wink calls 'God's domination-free order' in the One who suffers with us out of love and who enables us to name the destiny of the world – rather than to conquer it – 'in the name of the coming one'.[8]

Moving beyond Christendom

If this is so, and if I am reflecting hints that run throughout *Christian Mission in Western Society* as well as adding my own interpretation, then I am also articulating a different position on the significance of the church, Christians and Christianity for missionary theology than that reflected in the conclusion of Graeme Smith's introductory chapter. There he states:

> The identity of Christianity and Christian people are not of themselves important questions. We do not need to define who is Christian and who is not, nor what Christianity can or cannot be. Indeed we appear to have reached the end of the usefulness of the terms 'Christianity', 'churches' and 'gospel' in defining association with the life of God.

I can certainly concur with what that rules out – a Christianity of and for itself, *extra ecclesia nullam salus*, the restricting of God (even the God of Jesus Christ) to 'our' group or tribe. However, I still believe – along with René Girard and others of his ilk[9] – that the usefulness of gospel and church for our age are only just beginning to become properly visible as they are stripped of past pretensions.

Certainly the Western churches in their received Christendom form (compare Duncan B. Forrester and Hong Jung Lee) are in the process of outliving their usefulness. But as potential models of a new kind of deliberately anti-exclusionary community founded on a rejection of violence, a costly embracing of the outsider, a local embracing of the global and a Christ-like willingness to stake their lives with those crucified 'outside the gate' of our brave neo-liberal world, churches as praying, worshipping and witnessing communities may still be struggling with a way of coming into being again for this particular moment.

This is because, as William Eggen illustrates through his short and powerful 'liberating narrative',[10] as Ann Loades, Joe D. Aldred and Jay Kothare demonstrate through the fabric of everyday lives, and as Duncan Forrester and Hong Jung Lee assert by linking the small narratives of the gospel to the small narratives of daily existence in the face of the market metanarrative, the Christ-event is hugely subversive.[11] It creates what can only be called 'a divine reversal' of worldly power and expectations.[12] This being so, it needs embodying (collectively), nourishing and sowing.

In short, the idea of the Body of Christ, though not to be straightforwardly substituted for the church or Christianity in any particular form, requires some specificity in order to make its universalizing contribution. And it does this both by allying with those who share elements of its vision of 'a new heaven and a new earth' and by seeking to become in itself an expression of the Giver who sustains all and the countersign (Cross and Resurrection) that produced it.

Jesus Christ and the identity of mission

This in turn raises, as a key mission issue, Dietrich Bonhoeffer's abiding question, 'Who really is Jesus Christ for us today?'[13] Christology hovers tantalizingly around and beneath the surface of many of the contributions to this volume. In the case of Lynne Price, it is implicit. Yet, as often in missionary theology, the shape of the Christ being encountered and announced is none too clear to the bystander. In recent years there have been numerous confrontations between theologians defending or defining a variant of what Werner Ustorf summarizes as ecumenical 'Christocentric universalism' (which can take inclusive or exclusive forms) and the pluralist Christology of interreligious exponents such as John Hick. In the latest skirmishes on this well-worn territory – again, intra-Christian terrain of little immediate interest to a wider Western audience – 'the myth of pluralism' has gone into battle against 'the myth of

Christian uniqueness' and 'risking Christ for Christ's sake' (M. M. Thomas).[14] There have been important points scored on all sides, but little evidence that a 'debate' couched in these terms is of any practical use to Christian mission in any of its available guises. Nonetheless, the issues themselves cannot simply be sidelined. If the church is to persist in asserting the significance of Jesus Christ in a multireligious world, it is bound to give an account of what it means by that.

For many years now the exclusivist–inclusivist–pluralist paradigm (developed by Alan Race and others) has dominated practical Christology. The fact that, as can be seen in this book, most evocations of Christ in a missionary setting do not conform easily to these categorizations is but one sign that the terms of the debate now need to move on.

I would draw attention to several contributions to the discussion beyond this volume that offer signs of new insight and possibility. First, the Scottish systematic theologian Ruth Page has suggested a dramaturgical rendering of the encounter with God in Christ as 'the incarnation of freedom and love', which seeks to do justice both to the proper object of Christian devotion and to the needs of a plural, ambiguous world.[15]

Second, Peter Selby (in the context of a discourse about 'the language of faith and the debt of the world') has brought us back to the cutting edges of Bonhoeffer's original question.[16] This, he reminds us, embraces the issue of identity ('who?'), the challenge of solidarity ('us') and the need for discernment ('today') and finds these questions mirrored back to us in the Christ whom we meet both in the call to radical discipleship and in the climate of contemporary questioning. Marcus Borg and his associates take up a similar challenge.

Third, Paul Knitter has moved the debate in which he has been a significant protagonist forward considerably in his advocacy of 'a correlational, globally responsible theology of religions' issuing in a more 'Christic' postmodern approach to religion in the new millennium than his previous straightforwardly pluralistic position allowed for. 'The suffering other and the religious other belong together,' he has said. Against both traditional liberals and traditional conservatives, Knitter now argues that Christians can truly and faithfully bear witness to the universality, decisiveness and indispensability of Jesus in a fragmented world, but that this does not (on either biblical or other grounds) entail claiming him to be a sole, exclusive and totalizing revelation of God. As Richard Rohr has suggested in a more popular vein, 'My exclusive commitment to God in Christ finally brought me to the realization that the meaning of God in Christ is the end of all exclusivisms.' The trailblazer in the Roman Catholic world in this area has been Jacques Dupuis, along with the Jesuit Michael Barnes, who has deployed a conversational model in place of the conventional, bounded-set ones.[17]

The Bible in missiological perspective

Another fundamental question is the boundary and authority of 'the text' in the modern world. In the missionary encounter with the West (Newbigin et al.), what and whose is the script? By drawing our attention to the encounter between specific embodiments of the Christian message and different elements of the European literary heritage, Antonie Wessels (along with other contributors to this collection) forces upon us the vital question about what, in actual practice, constitutes 'scripture' in the world today.

Christians commonly claim that this has already been decided by the canonicity of their Bible. But such an assertion is challenged by the existence of several different canons of scripture in world Christianity. It is also threatened by deep historical and critical questions surrounding their formation and fixity, by the counter-claims of Jewish scholars towards a major part of what Christians see as the shared biblical heritage, and by the active presence in Western societies of other great religions claiming scriptural warrant for their own classic texts.

Wessels effectively widens such 'dilemmas of scripture' yet further, and in a missiological direction. He does this by showing how the engaged texts of Christianity (which, like all 'scriptures', create a world for their receivers and then exemplify how to act in it) must unavoidably contend with the texts of the beliefs and assumptions of a wider Western culture. These range from literary 'classics', the modern novel and scientific discourse through to advertising, the news media and cyber-culture.

Such 'texts' similarly codify and transmit (however untidily) the dominant, authoritative narratives by which people and communities live.

They are now far more influential and opinion-forming than many of the books, including the Bible, that claim direct and obvious religious authority. Precisely because they both empower and delimit the worlds of those persons and groups who use them, these 'texts of contemporary culture' can justifiably – though not uncontentiously – be described as constituting 'the text' for all who deeply inhabit their stories. And since they also infuse and modify the appropriation of the Bible within our churches, this might be said to include Christians, too.

So in any missionary encounter (that is, in any creative interaction, communication and tension between faith and culture) the hermeneutical challenge is not just to convey the meaning of the biblical text in the midst of competing Christian claims about it. It is also to engage this task in the arena of a much broader set of competing claims about which texts are truly held or seen to be 'scriptural' in contemporary Western life.

For these reasons, many would suggest, it can no longer be said straightforwardly (if it ever could) that the 'missionary task' with regard to the Bible is 'just to proclaim it' – as if its contents stood uncomplicatedly apart from the cultures in which they are transmitted and read. What Western Christians are confronted with instead is the theological task of discerning and performing the purposes of God amid the varied narratives of a visual, interactive, multiscriptural, intertextual society.

In this new setting the biblical text will continue to be at the core of Christian mission, of course. And the story of Jesus as the Crucified and Living One will remain its controlling centre. But where that might once have involved an a priori claim to textual and religious privilege, this can no longer be the case. In a multiscriptural environment, conversation must replace compulsion if we are not to do violence to each other, to our texts and (in a Christian context) to the gospel.[18]

Similarly, where previous biblical interpreters may have taken for granted the moral superiority and unassailable coherence of their founding documents, contemporary exegetes – conscious of the use of the Bible to legitimize colonialism, oppression, even holocaust – are required to acknowledge these texts to be both the bearer and subverter of revelation. For this reason, every act of interpretation becomes an ethical and spiritual task with profound consequences for the shape and mission of the church.[19]

As even a cursory look at the concrete use of the Bible in mission theory, literature and advocacy across the theological spectrum will confirm, we are still struggling to grasp such momentous questions. For the most part it seems that biblical texts are employed more to confirm prejudices and to win arguments than (say) to illuminate their role in shaping or questioning the identity and purpose of the church in specific contexts. Issues arising from the use and misuse of scripture in missionary encounter and their relation to the gospel–culture dynamic are therefore among the central questions for the churches as they enter a new millennium.[20] The insights and limitations of literary theory, the contextual practice in small communities of 'participatory Bible study' and the challenge of de/reconstruction all have a part to play in the sense of humble responsibility needed to receive, interpret and transmit the gift conveyed in our founding texts openly and faithfully.

Language, God and the religions

It is evident that the nature of Christian engagement with interreligious and interfaith questions, as well as with new religious movements and spiritualities, will be of considerable significance for the future of the churches' mission, not least in the West. In this book these concerns are reflected imaginatively and powerfully in Jay Kothare's contribution, even if questions can be raised about his particular use of the Celtic heritage. At a broader level, such critical and fruitful encounter is a consistent feature of new thinking coming through the recently concluded World Council of Churches' study programme 'Gospel and Cultures' (not to be confused with similar-sounding organizations in Britain and the United States inspired by Lesslie Newbigin).[21]

What we are only just beginning to register, however, is the common challenge that the 'religions of the book' face on the basic question of the meaning of God today. One person who has pushed this issue further than most is the Cambridge scholar Don Cupitt. In a whole raft of titles published since his landmark *Taking Leave of God* in 1980, Cupitt has been one of the chief European voices of the 'non-realism' that has swept continental philosophy and the vital fringes of American academia –

Mark C. Taylor is one who, along with D. Z. Philips, Thomas Altizer and others, has embraced the negative dialectical void at what some refer to as the 'nihilistic' end of postmodernity.

What these writers have in common is their commitment to religious expressivism, a view derived from the notion that language per se is 'outsideless'. Words describe only the inner world of the language-maker, so that talk of God, for instance, has no referent beyond itself. As Cupitt has put it: 'Our life has no outside. There is no beginning or end, no height or depth, no atom or foundation. There is only the manifest, and it is enough.' On this basis he has created what for many is an attractive religious philosophy 'in the absence of God'.[22]

Even if one takes the view, as I do, that the principal realist–non-realist dispute seriously misses the point, which is better summarized by the question 'What is the *nature* of reality?',[23] it is still remarkable how little attention it seems to receive in missiological circles – to judge from mission bibliographies and curricula, at least. There is much rhetoric about how objectionable relativism is, and how destructive post-structuralist linguistic philosophy is, but little genuine engagement with thinkers who are reflecting major trends in post-Christian spiritual perception.

This needs to change.[24] For it is rather sad that philosophers have been far quicker to discover the riches of the Christian mystical tradition than missiologists (Cupitt employs Meister Eckhart, for instance), and the possibility of apophatic mission is one that has barely been explored. While Christians in Europe are increasingly conscious of the gap between 'believing and belonging', there is less comprehension of 'spirituality without believing'. And where there is, the elusive category of 'religious experience' is all too easily used to avoid the nub of the problem.[25]

Explorations into God

Returning to the interreligious component of philosophical challenges to the deity who lies behind claims about the *missio dei*, it is worth articulating 'the problem of God' (popularized in John Robinson's best-selling *Honest to God*, published in 1963). This is less talked about but even more inescapable in Western society today, despite the persistence of aggressively conservative religion in the United States and its near equivalents in many parts of Europe.

Whatever the differences between them, the Jewish, Muslim and Christian religions share similar 'classical' traditions (all affected by Greek, particularly Aristotelian, philosophy) that hold a view of God as necessary, simple, eternal, immutable, infinite, omniscient, omnipotent, supremely valuable, incomprehensible – 'being' beyond all name and form. There are also, interestingly enough, similar ideas in elements of the Eastern tradition, such as the Hindu Upanishads. Yet these same religions also wish to speak of God – Yahweh, Allah, Abba, *Sachchidananda* – as tangibly manifested and affective in relation to the universe. Furthermore, in order to communicate faith, they have popular, familiar, street-level stories and ideas through which often pre-literate and informally educated believers have passed on powerful experiences that have shaped the tradition's understanding of God.

This has produced a three-fold tension. There are complex and abstract philosophical concepts pointing to the One who is forever covered in 'unapproachable light' (1 Timothy 6.16). There are warm, personal, confessional narratives showing that same God's demanding closeness to us. And there are also, it has to be said, crude, anthropomorphic images (Cupitt's 'Big Bloke' instead of the 'Big Bang'), which persist in the minds of 'cultured despisers' and unsophisticated believers alike – to a far greater degree than is sometimes acknowledged.

The internal problem of the Semitic religions (especially Judaism and Christianity, given their proximity to the questioning of the European Enlightenment) has therefore been whether there can be any presentable coherence between the God of the philosophers, the God of revealed religion and the various gods of popular piety. Can God be, simultaneously, wholly other and yet knowable, eternal and yet temporal, active yet impassable, complex yet simple, nowhere yet everywhere? And as soon as ancient cosmologies, which provided past coherence, collapse under the weight of scientific world-views, things begin to look even more intractable.

This, of course, is precisely what has happened. According to Bert Hoedemaker, unfulfilled Christian eschatological expectations produced a historicization of that vision into projects such as 'history', 'world' and 'science'. As modernity developed, it produced its own eschatological schemas, which in turn have reinhabited Christian thinking.

Similarly, I would add, the growing internal difficulties of theism in the face of these new impulses have been 'externalized' within our Western culture through the gradual emergence of secularity – forms of social life and thought that are not dominated by or accountable to prior religious authority, but which produce different processes of authorization. Philosophical empiricism, scientific materialism, technological pragmatism and linguistic non-realism all (in different and sometimes contradictory ways) have come to describe and animate the world we live in. And they all suggest that belief in a supreme value, power and source of being, namely God, is at best irrelevant and at worst irrational. The task of constructive theology (Hodgson, Farley, Page) against this backdrop is profoundly missionary, though it has not involved many missiologists as such.[26]

Mission theology, liberation and the globalization of difference

Meanwhile, political, moral, psychological and sociological critiques of the idea of God have also been forthcoming from Marx, Freud, Nietzsche, Foucault, various feminist theorists and others. In addition, we have the postmodern turn against metanarratives (overarching, controlling stories), which provided vehicles for both faith and reason in the modern era.

The overall result, compounded by a huge drift away from the historic religions in Western society, has been a massive crisis for traditional belief in God, whether of the classical or scriptural moulds. Such problems lie behind many of the concerns raised in *Christian Mission in Western Society*. Taken together, they constitute the biggest single intellectual and practical challenge to the narratives of the major religions in the last two millennia.

In the recent past it was suggested by some liberation theologians that such a diagnosis was a matter of complacent, affluent Western self-regard – the absorption of Western theology into the preoccupations of the agonistic 'non-believer' at the expense of the social 'non-person'

(Gutierrez and others). Now the tide is turning. As liberation theologians perceive the vulnerability of their own combination of biblical narrative and modern progressive thought (the failed 'historical project' of Exodus-inspired revolution), the power of Pentecostalism and, paradoxically, the growing urban secularity of many parts of Asia and Latin America, there is an increasing realization that the 'non-believer' and the 'non-person' are mutually reinforcing products of a market-led, consumer society. The task of liberation remains, but the analysis of the situation, the description of the task and the tools developed have proved inadequate.[27]

Similarly, Christian thinkers who seek refuge from what they reduce to 'the Western problem' by focusing on the growth of the churches in Africa and some parts of Asia, or who advocate an ever more determined reassertion of traditional forms of belief, are deluding themselves about the true scale and nature of globalization in its religious and cultural dimension. Doubt, diversity and difference are here to stay.

All this poses huge challenges for the current practice, thought and identity of the churches in Western society. Many of the essays in this volume have made the case for an open, critical engagement between Christianity and the culture of the West. It is surely clear, as Graeme Smith has emphasized, that such engagement requires us to embrace those life-giving elements of our societies that assist realistic hope for both the non-believer and the non-person, the existentially and the socio-economically alienated alike.

Just as rigorously, there must be a critique of their death-dealing features – which in turn necessitates the creation of communities of constructive resistance. This will involve fresh convergences within and beyond the churches, as the discerning of 'today' in the presence of God generates new missionary impulses. As Kirsteen Kim has argued, a theology of the Spirit – one of the lacks she identifies in David Bosch's magisterial *Transforming Mission* – is what will make an open yet faithful approach to others possible.[28]

Evangelization and human freedom

Jürgen Moltmann is among those who are willing to embrace the positive features of modernity and postmodernity while subjecting them (and the church in the light of the kingdom, or commonwealth, of God) to severe scrutiny. He has recently argued that mission involves a move beyond the mutual rationalisms of dogmatic modernism and religious fundamentalism. Proceeding on the basis of an ethic of life and a conversation among the religions, mission requires a re-reading and a re-orientation of Christian history.

Mission, says Moltmann, has proceeded in three stages. The first culminated in the creation of an *imperium*, the second involved the spread of the churches. Now the third involves participation in the evangelization of humanity – not its absorption into 'church', but dialogue and action aimed at disclosing the basis of its salvation. 'Christ came to bring life, not Christianity,' he says.[29]

One of the core questions that the church has to confront in its missionary encounter with Western culture is the issue of freedom. In his foreword to the English edition of Moltmann's *Theology and Joy*, David E. Jenkins suggests that this question is the one that most strongly links the question of God and the question of humanity.[30]

Echoing Bonhoeffer's unease about Barth's tendency towards a 'positivism of revelation', Jenkins reminds us that the traditional Christian picture of the total dependence of human beings on God has been severely undermined by the psychological view of dependency as a pathological state. On the other hand, the modern (Western) world is throwing up plenty of evidence about the pathologies of independence – a refusal to accept responsibility for the other, for our creatureliness and so on. Talk of interdependence is important but often masks the actual incomparability of the world with the transcendence of God.

The question we face, then, is 'Is there a liberating form of dependence?' Jenkins contends that a positive answer to this is at the heart of the offer of a gospel which is about the giftedness of life in the presence of God, the need for repentance and forgiveness, and the opportunity of a new start.

All this implies the continuing possibility of human community through reconciled difference, *pace* some pessimistic forms of postmodernism. For believers, that possibility exists not in the overwhelming efficacy of, say, communicative theory but through life understood in the presence of God – and in the maintenance of an eschatological horizon (Hoedemaker), albeit one founded on a different cosmology than that which has prevailed in Christian history to date.[31]

Economy and *ecclesia*

From these fundamental theological (and therefore missiological) questions about our founding texts, about Jesus Christ, and about God and freedom flow a number of other crucial challenges to mission practice and thinking in the West. We can only mention some of these here. Many are briefly referred to in this book.

One, relating to what – in use rather than in espoused theory – we value and worship, is the issue of engaging economic power, for which the West holds great responsibility in its relations with the South. The dominance of the market, the evolution of finance into a global network and the totality of the embrace of the money system (which not only commodifies every area of life but determines who is included and who excluded, and what things are 'worth') is a matter of profound missionary importance. Liberation theologians, speaking from the belly of the marginalized world, have rightly reminded the churches that 'where your wealth is, there is your heart also' (Jesus recorded by St Matthew).

Can Christian communities both commend practical interventions in the money-driven economy and practise some alternatives without succumbing to naïve anti-globalization? How can we hold together practical politics and eschatological faith? What is the future of ecumenical resource sharing? Do we need an economic theology of anti-idolatry? How do mission agencies and boards construct the financial basis of their international partnerships with equity and vision? Is there such a thing as effective 'globalization from below', and how do we make it happen? These are the central questions.

Another cluster of issues can be found around the genesis, reality and future of the churches. We have already noted the gauntlet thrown down to traditional ecclesiology by Graeme Smith. The extent to which women (Ann Loades), Black people (Joe Aldred) and other minorities such as lesbian and gay persons can exercise the freedom and responsibility of baptism in the Christian community depends, in all likelihood, upon a substantial re-visioning of the meaning of church. This, in turn, will affect the ability of the church to witness to 'communion' (in contrast to prevailing patterns of chaos and compulsion) as a plausible, salvific response to diversity in a plural environment.

In biblical terms, two images have dominated debate about the mission of the church in recent years. One is the so-called Great Commission in Matthew 28, the other the 'Nazareth Sermon' in Luke 4. Two paradigmatic texts that may need to play more of a role in the future of the Western churches are Matthew 5 (the Beatitudes – a picture of the 'new community' based on those who have been excluded or humbled) and Acts 15 (early Christians tackling the issue of how to combine Jewish and Greek cultural and religious elements in the church). Inculturation may be extensive, but it is far from complete.[32]

This also raises the question of Christian origins and doctrinal development as missionary issues. On the former, and paralleling the critical realism of Micheal MacCraith on early British and Irish Christianity,[33] Alan Le Grys has recently challenged the churches to rethink (and reconstruct) their rosy vision of the mission of the early church. Much of what has emerged as 'Christian mission' in modern times has relatively few precedents in Jewish antiquity, first-century practice or Jesus' own movement, he argues. The whole enterprise was much more uneven, ad hoc and context driven than we tend to suppose. In achievement-oriented cultures in which the church is a tiny minority, this can be liberating news. 'God can even use the mess of the church,' Le Grys goes on to remind us.[34]

This realism about our missionary origins and status is important for Christian communities trying to renegotiate their role on the edge of a Christendom system that appears to be in a state of disintegration. The biggest obstacles to revitalization are denial about the most evident features of our cultural contexts and denial of the decline of the church, according to Patricia Nimmo.[35] The relative disaggregation of large state churches in Europe is one of the major features of institutional life on our continent at the moment. In Britain, 42 per cent of the population profess no identifiable religious belief and only 12 per cent attend religious worship regularly. Half of those raised as Roman Catholics in the Netherlands now declare themselves to have no affiliation. In Sweden, church attendance is 4 per cent and dropping. At the same time, Nimmo points out (in common with a 1996 report from the Church of England and the ecumenical Churches' Commission on Mission), there has been a considerable expansion of informal 'popular' religion and the previously mentioned phenomenon of 'believing without belonging'. [36]

Mission on the global margins

The challenge implied here is not just to re-engage consciously with contemporary culture, but for the church to think through (as a missionary question) what it means to be a creative minority rather than a hegemonic majority, and how to apply this to programmes and possibilities for local church renewal.[37] The 'majoritarian' culture and ethos is one that comes naturally to many western churches. Either that or, as in the United States, the 'mini-empire' mentality that Loren Mead has called the 'Protestant version of Christendom' – 'majoritarian sectarianism'. [38] Mission partnerships with the minority churches of South Asia might therefore prove to be a vital link in rethinking Western church polity. The parallel questions about religious tolerance as both a virtue and a constraint cannot be avoided either.[39]

Here the matter of 'reception' should not be ignored as a model for ecclesial inculturation. Gillian Evans reminds us of the WCC Faith and Order definition of reception as 'the continuing process of the reinterpretation of the appropriation of the Gospel in new circumstances'.[40] As the churches struggle to continue their adaptation to the realities of Western culture and the fact of numerical decline, so education becomes more and more important – and reception rather than simple transmission becomes a vehicle for the renewal of mission. The aim is not to lose faith or to shrink it, but to re-engage Christian hope and rescale our institutions in the light of the tasks that have been given rather than in accordance with past expectations. Pentecostalism (hitherto regarded with suspicion in many ecumenical circles) and a re-visioned theology of the Spirit may have much to teach us in this area.

Finally, and most significantly, everything that has been said so far suggests the need for what Robert Schreiter has called a 'major refiguration' of the church and its mission as it seeks to take its part in a broad human discourse between an increasing number of 'locales' and 'the global'.[41] Here church-as-movement is as important, if not more important, than church-as-institution, he suggests. Religious and cultural differences in our world today must neither be reduced nor converged, but engaged practically on the basis of a positive Christian theology of plurality. This must be lucid and philosophically communicable in the contemporary world, not least the scientific world – yet it must also stay true to its biblical roots without absolutizing them. Above all, prophetic Christian faith, in critical alliance with those from other traditions and backgrounds, must reject the tendency of modernity/postmodernity to shrink into little more than a set of economic relations.

NOTES

1. See the Selected Bibliography at the end of this book and the list of Useful Organizations.
2. The editors are conscious that 'Western society' is a broad and elusive category. Apart from its primary geographical remit (the North Atlantic area), the features that we take to be common to 'the West' include urbanization, secularity in public life, marketization, individualization and pluralism. See also Jürgen Moltmann, *God for a Secular Society: The Public Relevance of Theology*, SCM, 1997.
3. Thankfully, the excellent Trinity Press International series Christian Mission and Modern Culture shows a bravery that defies this conservatism, though with a broad theological spread of contributors. Many of the key titles in this series are listed and asterisked in the Selected Bibliography.

4. For a sceptical response to interreligious concerns, see J. Andrew Kirk, *The Mission of Theology and Theology as Mission*, Trinity Press International, 1997, p. 45ff and *passim*.
5. Martin Prozesky wisely makes this point in *A New Guide to the Debate About God*, SCM, 1992, pp. 7–8.
6. See Keith Ward, *Religion and Revelation*, Oxford University Press, 1994, pp. 1–15.
7. Newbigin and his allies have tried to move missiology too far in this direction. In Britain the 'Radical Orthodoxy' school, often summarized as advocating a postmodern Augustinian synthesis, have produced a culture-rejecting trajectory within academic theology. So has Stanley Hauerwas (however stimulating his iconoclastic thought) in the United States. For a helpful critique, see Steven Shakespeare, 'The new Romantics', *Theology*, May/June 2000.
8. Bert Hoedemaker, 'Naming the world in the name of the coming one: changing relations between mission, modernity and eschatology', *EXCHANGE: Journal of Missiological and Ecumenical Research* 27(3), 1998.
9. René Girard is a literary critic and anthropologist. His critique of 'the scapegoat mechanism' as an archetype of the mimetic violence at the root of all civilizations hitherto has led him back to Christian faith, and in particular to the Gospel passion narratives as a decisive break with the whole sacrificial order that embodies it. For a narrative exposition of this see James Alison, *Living in the End Times*, SPCK, 1997.
10. See also his extraordinary article, 'Adam's (ir)religious finger: an African view on religion pointing beyond Barth and Rahner', *EXCHANGE* 26(2), 1997.
11. See also the committed 'de-totalitarianizing' theology of John Pohier, *God in Fragments*, SCM, 1985. Pohier points out that 'God is God, so God is not everything'.
12. Expounded in Simon Barrow, 'Encountering the other in Christ', *Christian* magazine, Passiontide 1998. See also David McCracken, *The Scandal of the Gospels: Jesus, Story and Offence*, Oxford University Press, 1994.
13. See Andreas Pangritz in John W. de Gruchy (ed.), *The Cambridge Companion to Dietrich Bonhoeffer*, Cambridge University Press, 1999, p. 134ff.

14. See John Hick and Paul F. Knitter (eds), *The Myth of Christian Uniqueness: Toward a Pluralistic Theology of Religions*, SCM, 1987; Gavin D'Costa (ed.) *Christian Uniqueness Reconsidered: The Myth of a Pluralistic Theology of Religions*, Orbis, 1990; and S. Mark Heim, *Salvations: Truth and Difference in Religion*, Orbis, 1995.
15. Ruth Page, *The Incarnation of Freedom and Love*, SCM, 1991. See also Stanley E. Porter, Michael A. Hayes, David Toombs (eds), *Images of Christ Ancient and Modern*, Sheffield Academic Press, 1997, and Lucien Richard, *Christ, the Self-Emptying of God*, Paulist Press, 1997, which recounts the Christological narrative of the kenotic church.
16. Peter Selby, *Grace and Mortgage: The Language of Faith and the Debt of the World*, Darton, Longman and Todd, 1997. See also Marcus Borg (ed.), *Jesus at 2000*, Westview, 1998, and Marcus Borg and N.T. Wright, *The Meaning of Jesus*, SPCK, 1999.
17. Paul F. Knitter, *Jesus and the Other Names: Christian Mission and Global Responsibility*, Oneworld, 1996; Richard Rohr, *Jesus' Plan for a New World*, St Paul, 1996. Also Leonard Swidler and Paul Mojzes (eds), *The Uniqueness of Jesus: A Dialogue with Paul Knitter*, Orbis, 1997; Jacques Dupuis, *Toward a Christian Theology of Religious Pluralism*, Orbis, 1999; Michael Barnes, *Christian Identity and Religious Pluralism: Religions in Conversation*, Darton, Longman and Todd, 1986.
18. See Wilfred Cantwell Smith, *What is Scripture?*, SCM, 1997, and Stephen E. Fowl, *Engaging Scripture*, Blackwells, 1998, for very different but equally illuminating stances on these questions. Also Paul Joyce in Frances M. Young (ed.), *Dare We Speak of God in Public?*, Mowbray, 1995, pp. 67–79. An excellent constructive approach to the use of biblical material is Walter Brueggemann, *The Bible and Postmodern Imagination: Texts Under Negotiation*, SCM, 1993.
19. Michael Prior, *The Bible and Colonialism: A Moral Critique*, Sheffield Academic Press, 1997, puts this point especially forcefully. As Peter Selby, among many others, suggests in *BeLonging: Challenge to a Tribal Church*, SPCK, 1995, the New Testament is an account of rival claims for the significance of the gospel. Moreover, the suppression of imprecatory psalms in a number of lectionaries, notably Anglican ones, is evidence of the ecclesiastical recognition that not everything in the Bible can be 'scripture'.

20. For a contrasting set of views, see Marion L. Soards, 'Key issues in biblical studies and their bearing on mission studies', *Missiology: An International Review*, January 1996.
21. The full range of WCC 'Gospel and Cultures' pamphlets are available through the World Council of Churches <www.wcc-coe.org> in Geneva. See S. Wesley Ariajah, *Gospel and Culture: An Ongoing Discussion Within the Ecumenical Movement*, WCC, 1995. Some of the issues are debated in the April 1997 issue *International Bulletin of Missionary Research*, 'Culture: The Ambiguous Ally of Mission'.
22. Don Cupitt, *The Long-legged Fly: A Theology of Language and Desire*, SCM, 1987, p. 160ff. Cupitt has recently suggested that as God has disappeared from everyday speech, so the old religious language, feelings and rituals have become refocused around the word 'life'. The consequences of this, of great importance to missiology, are expounded in a trilogy beginning with *The New Religion of Life in Everyday Speech*, SCM, 1999. See also Ursula King (ed.), *Faith and Praxis in a Postmodern Age*, Cassell, 1998, and Charles Winquist, *Desiring Theology*, University of Chicago Press, 1997.
23. This is a point made by Rowan Williams in his foreword to a fine collection, *God and Reality*, edited by Colin C. Crowder, Cassell, 1997. Grace Jantzen echoes it in *Becoming Divine: Toward a Feminist Philosophy of Religion*, Cambridge University Press, 1999.
24. A powerful challenge to the non-realists, albeit with dubious post-liberal claims to a theology that 'absorbs the world', is to be found in Sue Patterson, *Realist Christian Theology in a Postmodern Age*, Cambridge University Press, 1999. A stronger treatment of the issues is John Reader, *Beyond All Reason*, Aureus Publishing, 1997. Note the absence of such issues in a missiological collection such as William R. Barr (ed.), *Constructive Christian Theology in the Worldwide Church*, Eerdmans, 1997. A groundbreaking work in the area of missiology and epistemology is J. Andrew Kirk and Kevin J. Vanhoozer (eds), *To Stake A Claim: Mission and the Western Crisis of Knowledge*, Orbis, 1999.
25. See David Hay and Kate Hunt, *The Spirituality of People Who Don't Go to Church*, University of Nottingham, 2000.
26. See Edward Farley, *Divine Empathy: A Theology of God*, Fortress Press, 1997, and Peter Hodgson, *Winds of the Spirit: A Constructive Christian Theology*, SCM, 1995. Ruth Page's *Ambiguity and the Presence of God*, SCM, 1985, is

probably the most important recent example of confronting the zeitgeist head-on while still seeking to make the tradition of Christian thinking workable. See also her *Synergy in the Church*, SCM, 2000. Gordon D. Kaufman, *In the Presence of Mystery*, SCM, 1997, and Stewart Sutherland, *God, Jesus and Belief*, Blackwell, 1984, are more pessimistic – the latter less so in 'God and freedom,' in Colin Gunton(ed.), *God and Freedom*, T&T Clark, 1995.

27. For an exploration of liberation theology in a Western context, see Joerg Rieger (ed), *Liberating the Future: God, Mammon and Theology*, Fortress, 1998. The term 'liberation' is, of course, at one level an essentially modern one, carrying with it notions of advancement, progress and rational control. But I do not believe such ideological baggage hopelessly traps it.
28. Kirsteen Kim, 'The Holy Spirit in mission: where and how is the Spirit at work in religions, cultures and movements for liberation?', paper published on the Internet by the Churches' Commission on Mission <www.ccom.org.uk> or available from the author via the British and Irish Association of Mission Studies. See also David Bosch, *Transforming Mission: Paradigm Shifts in the Theology of Mission*, Orbis, 1991.
29. Moltmann, *God for a Secular Society*. See also, though in the form of a thoroughly modernist 'world uniting' project, Hans Kung (ed.), *Yes to a Global Ethic*, SCM, 1996.
30. David E. Jenkins, 'The liberation of "God"', in Jürgen Moltmann, *Theology and Joy*, SCM, 1983.
31. Bert Hoedemaker, 'Mission, unity and eschaton: a triadic relation', *Reformed World*, December 2000.
32. There is a substantial missiological literature on inculturation, a term much used in this volume, which focuses on the translatability and appropriate adaptation of the Christian message and community in changing cultural settings. It is to be distinguished from *a*cculturation, which implies accommodation rather than mutual critical dialogue. See also 'Contextualization: mission in the balance', *International Bulletin of Missionary Research*, January 1997.
33. See for comparison William van den Bercken, 'Early European conversion stories: the painful birth of Christian Europe', *EXCHANGE* 26(2), 1997.

34. Alan Le Grys, *Preaching to the Nations: The Origins of Mission in the Early Church*, SPCK, 1998, p. 189.
35. Pat Nimmo, 'Mission in Western society', unpublished paper from the former St Andrew's Hall, Selly Oak, Birmingham.
36. Mission Theology Advisory Group, *The Search for Faith and the Witness of the Church*, Church House Publishing, 1996.
37. See 'Turn to God: reflections on missionary renewal', *International Review of Mission*, October 1998.
38. Loren B. Mead, *The Once and Future Church*, Alban Institute, 1994. See also Stanley H. Skreslet, 'Impending transformation: mission structures for a new century', *International Bulletin of Missionary Research*, January 1999.
39. See the themed issue on 'Freedom of Religion', *EXCHANGE* 27(4), 1998.
40. Gillian Evans, *The Reception of the Faith: Reinterpreting the Gospel for Today*, SPCK, 1997. See also 'Translation and the fullness of Christ', *International Bulletin of Missionary Research*, October 1997.
41. See Robert Schreiter, *The New Catholicity: Theology Between the Local and the Global*, Orbis, 1998. Also 'Cutting edge issues in theology and their bearing on mission studies', *Missiology: An International Review*, January 1996.

Selected Bibliography

The bibliography includes key texts cited in each chapter plus a considerable amount of additional material on themes reflected in this volume. Most citations are from North Atlantic publishers.

An asterisk indicates a title in the Christian Mission and Modern Culture series published by Trinity Press International.

Joe D. Aldred, *Preaching With Power: Sermons by Black Preachers*, Cassell, 1999.

James Alison, *Living in the End Times*, SPCK, 1997.

Allan Anderson, *Pentecostals After a Century*, Sheffield Academic Press, 1999.

Gerald H. Anderson, Robert T. Cooke, Norman A. Horner and James M. Phillips (eds), *Mission Legacies: Biographical Studies of Leaders of the Modern Missionary Movement*, Orbis, 1994.

S. Wesley Ariajah, *Gospel and Culture: An Ongoing Discussion Within the Ecumenical Movement*, WCC, 1995.

William R. Barr (ed.), *Constructive Christian Theology in the Worldwide Church*, Eerdmans, 1997.

Simon Barrow, *The Churches Gathered and Dispersed in Witness: Reflections Stemming from the WCC Consultation on Mission and Ecclesiology, July 2000*, Churches Together in Britain and Ireland, 2000.

——— (ed.), *Expanding Horizons: Learning to be the Church in the World*, Church in Society Publications, 1995.

Zygmunt Bauman, *Life in Fragments: Essays in Post-Modern Morality*, Blackwell, 1995.

———, *Post-Modern Ethics*, Blackwell, 1993.

David Bosch, *Transforming Mission: Paradigm Shifts in the Theology of Mission*, Orbis, 1996.

———, *Believing in the Future: Toward a Missiology of Western Culture*, Trinity Press International, 1995. *

Ian Bradley, *Columba: Pilgrim and Penitent*, Wild Goose Publications, 1996.

Callum G. Brown, *The Death of Christian Britain: Understanding Secularisation, 1800–2000*, Routledge, 2001.

Walter Brueggemann, *The Bible and Postmodern Imagination: Texts Under Negotiation*, SCM, 1993.

Alexander Carmichael, *Carmina Gadelica: Hymns and Incantations from the Gaelic*, ed. by John MacInnes, Floris, 1992.

Thomas Owen Clancy and Gilbert Márkus, *Iona: the Earliest Poetry of a Celtic Monastery*, Edinburgh University Press, 1995.

John R. Cobb, Jr., *Transforming Christianity and the World: A Way Beyond Absolutism and Relativism*, Orbis, 1999.

Jane Collier, *From Complicity to Encounter: The Church and the Culture of Economism*, Trinity Press International, 1999. *

Ruth Conway, *Choices at the Heart of Technology*, Trinity Press International, 1999. *

Harvey Cox, *Fire from Heaven: The Rise of Pentecostal Spirituality and the Reshaping of Religion in the Twenty-first Century*, Cassell, 1996.

Kenneth Cragg, *The Secular Experience of God*, Trinity Press International, 1998. *

Colin C. Crowder (ed.), *God and Reality*, Cassell, 1997.

Don Cupitt, *The New Religion of Life in Everyday Speech*, SCM, 1999.

———, *After God: The Future of Religion*, Basic, 1997.

———, *The Long-legged Fly: A Theology of Language and Desire*, SCM, 1987.

Grace Davie, *Religion in Modern Europe: A Memory Mutates*, Oxford University Press, 2000.

———, 'Europe: the exception that proves the rule?', in Peter L. Berger (ed.), *The Desecularization of the World: Resurgent Religion and World Politics*, Eerdmans, 1999.

———, *Religion in Britain Since 1945: Believing Without Belonging*, Blackwell, 1993.

Oliver Davies, *Celtic Christianity in Early Medieval Wales*, University of Wales Press, 1996.

——— and Fiona Bowie (eds), *Celtic Christian Spirituality: An Anthology of Medieval and Modern Sources*, SPCK, 1995.

Esther de Waal, *A World Made Whole: Discovering the Celtic Tradition*, Fount, 1991.

Vincent Donovan, *The Church in the Midst of Creation*, SCM, 1991.

Jacques Dupuis, *Toward a Christian Theology of Religious Pluralism*, Orbis, 1999.

Diana I. Eck and Devaki Jain (eds), *Speaking of Faith: Cross-Cultural Perspectives on Women, Religion and Social Change*, The Women's Press, 1986.

Gillian Evans, *The Reception of the Faith: Reinterpreting the Gospel for Today*, SPCK, 1997.

Edward B. Farley, *Divine Empathy: A Theology of God*, Fortress Press, 1997.

Duncan B. Forrester, *Theology and Politics*, Blackwell, 1988.

Roswith I. H. Gerloff, *A Plea for British Black Theologies: The Black Church Movement in Britain in its Transatlantic Cultural and Theological Interaction*, Frankfurt, 1992.

René Girard, James G Williams (ed.), *The Girard Reader*, Crossroad, 1997.

Alan Le Grys, *Preaching to the Nations: The Origins of Mission in the Early Church*, SPCK, 1998.

Judith M. Gundry-Volf and Miroslav Volf, *A Spacious Heart: Essays on Identity and Belonging*, Trinity Press International, 1997. *

Jeffrey K. Hadden and Anson Shupe (eds), *Secularization and Fundamentalism Reconsidered: Religion and the Political Order*, New York, 1990.

John Douglas Hall, *The End of Christendom and the Future of Christianity*, Trinity Press International, 1997. *

Phillip E. Hammond (ed.), *The Sacred in a Secular Age: Toward Revision in the Scientific Study of Religion*, Berkeley, 1985.

Daphne Hampson, *After Christianity*, SCM, 1996.

Barry A. Harvey, *Another City: An Ecclesiological Primer for a Post-Christian World*, Trinity Press International, 1999. *

David Harvey, *The Condition of Postmodernity*, Blackwell, 1990.

Adrian Hastings, *A History of English Christianity 1920–1990*, SCM, 1991.

Vaclav Havel, *Living in Truth*, Faber, 1987.

David Hay and Kate Hunt, *The Spirituality of People Who Don't Go To Church*, University of Nottingham, 2000.

S. Mark Heim, *Salvations: Truth and Difference in Religion*, Orbis, 1995.

Máire Herbert, *Iona, Kells and Derry*, Four Courts Press, 1996.

Paul G. Hiebert, *The Missiological Implications of Epistemological Shifts: Affirming Truth in a Modern World*, Trinity Press International, 1999. *

Peter Hodgson, *Winds of the Spirit: A Constructive Christian Theology*, SCM, 1995.

Bert Hoedemaker, 'Mission, unity and eschaton: a triadic relation', *Reformed World*, December 2000.

———, *Secularization and Mission: A Theological Essay*, Trinity Press International, 1998. *

———, 'Naming the world in the name of the coming one: changing relations between mission, modernity and eschatology', *EXCHANGE: Journal of Missiological and Ecumenical Research* 27(3), 1998.

International Review of Mission, 'Open Space: The African Christian Diaspora in Europe and the Quest for Human Community' [themed issue], World Council of Churches, July 2000.

L. Isherwood and D. McEwan (eds), *An A to Z of Feminist Theology*, Sheffield Academic Press, 1996.

Grace Jantzen, *Becoming Divine: Toward a Feminist Philosophy of Religion*, Cambridge University Press, 1999.

David E. Jenkins, *The Contradiction of Christianity*, SCM, 1986.

———,'The Liberation of "God"', in Jürgen Moltmann, *Theology and Joy*, SCM, 1983.

Elizabeth A. Johnson, *She Who Is: The Mystery of God in Feminist Theological Discourse*, SCM, 1993.

Gordon D. Kaufman, *In the Presence of Mystery*, SCM, 1997.

Philip D. Kenneson, *Beyond Sectarianism: Re-Imagining Church and World*, Trinity Press International, 1999. *

Søren Kierkegaard, *Attack on Christendom*, Princeton University Press, 1968

———, *Training in Christianity*, Princeton University Press, 1944.

Ursula King (ed.), *Faith and Praxis in a Post-modern Age*, Cassell, 1998.

J. Andrew Kirk, *The Mission of Theology and Theology as Mission*, Trinity Press International, 1997. *

——— and Kevin J. Vanhoozer (eds), *To Stake a Claim: Mission and the Western Crisis of Knowledge*, Orbis, 1999.

Paul F. Knitter, *Jesus and the Other Names: Christian Mission and Global Responsibility*, Oneworld, 1996.

Alan Kreider, *The Change of Conversion and the Origin of Christendom*, Trinity Press International, 1999.

Steven J. Land, *Pentecostal Spirituality: A Passion for the Kingdom*, Sheffield Academic Press, 1993.

B. B. Lawrence, *Defenders of God: The Fundamentalist Revolt Against the Modern Age*, University of South Carolina Press, 1995.

Ann Loades (ed.), *Feminist Theology: A Reader*, SPCK, 1990.

Alasdair MacIntyre, *After Virtue: A Study in Moral Theory*, University of Notre Dame Press, 1981.

Bernice Martin, 'From pre- to postmodernity in Latin America: the case of pentecostalism', in P. Heelas (ed.), *Religion, Modernity and Postmodernity*, Oxford University Press, 1996.

M. E. Marty and R. S. Appleby (eds), *Fundamentalisms Observed*, University of Chicago Press, 1991.

Loren B. Mead, *The Once and Future Church*, Alban Institute, 1994.

Donald E. Meek, 'Surveying the Saints: Reflections on Recent Writings in "Celtic Christianity"', *Scottish Bulletin of Evangelical Theology*, Spring 1997.

———, 'Modern Celtic Christianity', in Terence Brown (ed.), *Celticism* (Studia Imagologica: Amsterdam Studies on Cultural Identity 8), 1996.

———, 'Modern Celtic Christianity: The Contemporary "Revival" and Its Roots', *Scottish Bulletin of Evangelical Theology*, Spring 1992.

J. B. Metz, *Faith in History and Society*, Burns and Oates, 1980.

John Milbank, *Theology and Social Theory: Beyond Secular Reason*, Blackwell, 1993.

Robinson A. Millwood, *Liberation And Mission*, Kent, 1997.

Mission Theology Advisory Group, *The Search for Faith and the Witness of the Church*, Church House Publishing, 1996.

———, *Good News in Our Times: The Gospel and Contemporary Cultures*, Church House Publishing, 1991.

Jürgen Moltmann, *God for a Secular Society: The Public Relevance of Theology*, SCM, 1997.

Hugh Montefiore (ed.), *The Gospel and Contemporary Culture*, Mowbray, 1992.

Michael Nazir-Ali, *Citizens and Exiles: Christian Faith in a Plural World*, United Church Press, 2000.

Lesslie Newbigin, *Truth and Authority in Modernity*, Trinity Press International, 1996. *

———, *Truth to Tell: The Gospel as Public Truth*, SPCK, 1991.

———, *The Other Side of 1984*, WCC, 1984.

H. Richard Niebuhr, *Christ and Culture*, Harper, 1951.

Oliver O'Donovan, *The Desire of the Nations: Rediscovering the Roots of Political Theology*, Cambridge University Press, 1996.

O'Hara Graff (ed.), *In the Embrace of God: Feminist Approaches to Theological Anthropology*, Orbis, 1995.

Ruth Page, *Synergy in the Church*, SCM, 2000.

———, *The Incarnation of Freedom and Love*, SCM, 1991.

———, *Ambiguity and the Presence of God*, SCM, 1985.

George Pattison, *Agnosis: Theology in the Void*, MacMillan, 1996.

Lynne Price, *Faithful Uncertainty: Leslie D. Weatherhead's Methodology of Creative Evangelism*, Peter Lang, 1996.

———, Juan Sepúlveda and Graeme Smith (eds), *Mission Matters*, Peter Lang, 1997.

Michael Prior, *The Bible and Colonialism: A Moral Critique*, Sheffield Academic Press, 1997.

Martin Prozesky, *A New Guide to the Debate About God*, SCM, 1992.

Konrad Raiser, *Ecumenism in Transition: A Paradigm Shift in the Ecumenical Movement*, WCC, 1991.

John Reader, *Beyond All Reason*, Aureus Publishing, 1997.

Joerg Rieger (ed), *Liberating the Future: God, Mammon and Theology*, Fortress, 1998.

Roland Robertson, 'Glocalization: time–space and homogeneity–heterogeneity', in Mike Featherstone and Scott Lash (eds), *Global Modernities*, Sage Publications, 1995.

Alan J. Roxburgh, *The Missionary Congregation, Leadership and Liminality*, Trinity Press International, 1997. *

Lamin Sanneh, *Religion and the Variety of Culture: A Study in Origin and Practice*, Trinity Press International, 1996. *

———, *Encountering the West: Christianity and the Global Cultural Process – the African Dimension*, Orbis, 1993.

———, *Translating the Message*, Orbis, 1989.

Robert Schreiter, *The New Catholicity: Theology Between the Local and the Global*, Orbis, 1998.

Gordon Scoville, *Into the Vacuum: Being the Church in an Age of Barbarism*, Trinity Press International, 1998. *

Peter Selby, *Grace and Mortgage: The Language of Faith and the Debt of the World*, Darton, Longman and Todd, 1997.

———, *BeLonging: Challenge to a Tribal Church*, SPCK, 1995.

Richard Sharpe (trans.), *Adomnán of Iona: Life of St Columba*, Penguin Books, 1995.

Wilbert R. Shenk, *Write the Vision: The Church Renewed*, Trinity Press International, 1995. *

Michael Simmons (ed.), *Street Credo: Churches and Communities*, Lemos & Crane, 2000.

Io Smith with Wendy Green, *An Ebony Cross: Being a Black Christian in Britain Today*, Marshall Pickering, 1989.

Stephen Toulmin, *Cosmopolis: The Hidden Agenda of Modernity*, University of Chicago Press, 1990.

Werner Ustorf, *Tales of Post-Christendom in Europe*, SMT, 1999.

———, *Mission in a Pluralist World*, Peter Lang, 1997.

William van den Bercken, 'Early European conversion stories: the painful birth of Christian Europe', *EXCHANGE: Journal of Missiological and Ecumenical Research* 26(2), 1997.

Peter van der Veer (ed.), *Conversion to Modernities: The Globalization of Christianity*, Routledge, 1996.

Keith Ward, *Religion and Revelation*, Oxford University Press, 1994.

Antonie Wessels, *Secularized Europe: Who Will Carry Off Its Soul?*, WCC, 1996.

———, *Europe: Was It Ever Really Christian?*, SCM, 1994.

Philip L. Wickeri, Janice K. Wickeri and Damayanthi M. A. Niles (eds.), *Plurality, Power and Mission: Intercontextual Theological Explorations on the Role of Religion in the New Millennium*, Council for World Mission, 2000.

Rowan Williams, *Lost Icons: Reflections on Cultural Bereavement*, T&T Clark, 2000.

———, *On Christian Theology: Challenges in Contemporary Theology*, Blackwell, 1999.

Jonathan R. Wilson, *Living Faithfully in a Fragmented World: Lessons for the Church from MacIntyre's After Virtue*, Trinity Press International, 1997. *

Walter Wink, *The Powers That Be: Theology for a New Millennium*, Doubleday, 1998.

Charles Winquist, *Desiring Theology*, University of Chicago Press, 1997.

Timothy Yates (ed.), *Mission: An Invitation to God's Future*, Cliff College Publishing, 2000.

———, *Christian Mission in the Twentieth Century*, Cambridge University Press, 1994.

Useful Organizations

BRITISH AND IRISH ASSOCIATION FOR MISSION STUDIES
Henry Martyn Centre, Westminster College
Cambridge CB3 0AA
E-mail: biams@martynmission.cam.ac.uk
Web: www.martynmission.cam.ac.uk/BIAMS.htm

CENTRE FOR MISSIOLOGY AND WORLD CHRISTIANITY
Graduate Institute for Theology and Religion
University of Birmingham
Elmfield House, Bristol Road
Selly Oak, Birmingham B29 6LQ
E-mail: mission@sellyoak.ac.uk
Web: www.bham.ac.uk/theology/cmwc.htm

CENTRE FOR THEOLOGY AND PUBLIC ISSUES
New College, University of Edinburgh
Mound Place
Edinburgh EH1 2LX
Web: www.div.ed.ac.uk/research/public_issues/ctpidetail.html

CHURCHES' COMMISSION ON MISSION
Churches Together in Britain and Ireland
Inter-Church House, 35–41 Lower Marsh
London SE1 7SA
E-mail: ccom@ctbi.org.uk
Web: www.ccom.org.uk

CONFERENCE OF EUROPEAN CHURCHES
PO Box 2100
150 route de Ferney
1211 Geneva 2
Switzerland
E-mail: reg@cec-kek.org
Web: www.cec-kek.org/English/index.html

COUNCIL FOR WORLD MISSION
Ipalo House, 32–34 Great Peter Street
London SW1P 2DB
E-mail: council@cwmission.org.uk
Web: www.cwmission.org.uk

CURRENTS IN WORLD CHRISTIANITY PROJECT
Westminster College
Cambridge CB3 0AA
E-mail: cwc@divinity.cam.ac.uk
Web: www.divinity.cam.ac.uk/CARTS/cwc/default.html

GLOBAL CONNECTIONS
Web: www.globalconnections.co.uk

INTERNATIONAL ASSOCIATION FOR MISSION STUDIES
Secretary: Peter Bangsvej
1D - DK-2000 Frederiksberg
Copenhagen, Denmark
E-mail: secretary@missionstudies.org
Web: www.missionstudies.org

INTERNATIONAL RESEARCH INSTITUTE INTO SPIRITUALITY AND CHANGE
c/o University of Wales
Bangor
Gwynedd LL57 2DG
Web: www.geocities.com/irisc_uk

KIMMAGE MISSION INSTITUTE
Institute of Theology and Cultures
Whitehall Road
Dublin 12
Web: www.kmitc.ie

MISSIONARY INSTITUTE LONDON (ROMAN CATHOLIC)
Holcombe House , The Ridgeway
London NW7 4HY
Web: www.mdx.ac.uk/www/religion/

OXFORD CENTRE FOR MISSION STUDIES
P.O. Box 70
Oxford 0X2 6HB
E-mail: OCMS@ocms.ac.uk
Web: www.ocms.ac.uk

WORLD COUNCIL OF CHURCHES
(*International Review of Mission*)
150 route de Ferney
1211 Geneva 2
Switzerland
Web: www.wcc-coe.org/wcc/what/mission/index-e.html